*And—if you, or any of your colleagues, wish to order additional copies of Carbohydrate Intolerance in Infancy, edited by* **Fima Lifshitz**, *simply fill out the coupon below.*

-------------------------------- ORDER FORM --------------------------------

Mrs. Eridania Perez, Promotion Department
**MARCEL DEKKER, INC.**
270 Madison Avenue
New York, New York 10016

☐ Please send me _____ copy(ies) of *Clinical Disorders in Pediatric Gastroenterology and Nutrition,* edited by **Fima Lifshitz**, at \$44.50* per volume.

☐ Please send me _____ copy(ies) of *Pediatric Nutrition: Infant Feedings— Deficiencies—Diseases*, edited by **Fima Lifshitz**, at \$44.50* (prepublication price) per volume.

☐ Please send me _____ copy(ies) of *Carbohydrate Intolerance in Infancy*, edited by **Fima Lifshitz**, at \$35.00* per volume.

    *\*(add \$1.50 for postage and handling per volume.)*

☐ Please add my name to your mailing list to receive information about forthcoming books of related interest.

I enclose payment by ☐ check ☐ money order ☐ credit card

☐ Visa ☐ MasterCard _____ Exp. Date: _____

    MasterCard 4 digit Interbank number _____

Signature _____
               *(must be signed for credit card payment)*

Name _____

Address _____

City _____

State _____ Zip _____

*New York State residents should add appropriate sales tax.*
*Payments must be made in U.S. currency.*

Form No. 82-6547                    Printed in U.S.A.

# Infant Feedings–Deficiencies–Diseases

## CONTENTS

**ISBN: 0–8247–1430–X**

\* *Clinical Disorders in Pediatric Nutrition* is a series of individual volumes under the general editorial direction of Fima Lifshitz, M.D., Cornell University Medical College, New York, New York, New York and North Shore University Hospital, Manhasset, New York.

# Clinical Disorders in Pediatric Gastroenterolog

edited by **FIMA LIFSHITZ**
*Cornell University Medical College, New York, New York*
and *North Shore University Hospital, Manhasset, New York*

1980    464 pages, illustrated
$44.50 *(Price is 20% higher outside the U.S. and Canada)*

*"The general pediatrician, in his endeavor to keep abreast of developments in pediatric specialties, will welcome this volume. . . . To produce a satisfactory amalgam of general reviews and papers on specific subjects, which may be as esoteric as mitochondrial function in relatively rare disorders, is very difficult. This volume succeeds. . .*

*"Throughout, the text is commendably clear, the bibliography is extensive, and the electron-micrographs are of very high quality. The well-illustrated paper on chronic liver disease by Mervin Silverberg and Ellen Kahn from Cornell is particularly good.*

*"Amidst the contributions on high technology are papers on malnutrition and primitive communities, including a fascinating study by Ulysses Fagundes-Neto on Brazilian Indians. . .*

*". . . this volume is at its best when dealing with the broader aspects of nutritional problems and must certainly commend itself to general pediatricians, although the systems specialists would doubtless find much to his taste here. I awaid with interest Volume II."*

—**A. P. Cole**, *Department of Pediatrics,*
*Worchester Royal Infirmary,*
***THE LANCET*** (Jan., 1981)

# ɉy and Nutrition (Pediatric Series, Volume 1)

## CONTENTS

ISBN: 0–8247–6954–6

*see over* ▶

# Pediatric Nutrition

## (Clinical Disorders in Pediatric Nutrition Series, Volume 2)*

edited by **FIMA LIFSHITZ**
*Cornell University Medical College, New York, New York*
and *North Shore University Hospital, Manhasset, New York*

October, 1982    640 pages (tentative), illustrated
$44.50 (prepublication price)
*(Price is 20% higher outside the U.S. and Canada.)*

### From the Foreword—

*"This symposium has brought together a distinguished panel of contributors who focus on the various aspects of nutrition in health and disease states. The North Shore University Hospital faculty, joined by national and international experts in the field, provides students, practitioners, and academicians with the most current data in each area.*

*"At a time when the teaching of nutrition in most medical schools and hospitals is still in its formative years, this textbook will be a welcome addition to the library of everyone concerned with the delivery of health care to infants, children, and adolescents."*

—**Mervin Silverberg, M.D.,** *Professor of Pediatrics, Cornell University Medical College*

*Pediatric Nutrition: Infant Feedings—Deficiencies—Diseases* fully covers the most recent developments, advances and findings in pediatric nutrition, emphasizing current concepts in infant feedings, as well as the pathophysiology and management of frequently encountered disorders in pediatric nutrition.

Interdisciplinary in scope, the subjects in each section of this outstanding monograph are explored from a clinical perspective by eminent authorities in the field; the 43 contributors to *Pediatric Nutrition: Infant Feedings—Deficiencies—Diseases* provide pediatricians, neonatalogists, nutritionists, gastroenterologists, microbiologists, biochemists, and others dealing with various childhood nutritional disorders with the finest, comprehensive research reference available today.

# Carbohydrate Intolerance in Infancy

# Clinical Disorders in Pediatric Nutrition

**Editor: Fima Lifshitz**
Cornell University Medical College, New York, New York
North Shore University Hospital, Manhasset, New York

Other Volumes in Preparation

# Carbohydrate Intolerance in Infancy

edited by
## Fima Lifshitz

Cornell University Medical School
New York, New York
North Shore University Hospital
Manhasset, New York

MARCEL DEKKER, INC.

New York • Basel

**Library of Congress Cataloging in Publication Data**
Main entry under title:

Carbohydrate intolerance in infancy.

   (Clinical disorders in pediatric nutrition ; v. 1)
   Includes bibliographical references and index.
   1. Carbohydrate metabolism disorders in children.
2. Infants—Diseases. I. Lifshitz, Fima, [date].
II. Series. [DNLM: 1. Carbohydrate metabolism, Inborn
errors. W1 CL694I v.1 / WD 205.5.C2 C264]
RJ399.C3C37       618.92'3998       82-5107
ISBN 0-8247-1747-3             AACR2

MARCEL DEKKER, INC.
270 Madison Avenue, New York, New York 10016

Current printing (last digit):
10  9  8  7  6  5  4  3  2  1

PRINTED IN THE UNITED STATES OF AMERICA

# DEDICATION

Dr. Horacio Toccalino, Argentinean pediatrician, was a modern pioneer of pediatric gastroenterology and nutrition in South America. He served at The "Alejandro Posadas" Polyclinic in Buenos Aires, Argentina. In the early sixties Horacio Toccalino started his career at the Hospital de Niños of Buenos Aires, where he studied food intolerances which affected a large number of his patients. Specifically, he worked on carbohydrate intolerance in both acute and chronic diarrhea, with special emphasis on secondary disaccharidase deficiencies and the bacterial overgrowth syndrome in children with malnutrition and diarrhea. Later he studied the absorption of potential antigens through the small intestine as a cause of food allergy. Thus, years before these subjects attained general interest, he was pioneering the field covered in this book.

Dr. Toccalino was a man of fascinating personal characteristics which gave him charisma. His extremely remarkable personality, enterprising character, permanent desire to teach, involve, and stimulate young doctors in research, and his sincere friendship with his students were his most notable characteristics. All of these personal attributes gave him a great power of attracting numerous people of unquestionable natural leadership; thus, he trained many of the pediatric gastroenterologists in South America. Unfortunately, he died on December 28, 1977, at 45 years of age at the apex of his professional career. In spite of his early death, he carried out work sufficiently important to have his name perpetuated in the history of pediatric gastroenterology and nutrition. His philosophy of work is embodied in the Latin American Society of Pediatric Gastroenterology and Nutrition, which he founded in 1974.

Ulysses Fagundes-Neto
Fima Lifshitz

# CONTRIBUTORS

**Eduardo Cichowicz-Emmanuelli, M.D.** Fellow, Pediatric Gastroenterology, Department of Pediatrics, University of Oklahoma Health Sciences Center, and Children's Memorial Hospital, Oklahoma City, Oklahoma

**David A. Cook, Ph.D.** Director Nutritional Science, Mead Johnson Nutritional Division, Evansville, Indiana

**Angel Cordano, M.D., M.P.H., F.A.A.P.** Director, Pediatric Nutrition, Mead Johnson Nutritional Division, Evansville, Indiana

**Ulysses Fagundes-Neto, M.D.** Assistant Professor of Pediatrics, Escola Paulista de Medicina, and Chief, Division of Pediatric Gastroenterology and Nutrition, Sao Paulo, Brazil

**Richard J. Grand, M.D.** Associate Professor of Pediatrics, Harvard Medical School, and Chief, Division of Gastroenterology and Nutrition, The Children's Hospital Medical Center, Boston, Massachusetts

**Leo A. Heitlinger, M.D.** Fellow, State University of New York at Buffalo, and Division of Pediatric Gastroenterology and Nutrition, The Children's Hospital at Buffalo, Buffalo, New York

**Harold W. Hermann, M.D.** Vice President and Medical Director, Mead Johnson Nutritional Division, Evansville, Indiana

**Ian H. Holmes, Ph.D.** Reader in Microbiology, University of Melbourne, Parkville, Victoria, Australia

**Maureen M. Jonas, M.D.** Research Fellow in Pediatrics, Harvard Medical School, and Fellow in Pediatric Gastroenterology and Nutrition, The Children's Hospital Medical Center, Boston, Massachusetts

**Emanuel Lebenthal, M.D.** Professor of Pediatrics, State University of New York at Buffalo, and Chief, Division of Gastroenterology and Nutrition, The Children's Hospital at Buffalo, Buffalo, New York

**P. C. Lee, Ph.D.** Associate Professor of Pediatrics and Biochemistry, State University of New York at Buffalo, and The Children's Hospital at Buffalo, Buffalo, New York

**Carlos H. Lifschitz, M.D.** Instructor of Pediatrics, Baylor College of Medicine, and Consultant, Pediatric Gastroenterology and Nutrition, Texas Children's Hospital, Houston, Texas

**Fima Lifshitz, M.D.** Professor of Pediatrics, Cornell University Medical College, New York, and Associate Director of Pediatrics and Chief, Division of Pediatric Endocrinology, Metabolism and Nutrition, Chief, Pediatric Research, North Shore University Hospital, Manhasset, New York

**Robert K. Montgomery, Ph.D.** Research Associate, Harvard Medical School, and Research Associate in Medicine, The Children's Hospital Medical Center, Boston, Massachusetts

**Buford L. Nichols, Jr., M.D.** Professor of Pediatrics and Physiology, Baylor College of Medicine, and Chief of Pediatric Nutrition and Gastroenterology, Texas Children's Hospital, Houston, Texas

**Veda N. Nichols, R.N., M.P.H.** Research Assistant in Pediatrics, Baylor College of Medicine, and Pediatric Gastroenterology and Nutrition, Texas Children's Hospital, Houston, Texas

**Jay A. Perman, M.D.** Assistant Professor of Pediatrics, University of California, San Francisco, and Associate Chief, Pediatric Gastroenterology Unit, University of California Hospital, San Francisco, California

**Thomas M. Rossi, M.D.** Assistant Professor of Pediatrics, State University of New York at Buffalo, and Division of Gastroenterology and Nutrition, The Children's Hospital at Buffalo, Buffalo, New York

**Saul Teichberg, Ph.D.** Assistant Professor of Pediatrics, Cornell University Medical College, New York, and Head, Electron Microscopy, North Shore University Hospital, Manhasset, New York

**Ramon Torres-Pinedo, M.D.** Professor of Pediatrics, University of Oklahoma, and Chief, Pediatric Gastroenterology Section, Children's Memorial Hospital, Oklahoma City, Oklahoma

**John A. Walker-Smith, M.D., F.R.A.C.P., F.R.C.P.** Reader in Pediatric Gastroenterology, Academic Department of Child Health, Queen Elizabeth Hospital for Children, London, England

**Raul A. Wapnir, Ph.D.** Professor of Biochemistry in Pediatrics, Cornell University Medical College, New York, and Head, Special Studies Laboratory, North Shore University Hospital, Manhasset, New York

**John B. Watkins, M.D.** Associate Professor of Pediatrics, University of Pennsylvania School of Medicine, and Chief, Division of Gastroenterology and Nutrition, The Children's Hospital of Philadelphia, Philadelphia, Pennsylvania

# FOREWORD

Since the beginning of this century, protein feedings and formulas, with simple sugars or sugar-free, have been utilized for the management of diarrhea. It was in the early 1900s that Finkelstein, in Germany, published his observations about the failure of selected infants to tolerate complex sugars, especially after acute diarrhea. Even earlier, empirical dietary changes were utilized for the nutritional rehabilitation of infants with diarrhea and other illnesses. Since those astute early clinical observations, researchers have made impressive gains in the knowledge of infant feedings in health and disease states. Application of this knowledge has helped in some regions of the world to decrease the mortality rate, secondary to severe diarrhea, to a nearly irreducible point. However, much more remains to be learned about the proper nutritional rehabilitation of infants that are premature or suffer from several diseases, including acquired monosaccharide intolerance and cow's milk protein hypersensitivity.

In response to research findings through the past five decades, a number of special formulas for infant feedings have been made available to medical practitioners. In 1911, Mead Johnson introduced its first product, Dextri-Maltose, to help physicians in the dietary rehabilitation of infants who were not able to tolerate milk sugar, as well as those who were not thriving appropriately. The carbohydrate content is the single most important formula ingredient in determining the acceptance and tolerance of the product. Furthermore, a number of infant formulas are now available which contain different types and concentration of other ingredients, including protein and fat. Thus, for rational nutritional rehabilitation, the pediatrician must be familiar with all the possible alterations in specific and generalized dietary intolerances that may occur. Therefore, the pediatrician must also be familiar with the different formulas available for proper prescription in specific instances.

This book focuses on the most recent advances in the knowledge of carbohydrate intolerance in infancy. This most important aspect of infant nutrition and pediatric gastroenterology is reviewed from the vantage point of many well-known experts in the field. Their collective efforts update our knowledge in carbohydrate digestion and tolerance in infancy and, therefore, constitute an important contribution for all those who care for infants. Dr. Lifshitz deserves our thanks for editing this book by a distinguished panel of experts.

**Angel Cordano**

# SYMPOSIUM REFLECTIONS

In this book we have an excellent mixture of results, from clinical and applied research, on the subject of carbohydrate intolerance in infancy, making the contents informative to students of nutrition and pediatrics alike. To the contributors of this book we owe a debt of gratitude.

I am thrilled at the attention being given to the subject of carbohydrate malabsorption, including monosaccharide absorptive defects. In Chapter 2 (Veda N. Nichols) there is a summary of factors which have been found to be higher in incidence in infants with acquired monosaccharide intolerance (AMI). While reading that information, I recalled a classic volume published by Miller and Merritt in 1979.* They summarized maternal practices and their effect upon fetal growth and development. Most of their factors are paralleled by those identified in the AMI patient group. This leads me to conclude that (a) perhaps obstetricians should be included in future seminars on the prevention of diarrhea, malnutrition, and/or acquired monosaccharide intolerance, and (b) infants are not all the same when delivered, but subtle changes may occur in their molecular biological function due to gestational exposures which may result, among other hazards, in increased susceptibility to carbohydrate intolerance in infancy.

I pose for this august group two questions which when answered will make this symposium's results increasingly applicable by the generalist and pediatrician. (a) What is the difference in the risk of generating an immune response to dietary antigens when a protein hydrolysate diet compared to an intact protein diet is used as the first *enteral* feeding to diarrheal patients? (b) How can we clarify the role of bacteria, viruses, antibiotics, enzyme deficits, and allergy to tailor the therapy to the individual patient who has had protracted diarrhea with resultant intestinal mucosa damage?

I trust that the information exchanged in this book will stimulate each of us to further pursuits in search of answers to questions raised regarding carbohydrate intolerance in infancy.

Harold W. Hermann

*Miller, H. C., and Merritt, T. A. (1979). *Fetal Growth in Humans,* Year Book Medical Publishers, Chicago.

*Knowledge is of two kinds. We know a subject ourselves or we
know where we can find information upon it.* (Samuel Johnson)

The subject of carbohydrate intolerance in infancy refers to the alterations
which result from carbohydrate malabsorption. It is not to be confused with
the subject of carbohydrate intolerance which pertains to diabetes mellitus
and/or impaired carbohydrate metabolism. In the past, the latter was referred
to as "glucose intolerance" manifested by hyperglycemia and glycosuria.
Today this syndrome is referred to as "impaired glucose tolerance" of various
types. Thus, this modern nomenclature clearly distinguishes it from the alterations in carbohydrate absorption leading to carbohydrate intolerance,
which is the subject of this book.

Since carbohydrates provide 40–50% of the total calories ingested by infants, there must be an adequate digestion and absorption of these foodstuffs to attain optimum growth and development. Unabsorbed carbohydrates may lead to malnutrition and diarrhea as well as other gastrointestinal
alterations. *Carbohydrate Intolerance in Infancy* brings together the state-of-
the-art knowledge by 23 recognized experts in this field. A particular emphasis is made on the acquired form of carbohydrate intolerance which frequently complicates diarrheal disease of infancy. The presence of carbohydrate intolerance is an important issue to be considered in the nutritional
rehabilitation of the large number of patients who are affected by diarrheal
disease. The epidemiology and pathophysiology of the most severe form of
this complication, namely, acquired monosaccharide intolerance, are discussed
in detail. These patients constitute the majority of infants with chronic diarrhea in hospital wards in developed countries.

The frequent association of carbohydrate intolerance with rotavirus infection and the current state of the "lactase hypothesis" regarding the infectivity
of this virus is also reviewed. The problem of lactose intolerance, lactose malabsorption, and lactase deficiency in infancy is addressed in detail since
lactose, the carbohydrate found in milk, is broadly consumed from birth.
However, other intestinal oligodisaccharidase deficiencies and other carbohydrate intolerance syndromes are also reviewed. These include sucrase-isomaltase deficiency, resulting in sucrose intolerance, and starch intolerance, which
is important in the planning of supplementation with solids or other foodstuffs in infancy. The clinical role of carbohydrate intolerance in the premature infant and in other nondiarrheal syndromes is also discussed.

The dual role of intestinal microflora in the syndrome of carbohydrate intolerance is brought to light. On the one hand, proliferation of fecal and colonic bacteria resulting from malabsorbed carbohydrates may be injurious to the bowel. On the other hand, colonic flora may assist in the metabolism of unabsorbed carbohydrates and alleviate some of the symptoms of carbohydrate intolerance. The kinetic effects of malabsorbed carbohydrates on water secretion and the possible modes of correcting these derangements are reviewed.

The possible relationships between carbohydrate intolerance and protein hypersensitivity are examined. This topic includes reviews of the clinical association of lactose intolerance with cow's milk protein hypersensitivity, the potential role of unabsorbed lactose in stimulating intestinal macromolecular absorption that could lead to antigen uptake, and the production of hypersensitivity in a susceptible host, as well as the role of oligodisaccharides in soy protein intolerance.

Finally, the use of breath hydrogen testing in diarrheal disease for the diagnosis of carbohydrate intolerance, and the use of different infant formulas available for treatment of carbohydrate intolerance are discussed.

The recent advances in our understanding of carbohydrate intolerance in infancy are many, but much remains to be learned. The symposium held at Key Largo, Florida, in January 1982, sponsored by Mead Johnson Nutritional Division, brought together the contributors of this book in an attempt to integrate current knowledge and to disseminate it to the practicing physician and to others who care for infants.

I am grateful to Dr. Angel Cordano and Mr. David Wallace as well as to all other directors of Mead Johnson for all their efforts and support in organizing this symposium and in the publication of this volume. I also acknowledge the contribution of my former and present associates who have published with me much of our work in this field, Drs. Gerald H. Holman, Pedro Coello-Ramirez, Gillermo Guttierrez Topete, Raul A. Wapnir, Saul Teichberg, Mrs. Silvia Diaz Bensussen, and Mary Ann Bayne. Similarly, I want to thank those who behind the scenes have been instrumental in allowing us to pursue this work: Drs. Herbert C. Miller, Gonzalo Gutierrez Trujillo, and Mervin Silverberg. For secretarial assistance thanks to Jan M. Coyle, Cynthia Aquila, and Lauren Strand.

Progress to date on the subject of carbohydrate intolerance in infancy, as documented in this book, is impressive. However, we are only at the threshold of the acquisition of greater knowledge in infant nutrition. Those who wish to learn may find in this volume substantive information which may help in the nutritional rehabilitation and the care of their patients.

**Fima Lifshitz**

# CONTENTS

# CARBOHYDRATE INTOLERANCE IN INFANCY

# PERSPECTIVES OF CARBOHYDRATE INTOLERANCE IN INFANTS WITH DIARRHEA

FIMA LIFSHITZ
*Cornell University Medical College, New York
and North Shore Univesrity Hospital, Manhasset, New York*

Milk is the major food of infancy. Therefore, lactose, the carbohydrate found in milk, is broadly consumed from the time of birth. However, it is well known that there may be lactose malabsorption in the immediate neonatal period and beyond 3-5 years in many ethnic groups (1,2). This is due to a widespread selective ontogenetic lactase deficiency now considered to be the normal state of mankind (3,4). In mammals the ontogenetic changes in intestinal lactase activity from high levels at birth, to decreased levels at the time of weaning, diminishing to trace levels in the adult has been known to occur since the early part of this century (Chapters 4, 6). It was then recognized that younger calves had a greater concentration of lactase activity in the small intestine than older ones (5,6). This ontogenetic sequence of events, with low adult lactase levels, occurs in all but a few ethnic and racial groups of mankind. They are the minority of the world's population and include some caucasians from Europe, Mongols of Central Asia, and some African tribes (1-4). These people tolerate lactose after childhood, and their small intestinal lactase activity during adulthood is similar to the levels found in infancy.

In individuals with ontogenetic lactase deficiency, lactose malabsorption is usually a clinically insignificant problem. This applies to both adults and newborn infants who may drink intermediate levels of milk without any symptoms (7,8) (Chapters 4 and 5). In contrast, in patients with acquired or secondary intestinal surface oligodisaccharidase deficiencies, due to jejunal mucosal damage induced by a large number of disease processes, there is often carbohydrate intolerance (9-11). Under these conditions there is usually a rapid disappearance of lactase with secondary lactose intolerance, and eventually, a slow reappearance of lactase and lactose tolerance after recovery from the initial insult (Chapter 6). The most frequent alteration in infancy which is associated with acquired carbohydrate intolerance is diarrheal disease (12). This association was first recognized in the early 1900s in infants who could not tolerate cow's milk formula following gastroenteritis (13-15). At that time it was postulated that milk intolerance following gastroenteritis was due to some deficit in the ferments necessary for the hydrolysis of lactose. Today we know that carbohydrate intolerance is a ubiquitous complication of diarrheal disease and that it may cause a large number of deleterious alterations (16). When carbohydrate intolerance occurs, dietary treatment is usually necessary for clinical improvement (12).

Thus, acquired lactose intolerance secondary to infectious gastroenteritis in infants poses important questions concerning proper feeding regimens. The Committee on Nutrition of the American Academy of Pediatrics has recommended that malnourished infants, not on human milk, should be fed a lactose-free diet as the initial feeding during severe diarrhea (17). However, the recommendation to restrict dietary foodstuffs may lead to other complications. For example, cow's milk substitutes like soy may have a high allergenicity (Chapter 13), and its prolonged use may also result in other nutritional complications (18,19). Moreover, a therapeutic recommendation for a group of patients in this country may be a most difficult taks to implement elsewhere; lactose-free diets may not be readily available where diarrheal disease and malnutrition are most prevalent. Therefore, the manner in which the nutritional needs of these patients are safely and effectively met during the acute phase of diarrhea as well as during recovery requires more attention.

In this chapter a review is made of some of the factors that influence the clinical expression and the degree of carbohydrate intolerance in diarrheal disease of infancy. The consequences of cow's milk feedings during the acute stage of illness and after recovery is also assessed. This is done in order to provide guidelines to the clinician for the nutritional management of infants with diarrheal disease. The reader is referred elsewhere for other comprehensive reviews of the subject (8–11,16).

## Carbohydrate Intolerance in Diarrheal Disease

### Clinical Expression

Acquired carbohydrate intolerance is a clinical syndrome characterized by diarrhea with acid stools and carbohydrate in feces. It is a very frequent sequelae of acute gastroenteritis and it has been observed in 78% of a large group of infants with severe diarrhea (12), as well as in infants with mild gastroenteritis which did not lead to dehydration (20). There is a great variation in the clinical expression of this syndrome. Patients with gastroenteritis have different degrees of carbohydrate malabsorption and the symptoms may also differ (21). Even the same patient may vary in his capacity to tolerate carbohydrates at different stages of the duration of the illness (12) (Chapter 11). Some of the reported differences in degree of malabsorption may be attributed to the sensitivity of the tests to diagnose carbohydrate intolerance. The use of simple semiquantitative methods to measure the presence of reducing substances, glucose, and the pH of the stools may be fraught with error produced by testing nonfresh stool specimens (22). In milder cases of carbohydrate intolerance, there may be diarrhea without excretion of acid stools and/or carbohydrates in feces (12). More sensitive diagnostic methods, such as measurements of breath hydrogen excretion, may improve the sensitivity and surveillance of carbohydrate intolerance in infancy (Chapter 3).

Carbohydrate intolerance in infants with diarrhea is usually specific for lactose. This may be due to the fact that lactase is the most vulnerable jejunal enzyme; it is the most superficial of the brush-border oligodisaccharidases, its activity is rate limiting for the absorption of lactose, and its concentrations are considerably lower than other brush-border enzymes (23). However, lactose intolerance may also be due to the possible relationship between rotavirus, which frequently causes diarrhea in infancy, and intestinal lactase, which may be the receptor for infantile gastroenteritis viruses (Chapter 7).

Carbohydrate intolerance in infants with diarrhea may also involve other disaccharides and at times it may even include all carbohydrates (12,24) (Chapter 6). The degree of carbohydrate intolerance to the different dietary disaccharides and/or monosaccharides is more inclusive and more severe in children with severe diarrhea with underlying malnutrition than it is in well-nourished patients with mild diarrhea (20). Usually the problem is temporary with complete recovery after improvement of the disease. However, at times it may be associated with, or be the cause of, chronic diarrhea and monosaccharide intolerance (24) (Chapters 2 and 8).

Pathophysiology

The major cause of diarrhea in carbohydrate malabsorption is the presence of osmotically active carbohydrate and fermentative products within the lumen of the bowel (Chapter 9). It has been shown that 42–75% of a lactose load is recovered in the ileum of a lactase-deficient individual, whereas only 8–10% may be present in normal controls (25). The osmotic load of the unabsorbed carbohydrate results in secretion of fluid and electrolytes into the small intestinal lumen (26). Thus the volume of the chyme increases (27). In addition, there is a loss of mucosal cells and intestinal disaccharidases (28). Even under isotonic conditions, the presence of unabsorbed lactose may interfere with intestinal absorption (Chapter 9) and may be associated with proliferation of fecal and colonic bacteria in the upper segments of the small intestine (Chapter 10). Moreover, intestinal bacterial fermentation of the unabsorbed carbohydrates further increases the osmotic pressure and produces large quantities of hydrogen gas and organic acids (29). Increased intestinal volume may also lead to motility alterations and exacerbate diarrhea (26). Therefore, the liquid stools seen in carbohydrate intolerance are characterized by an acid pH due to organic acids, and by the presence of unabsorbed sugar. Also there may be a high level of $H_2$ production (Chapter 3). The elimination of the unabsorbed sugar from the diet very often breaks the cycle and a lessening of the diarrhea results regardless of the etiology of the disease.

Factors Influencing the Degree of Carbohydrate Intolerance

The factors that tend to minimize or maximize the problem of carbohydrate intolerance are shown in Figure 1. Variations in the degree of damage produced by the intestinal infection, the type and quantity of feedings, the

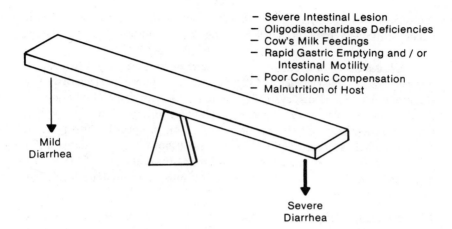

- Severe Intestinal Lesion
- Oligodisaccharidase Deficiencies
- Cow's Milk Feedings
- Rapid Gastric Emptying and / or
  Intestinal Motility
- Poor Colonic Compensation
- Malnutrition of Host

Mild
Diarrhea

Severe
Diarrhea

**Figure 1** Factors that tend to minimize or maximize carbohydrate intolerance in diarrheal disease.

effectiveness of compensatory mechanisms of the host, and the bacterial flora, present at any one time, will minimize or maximize the degree of carbohydrate intolerance.

*Intestinal Lesion*   Once intestinal mucosal integrity is altered by any agent which induces diarrheal disease, the result is depression of brush-border oligodisaccharidases and intestinal transport derangements which may lead to carbohydrate intolerance involving one or several dietary sugars (30,31). Diarrhea resulting from intestinal infection with organisms which invade the jejunal mucosa, and disrupt the enterocyte producing an inflammatory response, is more likely to be associated with carbohydrate intolerance (30, 31). In contrast, when the disease is produced by enterotoxins which do not damage the jejunal epithelium, there may be no major alteration in carbohydrate absorption. Carbohydrate intolerance in infancy is often seen in rotavirus-induced diarrhea. This may be due to viral infection of gut epithelium rich in lactase, inducing functional and morphological damage of the small intestine (Chapter 7). Jejunal mucosal damage in diarrheal disease may also result from products of jejunal bacterial metabolic activity acting upon foodstuffs and host secretions. Among the bacterially generated factors which are injurious to the small intestine are deconjugated bile salts, short-chain organic acids, hydroxy fatty acids, and alcohol (30).

Small intestinal mucosal lesions in diarrheal disease may also result in luminal hyperosmolar gradients (32), and from protein hypersensitivity (33) (Chapters 11-13). Other systemic complications, such as dehydration and shock, may also play a role inducing small bowel injury. Similarly, the presence of generalized protein calorie malnutrition or specific nutritional deficiencies, that is, iron, may also lead to small bowel mucosal damage (34-36). Whatever the mechanism, severe intestinal mucosal damage with marked intestinal disaccharidase deficiencies will maximize carbohydrate intolerance in diarrheal disease.

*Feedings*  It has long been recognized that feedings play an important role in the evolution of diarrheal disease. A patient with diarrhea may improve his stool losses with fasting, and the elimination of unabsorbed carbohydrate usually results in amelioration of diarrhea regardless of the primary etiology of the disease (12,37). It is also known that infants fed human milk have a decreased incidence and severity of diarrhea and carbohydrate intolerance (38-41). On the other hand, unmodified cow's milk feedings lead to more severe intolerance to milk and/or carbohydrate intolerance (12-15). Recent evidence suggests that feedings with more processed, modern, low-solute cow's milk may improve tolerance in postenteritis of infancy (Chapter 11). The amount and frequency of formula feedings may also influence the response of the patient. A constant nasogastric administration of milk formulas may improve tolerance as compared with oral bolus feedings (42). The amount, concentration, and quantity of cow's milk formula feedings may determine the presence and the severity of lactose intolerance and other complications such as metabolic acidosis (43). "Overfeeding" and hyperosmolar feedings have been associated with severe complications resulting from carbohydrate intolerance such as necrotizing enterocolitis (44-46). It has long been known that pneumatosis intestinalis and monosaccharide intolerance is more frequent among infants with diarrhea who have lactose intolerance and continue being fed lactose-containing milk formulas (24,47).

Feedings may also exert an indirect influence, which may minimize or maximize carbohydrate intolerance, through alterations in intestinal absorption and disaccharidase activities (48). The type of oligodisaccharidase deficiencies secondary to diarrheal disease may be related to the dietary manipulations that such patients receive during their illness. Under experimental conditions of chronic hyperosmotic diarrhea in rats, the intestinal oligodisaccharidases were altered in relation to the specific disaccharide represented in the diet (49). Feedings may also influence the general health of the patient with diarrhea. These patients may have a more rapid recovery and a better body weight when fed, as compared with those who are fasted (50). Similarly, feedings per se have a positive effect on intestinal function and structure even when nutrition is kept up by parenteral nutrition (42). In Chapter 9 evidence is presented regarding other compensatory mechanisms whereby the intestine may improve water fluxes across the intestine by lumenal glucose and/or amino acids despite the presence of unabsorbed lactose. The principles of this phenomenon have long been recognized and utilized for oral rehydration therapy in diarrheal disease. Thus, feedings per se, as well as intake of specific food components, may influence the clinical expression of carbohydrate intolerance in infants with diarrhea.

*Gastric Emptying and Intestinal Motility*   The effects of gastric emptying and intestinal motility on carbohydrate intolerance in diarrheal disease have not been clearly defined. It has been shown that lactose empties from the stomach faster in subjects with lactase deficiency that equivalent loads of other carbohydrates (51). Therefore, the possibility exists that cow's milk formulas containing lactose might empty more rapidly in conditions of hypolactasia than do other sugar-containing formulas. One might speculate that rapid gastric emptying may play a role in the development of carbohydrate intolerance in infants with diarrhea who were fed cow's milk formulas. In other conditions, such as after gastric surgery, when gastric emptying of liquids is rapid, lactose malabsorption may be unmasked (52,53). In addition, rapid intestinal transit has been found when there is unabsorbed lactose in the intestinal lumen (26,54,55). However, the question of whether the altered intestinal transit in diarrheal disease may itself further impair absorption of lactose and fluid has not been answered. The effects of different formula feedings on these parameters also remain to be evaluated.

*Colonic Compensation*   There may be colonic compensation resulting in amelioration of carbohydrate intolerance (Chapters 4 and 10). Enteric microflora may play both harmful and beneficial roles in the intestinal ecosystem. There may be types of colonic bacterial flora which assist in the hydrolysis of the unabsorbed carbohydrate and alleviate some of the symptoms of carbohydrate intolerance (56). The colon also has the ability to absorb gaseous by-products of lactose fermentation. Finally, colonic reabsorption of water and electrolytes plays a role in determining the presence and severity of diarrhea (57,58). However, how these properties of colonic function may be affected in diarrheal disease of infancy has not been determined.

*General Host Factors*  There may be general host factors such as age and nutrition which may influence the presence or absence of carbohydrate intolerance. Age and the nutritional status of the patient are important factors in determining whether diarrhea occurs and its severity (59). In a malnourished host there are numerous abnormalities in the digestive absorptive function which may result in carbohydrate intolerance and diarrheal disease (60, 61). The type of malnutrition is also important; children with Kwashiorkor may have more severe abnormalities of the small intestine and disaccharidase deficiencies than those with marasmus (35,35).

## Consequences of Milk Feedings in Diarrheal Disease

Human breast milk feedings should be continued in infants with diarrhea since they usually tolerate these feedings well (38–41). Moreover, human milk provides other immunological advantages that may help in the treatment of infectious diarrhea (62). Only very rarely may there be intolerance to human milk in diarrheal disease (63,64). Therefore, the pediatrician must weigh carefully the use of these feedings and permit consumption in accordance with clinical courses. In contrast, the soundness of using cow's milk in patients with acute gastroenteritis should be questioned (17), since these patients often have carbohydrate intolerance, their disease is more severe and is prolonged by milk feedings (12). It is almost 15 years since we did a prospective study to evaluate the outcome of infants with diarrhea while fed cow's milk formula (12). In this study there were 332 infants with severe gastroenteritis who were fed cow's milk formula as follows: in 128 of these patients a lactose-free formula, with an alternate carbohydrate, was substituted in the first 3 weeks of diarrhea when the severity of the disease did not permit the physician to continue feedings. The remaining 204 infants received milk for up to 3 weeks of their illness. Dietary treatment was given to the 67 of the 204 who continued with diarrhea after that period of time.

The duration and the severity of diarrhea was positively correlated with the capacity to tolerate lactose during the illness (Fig. 2). The patients who were able to tolerate lactose had a short diarrheal illness, and all but two recovered uneventfully while receiving a milk formula within less than 3 weeks of diarrhea. In contrast, the lactose-intolerant infants had a more severe diarrheal course which lasted longer; often their illness did not improve until milk formula feedings were changed to a formula with a different carbohydrate source. One-third of the infants with mild and two-thirds of those with severe

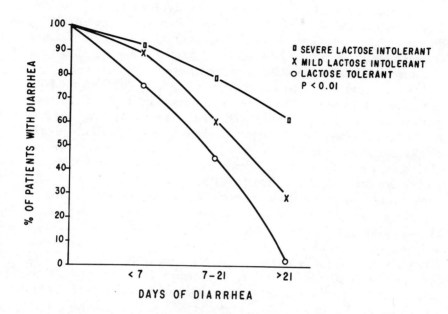

**Figure 2**  Duration of diarrhea in patients receiving milk formula. The percentages of patients who persisted with loose stools at different time intervals, corrected for the number of infants who died or who were removed for dietary therapy at each interval. Of 77 lactose-tolerant patients (o—o), 3 died before the diarrhea ceased and 2 were given dietary treatment after 21 days. Of 195 infants with mild lactose intolerance (x—x), 3 died before recovery and 81 were given dietary treatment. Of 60 patients with severe lactose intolerance (□—□), 2 died and 45 required dietary treatment. The proportions of patients with persistent diarrhea in each group were significantly different from one another ($P<0.01$). Dietary treatment before 3 weeks of diarrhea was required when the disease was severe. Further details of this study are discussed elsewhere (12).

lactose intolerance had diarrhea for more than 3 weeks while on milk formula. Moreover, all patients who required dietary treatment during the first 3 weeks of their illness were infants who exhibited lactose intolerance. However, it is worth pointing out that there were spontaneous recoveries in many patients who were lactose intolerant even while receiving a milk formula. This is not surprising, since it is known that diarrheal disease is often a self-limiting disorder, but the data does provide evidence of the high cost of milk formula feedings in infantile gastroenteritis, since the diarrhea is more prolonged and more severe in those who exhibit lactose intolerance.

The high frequency of lactose intolerance has been confirmed in infants with mild gastroenteritis (20), as well as in many other groups of diarrheal patients throughout the world (65–69). These observations have also confirmed the deleterious role of lactose in gastroenteritis, particularly in malnourished children with diarrhea. Moreover, the use of a lactose-free formula as an initial choice for infants less than 1 year of age with acute gastroenteritis has significantly reduced the duration and severity of diarrhea (70). We think it is reasonable that the severity and duration of diarrhea is correlated with the presence of carbohydrate intolerance. The volume of water excreted by patients with unabsorbed carbohydrates may be up to three times that of an isotonic solution of the carbohydrate present in the bowel (26). Therefore, diarrhea will persist for as long as unabsorbed carbohydrate is present in the diet; when this is eliminated, or when improvement in the intestinal absorption occurs due to improvement of the illness, a prompt recovery of diarrhea may ensue. The loss of fluid and electrolytes induced by milk formula feedings is also accompanied by generation of an excess of hydrogen ions and organic acids due to a bacterial carbohydrate fermentation. This may stimulate excretion and loss of bicarbonate inducing metabolic acidosis, the hallmark of severe diarrheal disease (43).

The losses of unabsorbed carbohydrates while fed milk formula in diarrheal disease of infancy may also account for considerable caloric deficits; 40–50% of the total calories are derived from dietary carbohydrates. Therefore, the general nutritional status of an infant with carbohydrate intolerance is at stake. Even if the diarrhea is mild, the presence of lactose intolerance is associated with significant body weight deficits (20), the presence of unabsorbed carbohydrates and diarrhea also enhances fat and nitrogen losses (71), further compromising the nutritional status of the host, particularly in infants with marginal dietary intakes.

Continuing dietary intolerance and nutrient losses not only impair the infant's ability to recover from the intestinal illness, but also may increase the susceptibility to other conditions and further deteriorate intestinal function. Clinically, this may result in pneumatosis intestinalis (47), and in aggravation of diarrhea and carbohydrate intolerance (12,24). A patient with lactose intolerance may become intolerant to other disaccharides, and if the diarrhea persists for a longer period, then monosaccharide intolerance may ensue (Chapter 8). Additionally, there may be a relationship between lactose intolerance in diarrheal disease and the development of milk protein hypersensitivity as discussed in detail in Chapters 11–13.

## Final Considerations

The above data linking cow's milk feedings with the development of many complications of diarrheal disease of infancy raises issues of interest. The need to meet the nutritional requirements of an infant with diarrhea may introduce risks which may even be greater than the disease itself. On the other hand, failure to provide adequate nutrition because of inappropriate diets or prolonged "bowel rest" may result in a high nutritional cost at a critical stage in the development of the infant. Meeting the nutritional requirements of patients with gastroenteritis and during the immediate recovery period in a safe and effective manner deserves more attention. The pediatrician, nutritionist, and other health-related personnel must take up this challenge in a rational and scientific fashion.

Patients who have severe diarrhea and who excrete stools of an acid pH and containing carbohydrates must be treated promptly to avoid complications. However, since there may be variations in the clinical expression of the syndrome, which result from variations in any one of several factors involved in the absorption and metabolism of carbohydrates as discussed above, there may be patients who require dietary treatment even when no overt signs of carbohydrate intolerance are documented. By means of the breath hydrogen testing, it may be feasible to demonstrate carbohydrate malabsorption complicating diarrheal disease in these cases (Chapter 3), so that a prompt diagnosis and treatment is instituted. The use of a lactose-free formula as the initial feeding for infants with gastroenteritis who are not on breast milk is recommended (17), since lactose intolerance is a very frequent complication (12,20,65–69). This simple dietary elimination of lactose may result in a decreased severity and duration of the diarrhea (70), at the onset, before other complications develop. This is important to improve the eventual outcome of the disease, as it is not known why some patients with diarrhea recover uneventfully while others progress to monosaccharide intolerance (12,

24) and other complications (16). The elimination of lactose from the diet of these patients should be for a brief period, since carbohydrate tolerance is recovered rapidly once there is improvement of the disease (31). Moreover, the elimination of dietary carbohydrates for prolonged periods may, in itself, perpetuate altered carbohydrate absorption (49); the presence of lactose in the diet may be necessary for restoration of normal bowel flora which may oppose potentially enteropathogenic infections.

The infant formulas available for management of carbohydrate intolerance are reviewed in Chapter 16 and elsewhere (72). The nutritional management of infants with diarrhea, including feeding strategies, is also reviewed in detail elsewhere (73). However, it is worth pointing out that those recommendations should be limited to infants receiving cow's milk formulas as those who receive human milk exhibit an improved tolerance even when sick with diarrhea (38-41). Further studies should be done to ascertain the reasons for the decreased incidence of lactose intolerance, despite the high lactose content, of human milk. This is important to develop more "humanized milk" formulas for infants who are not fortunate enough to be breast-fed. There is evidence that the more processed modern formulas have already improved "tolerance" during diarrhea as compared with previous cow's milk formulas (Chapter 11). On the other hand, soy protein formulas which are lactose-free could also be allergenic (Chapter 13). Similarly, further studies must be done to learn how to supply appropriate formula substitutes for the rehabilitation of infants with diarrhea, especially when breast milk feedings are not feasible. The implementation of dietary lactose elimination may be a most difficult undertaking where malnutrition and diarrhea are most prevalent.

## References

1. Paige, D. M., and Bayless, T. M. (1981). Lactose digestion. Clinical and nutritional implications. Johns Hopkins Univ. Press, Baltimore.
2. Johnson, J. D., Kretchmer, N., and Simoons, F. J. (1974). Lactose malabsorption: its biology and history. *Adv. Pediatr. 21*:191–237.
3. Simoons, F. J., Johnson, J. D., and Kretchmer, N. (1977). Perspective on milk-drinking and malabsorption of lactose. *Pediatrics 59*:98–110.
4. Kretchmer, N. (1972). Lactose and lactase. *Sci. Am. 227* (4):70–78.
5. Mendel, L. B., and Mitchell, P. H. (1907). Chemical studies on growth. I. The inverting enzymes of the alimentary tract, especially in the embryo. *Am. J. Physiol. 20*:81–95.

6.  Plimmer, R. H. A. (1907). On the presence of lactase in the intestine of animals and on the adaptation of the intestine to lactose. *J. Physiol. (Lond.) 35*:20–31.
7.  Lisker, R., Aguilar, L., and Zavala, C. (1978). Intestinal lactase deficiency and milk drinking capacity in the adult. *Am. J. Clin. Nutr. 31*: 1499–1503.
8.  Lifshitz, F. (1980). Carbohydrate malabsorption. In *Clinical Disorders in Pediatric Gastroenterology and Nutrition,* F. Lifshitz (Ed.), Marcel Dekker, New York, pp. 229–246.
9.  Lifshitz, F. (1977). Carbohydrate problems in paediatric gastroenterology. *Clin. Gastroenterol. 6*:415–429.
10. Lifshitz, F. (1980). Secondary carbohydrate intolerance in infancy. In *Clinical Disorders in Pediatric Gastroenterology and Nutrition,* F. Lifshitz (Ed.), Marcel Dekker, New York, pp. 327–340.
11. Lifshitz, F. (1982). Disaccharide intolerance. In *Food Intolerance,* R. K. Chandra (Ed.), Elsevier-North Holland, Amsterdam, in press.
12. Lifshitz, F., Coello-Ramirez, P., Gutierrez-Topete, G., and Cornado-Cornet, M. C. (1971). Carbohydrate intolerance in infants with diarrhea. *J. Pediatr. 79*:760–767.
13. Jacobi, A. (1901). Milk sugar in infant feeding. *Trans. Am. Pediatr. Soc. 13*:150–160.
14. Finkelstein, H., and Meyer, L. F. (1911). Zur Tecknik und Indikation der Ernahrung mit Eiweissilch. *Munch. Med. Wochenschr. 58*:340–345.
15. Howland, J. (1921). Prolonged intolerance of carbohydrates. *Trans. Am. Pediatr. Soc. 33*:11–19.
16. Lifshitz, F. (1981). Acquired carbohydrate intolerance in children: Clinical manifestations and therapeutic recommendations. In *Lactose Digestion. Clinical and Nutritional Implications,* D. M. Paige and T. M. Bayless (Eds.), Johns Hopkins Univ. Press, Baltimore.
17. Barness, L. (Ed.). (1979). *Pediatric Nutrition Handbook,* American Academy of Pediatrics, Evanston, Ill., p. 385.
18. Hoff, N., Haddad, J., Teitelbaum, S., McAlister, W., and Hillman, L. S. 25-Hydroxyvitamin D serum concentrations in rickets of extremely premature human infants. *J. Pediatr. 94*:460–466.
19. Borum, P. R. (1981). Possible carnitine requirement of the newborn and the effect of genetic disease on the carnitine requirement. *Nutr. Rev. 39*: 385–390.
20. Kumar, V., Chandrasekaran, R., and Bhaskar, R. (1977). Carbohydrate intolerance associated with acute gastroenteritis. *Clin. Pediatr. 16*:1123–1127.

21. Torun, B., Solomons, N. W., and Viteri, F. E. (1979). Lactose malabsorption and lactose intolerance: implications for general milk consumption. *Arch. Lat. Am. Nutr.* 29:445–494.

22. Lifshitz, F. (1975). Clinical studies in diarrheal disease and malnutrition associated with carbohydrate intolerance. *Proc. IX International Congress Nutrition,* A. Chavez, H. Bourges, and S. Gasta (Eds.), S. Karger, Basel, pp. 173–181.

23. Gray, G. M. (1975). Carbohydrate digestion and absorption. Role of the small intestine. *N. Engl. J. Med. 292*:1225–1230.

24. Lifshitz, F., Coello-Ramirez, P., and Gutierrez-Topete, G. (1970). Monosaccharide intolerance and hypoglycemia in infants with diarrhea. I. Clinical course of 23 cases. *J. Pediatr. 77*:595–603.

25. Bond, J. H., and Levitt, M. D. (1976). Quantitative measurement of lactose absorption. *Gastroenterology 70*:1058–1062.

26. Launiala, K. (1968). The effect of unabsorbed sucrose and mannitol on the small intestinal flow rate and mean transit time. *Scand. J. Gastroenterol. 39*:665–671.

27. Christopher, N. L., and Bayless, T. M. (1971). Role of the small bowel and colon in lactose-induced diarrhea. *Gastroenterology 60*:845–852.

28. Teichberg, S., Lifshitz, F., Pergolizzi, R., and Wapnir, R. A. (1978). Response of rat intestine to a hyperosmotic feeding. *Pediatr. Res. 12*: 720–725.

29. Ingelfinger, F. J. (1967). Malabsorption: The clinical background. *Fed. Proc. 26*:1388–1390.

30. Lifshitz, F. (1977). The enteric flora in childhood disease—diarrhea. *Am. J. Clin. Nutr. 30*:1811–1818.

31. Lifshitz, F., Coello-Ramirez, P., and Contreras-Gutierrez, M. L. (1971). The response of infants to carbohydrate oral loads after recovery from diarrhea. *J. Pediatr. 79*:612–617.

32. Teichberg, S., Lifshitz, F., Pergolizzi, R., and Wapnir, R. A. (1978). Response of rat intestine to a hyperosmotic feeding. *Pediatr. Res. 12*: 720–725.

33. Iyngkaran, N., Abdin, Z., Davi, K., Boey, C. G., Prathrap, K., Yadar, M., Lam, S. K., and Puthucheary, S. D. (1979). Acquired carbohydrate intolerance and cow's milk protein-sensitive enteropathy in young infants. *J. Pediatr. 95*:373–378.

34. Stanfield, J. P., Hutt, M. S. R., and Tunnicliffe, R. (1965). Intestinal biopsy in Kwashiorkor. *Lancet 2*:519–523.

35. Brunser, O., Reid, A., and Monckeberg, R. G. F. (1968). Jejunal mucosa in infant malnutrition. *Am. J. Clin. Nutr. 21*:976–983.

36. Sriratanaban, A., and Thayer, W. R. (1971). Small intestinal disaccharidase activities in experimental iron and protein deficiency. *Am. J. Clin. Nutr. 24*:411–415.

37. Burke, V., Kerez, K. R., and Anderson, C. M. (1965). The relationship of dietary lactose to refractory diarrhea in infancy. *Aust. Pediatr. J. 1*: 147–160.

38. Woodbury, R. M. (1922). The relation between breast and artificial feeding and infant mortality. *Am. J. Hyg. 2*:668–687.

39. Mata, L. J., and Urrutia, J. J. (1971). Intestinal colonization of breast fed children in a rural area of low socioeconomic level. *Ann. N.Y. Acad. Sci. 176*:93–109.

40. Okuni, M., Okinaga, K., and Baba, K. (1972). Studies on reducing sugars in stools of acute infantile diarrhea, with special reference to differences between breast-fed and artificially fed babies. *Tohoku J. Exp. Med. 107*: 395–402.

41. Brown, K. H., Parry, L., Khatun, M., and Ahmed, M. G. (1979). Lactose malabsorption in Bangladesh village children: relation with age, history of recent diarrhea, nutritional status and breast feeding. *Am. J. Clin. Nutr. 32*:1962–1969.

42. Green, H. L., McCabe, D. R., and Merenstein, G. B. (1975). Protracted diarrhea and malnutrition in infancy: changes in intestinal morphology and disaccharidase activities during treatment with total intravenous nutrition or oral elemental diets. *J. Pediatr. 87*:695–704.

43. Lugo-de-Rivera, C., Rodriguez, H., and Torres-Pinedo, R. (1972). Studies on the mechanism of sugar malabsorption in infantile infectious diarrhea. *Am. J. Clin. Nutr. 25*:1248–1253.

44. Willis, D. M., Chabot, J., Radde, I. C., and Chance, G. W. (1977). Unsuspected hyperosmolality of oral solutions contributing to necrotizing enterocolitis in very-low-birth-weight infants. *Pediatrics 60*:535–538.

45. Book, L. S., Herbst, J. J., Atherton, S. O., and Jung, A. L. (1975). Necrotizing enterocolitis in low-birth-weight infants fed an elemental formula. *J. Pediatr. 87*:602–605.

46. Goldman, H. I. (1980). Feeding and necrotizing enterocolitis. *Am. J. Dis. Child. 134*:553–555.

47. Coello-Ramirez, P., Gutierrez-Topete, G., and Lifshitz, F. (1970). Pnematosis intestinalis. *Am. J. Dis. Child. 120*:3–9.

48. Knudsen, K. B., Bellamy, H. M., Lelocq, F. R., Bradley, E. M., and Welsh, J. D. (1968). Effect of fasting and refeeding on the histology and disaccharidase activity of the human intestine. *Gastroenterology 55*:46.

49. Pergolizzi, R., Lifshitz, F., Teichberg, S., and Wapnir, R. A. (1977). Interaction between dietary carbohydrates and intestinal disaccharidases in experimental diarrhea. *Am. J. Clin. Nutr. 30*:482–489.

50. Chung, A. W., and Viscorova, B. (1948). The effect of early oral feeding versus early oral starvation on the course of infantile diarrhea. *J. Pediatr. 33*:14.

51. Welsh, J. D., and Hall, W. H. (1977). Gastric emptying of lactose and milk in subjects with lactose malabsorption. *Am. J. Dig. Dis. 22*:1060–1063.
52. Bank, S., Barbezat, G. O., and Marks, I. N. (1966). Postgastrectomy steatorrhea due to intestinal lactase deficiency. *South Afr. Med. J. 40*: 597–599.
53. Gudmand-Hoyer, E. (1969). Lactose malabsorption after gastric surgery. *Digestion 2*:289–297.
54. Bond, J. H., and Levitt, M. D. (1975). Investigation of small bowel transit time in man utilizing pulmonary hydrogen ($H_2$) measurements. *J. Lab. Clin. Med. 85*:546–555.
55. Debongnie, J. C., Newcomer, A. D., McGill, D. B., and Phillips, S. F. (1979). Absorption of nutrients in lactase deficiency. *Dig. Dis. Sci. 24*: 225–231.
56. Gallagher, C. R., Molleson, A. L., and Caldwell, J. H. (1974). Lactose intolerance and fermented dairy products. *J. Am. Diet. Assoc. 65*: 418–419.
57. Bond, J. H., and Levitt, M. D. (1976). Fate of soluble carbohydrate in the colon of rats and man. *J. Clin. Invest. 57*:1158–1164.
58. Ruppin, H., Bar-Meir, S., Soergel, K. H., Wood, C. M., and Schmitt, Jr., M. G. (1980). Absorption of short chain fatty acids by the colon. *Gastroenterology 78*:1500–1507.
59. Gordon, J. E. (1971). Diarrheal disease of early childhood—world wide scope of the problem. Part 1. Factors determining host susceptibility and response to neonatal gastroenteritis. *Ann. N.Y. Acad. Sci. 176*: 9–15.
60. Fagundes-Neto, U. (1980). Malnutrition and the intestine. In *Clinical Disorders in Pediatric Gastroenterology and Nutrition,* F. Lifshitz (Ed.), Marcel Dekker, New York, pp. 249–266.
61. Lifshitz, F., Teichberg, S., and Wapnir, R. A. (1981). Malnutrition and the intestine. In *Nutrition and Child Health Perspectives for the 1980's,* R. C. Tsang and B. L. Nichols (Eds.), Alan R. Liss, New York, pp. 1–24.
62. Coello-Ramirez, P., Garcia-Cortes, M. J., Diaz-Bensussen, S., Domingues-Camacho, C., and Zuniga, V. (1977). Tratamiento con calostro humano a ninos con gastroenteritis infecciosa prolongada. *Bol. Med. Hosp. Inf. 34*:487–506.
63. Goel, K., Lifshitz, F., Kahn, E., and Teichberg, S. (1978). Monosaccharide intolerance and soy-protein hypersensitivity in an infant with diarrhea. *J. Pediatr. 93*:617–619.
64. King, F. (1972). Intolerance to lactose in mother's milk. *Lancet 2*:335.
65. Chandrasekaran, R., Kumar, V., Walia, V. N. S., and Moorthy, B. (1975). Carbohydrate intolerance in infants with acute diarrhea and its complications. *Acta. Paediatr. Scand. 64*:483–488.

66. Mokhtar, N. A., and Ghaly, I. M. (1974). Lactose intolerance, a cause of recurrent diarrhea in Kuwait. *Gaz. Egypt. Paediatr. Assoc.* 22:113–118.
67. Solomons, N. H., Viteri, F. E., and Rosenberg, I. H. (1978). Development of an interval sampling hydrogen ($H_2$) breath test for carbohydrate malabsorption in children: evidence for a circadian pattern of breath $H_2$ concentration. *Pediatr. Res. 12*:816–823.
68. Bowie, M. D., Brinkman, G. L., and Hansen, J. D. L. (1965). Acquired disaccharide intolerance in malnutrition. *J. Pediatr. 66*:1083–1091.
69. James, W. P. T. (1970). Sugar absorption and intestinal motility in children when malnourished and after treatment. *Clin. Sci. 39*:305–318.
70. Dagan, R., Gorodisher, R., Moses, S., and Margolis, C. (1980). Lactose-free formula for infantile diarrhea. *Lancet 1*:207.
71. Paige, D. M., and Graham, G. G. (1972). Nutritional implications of lactose malabsorption. *Pediatr. Res. 6*:329.
72. Cook, D., and Sarrett, H. P. (1982). Design of infant formulas for meeting normal and special needs. In *Clinical Disorders in Pediatric Nutrition,* F. Lifshitz (Ed.), Marcel Dekker, New York, in press.
73. Lifshitz, F. (1982). Nutritional management of diarrheal disease. In *Manual of Clinical Nutrition,* V. Young, G. Owens, H. Jacobson, R. Sherwin, D. Paige, and N. Solomon (Eds.), Nutrition Publications, Washington, D.C., in press.

# 2

# EPIDEMIOLOGY OF ACQUIRED MONOSACCHARIDE INTOLERANCE

VEDA N. NICHOLS
*Baylor College of Medicine*
*and Texas Children's Hospital, Houston, Texas*

The most prevalent form of severe malnutrition in infants admitted to the Pediatric Service at Ben Taub General Hospital is associated with chronic diarrhea and acquired monosaccharide intolerance (AMI). Ben Taub serves a low-income population with a racial distribution of 30% black, 50% Hispanic, and 20% white. AMI is a form of chronic diarrhea that is relieved by fasting and is characterized by the recurrence of diarrhea after feeding any form of dietary carbohydrate, including monosaccharides (1). After a diagnostic challenge with an oral glucose load, the patients with AMI develop severe, watery, glucose-positive diarrhea with a pH less than 5.5. With total parenteral nutrition and gradual reintroduction of monosaccharides and disaccharides into the diet, these children regain normal gastrointestinal function and nutritional status (1-3). The pathogenesis of AMI disease is unknown; however, Klish and co-workers have shown that the glucose malabsorption is proportional to the reduction in surface area of the small bowel mucosa (4). Because little is known of the pathogenesis of this disease and because of its significance to the practical pediatric management of chronic diarrhea and malnutrition in hospitalized patients, a prospective epidemiological study is being conducted to (a) describe the occurrence of acute severe diarrhea associated with acquired monosaccharide intolerance (AMI) in malnourished infants less than 3 months of age, (b) compare the nutritional status of the children with AMI with the nutritional status of the children who do not develop AMI, (c) identify the key epidemiological characteristics of the AMI patient in order to recognize the high risk factors in the genesis of the disorder, and (d) compare the sources of disease in the children with AMI with patients free from AMI.

### Population at Risk for AMI

Ninety patients 3 months of age or less with diarrhea examined at the pediatric outpatient or inpatient section of Ben Taub General Hospital were entered into the study with the informed consent of the parents. Information concerning history of the illness, feeding history, home and family conditions, pregnancy of the mother, and newborn history was obtained. A nutritional assessment was done and a stool sample was collected for bacterial and viral pathogens. A patient was considered to have AMI if diarrhea with acid stools and carbohydrate in feces occurred when feedings were given (1,2). Of the 90 patients with diarrhea, 10 had AMI. Of the 80 patients with diarrhea and no AMI, 4 were found to have *Salmonella* in their stools, and *Campylobacter* was isolated in 2. We did not find *Shigella* or *Yersinia* in any stool samples. Rotavirus was found by electron microscopy in the stool specimens of 7 patients. The rotazyme was positive for 7 additional patients; of the 10 patients with AMI, only 2 had an etiological diagnosis, namely rotavirus identified by rotazyme test.

Some of the pertinent findings of the Ben Taub population are shown in Table 1. As stated earlier, the overall racial distribution is 30% black, 50% Hispanic, and 20% white. In the study reported, however, 90% of the AMI patients were black and 10% were Hispanic (Table 1).

Sixty-six percent of the AMI mothers were single or divorced and 63% of the AMI fathers were employed. There were no differences in the AMI and non-AMI groups in regard to the mothers working during pregnancy or at the time of admission. Very few mothers were employed.

**Table 1**   Patient Distribution in Relation to Sex, Race, Marital
Status of Mother, Employment, and Prenatal History

|  | AMI<br>% | non-AMI<br>% |
|---|---|---|
| Sex |  |  |
| Male | 78 (7) | 64 (62) |
| Female | 22 (2) | 35 (29) |
| Ethnic groups |  |  |
| Black | 90 (9) | 43 (35) |
| Hispanic | 10 (1) | 41 (33) |
| White | 0 | 14 (11) |
| Marital status |  |  |
| Single | 55 (5) | 45 (35) |
| Divorced | 11 (1) | 0 |
| Separated | 0 | 8 ( 6) |
| Widowed | 0 | 1 ( 1) |
| Married | 33 (3) | 45 (34) |
| Father employed |  |  |
| Yes | 63 (5) | 76 (44) |
| No | 37 (3) | 24 (14) |
| Prenatal care |  |  |
| Regularly | 66 (6) | 60 (44) |
| Occasionally | 11 (1) | 28 (21) |
| None | 22 (2) | 12 ( 9) |
| Prenatal WIC enrollment |  |  |
| Yes | 38 (3) | 36 (26) |
| No | 62 (5) | 64 (47) |
| Anemia during pregnancy |  |  |
| Yes | 50 (4) | 21 (15) |
| No | 50 (4) | 79 (55) |
| Some consumption of alcohol<br>during pregnancy |  |  |
| Yes | 40 (4) | 13 ( 9) |
| No | 60 (6) | 87 (63) |
| Gestational age |  |  |
| Full-term | 100 (7) | 82 (32) |
| Premature or small for date | 0 | 18 ( 7) |
| Infants with one or more<br>siblings |  |  |
| Yes | 90 (9) | 68 (52) |
| No | 10 (1) | 32 (25) |

(n) = number of observations.

Table 2   Data of Patients with Acquired Monosaccharide Intolerance
Compared with Data of Non-AMI Diarrhea Patients

|  | AMI mean ± SD | non-AMI mean ± SD |
|---|---|---|
| Total number of years completed in school | | |
| Mother | 10.8 ± 2.1 | 9.3 ± 2.9 |
| Father | 11.4 ± 1.0 | 10.5 ± 2.6 |
| Mother's age at time of admission to study | 21.8 ± 3.2 | 22.5 ± 5.3 |
| Number of pregnancies | 3.1 ± 2.0 | 2.5 ± 1.8 |
| Mother's weight at time of admission to study (kg) | 55.9 ± 7.5 | 62.9 ± 13.8 |
| Weight gain during pregnancy | 10.2 ± 4.0 | 15.1 ± 5.8 |
| Weight gain for infants per day since birth (g) | −5.5 ± 11.4 | 1.01 ± 26.7 |
| Number in household less than 2 years of age | 1.2 ± 1.1 | 0.5 ± 0.7 |
| Number of persons in house with diarrhea in the past 2 weeks | 1.2 ± 1.1 | 0.4 ± 0.8 |
| Total number of persons in household | 5.8 ± 0.84 | 5.0 ± 2.6 |

The total number of years completed in school was 10.8 ± 2.1 for the mothers of the AMI infants and 9.3 ± 2.9 for the mothers of the non-AMI infants. The fathers of the AMI infants had completed 11.4 ± 1.0 years of school and the non-AMI fathers had finished 10.5 ± 2.6 years of school as seen in Table 2.

The AMI patients came from larger families living in more crowded conditions than the non-AMI group. Ninety percent of the AMI infants had one or more siblings. The mean number of persons in the household less than 2 years of age was 1.2 ± 1.1 from the AMI group, and the mean total number of persons in the household was 5.8 ± 0.84 for the AMI patients and 5.0 ± 2.6 for the non-AMI patients (Table 2). There also was a higher frequency of diarrhea in the households of the AMI patients in the 2 weeks prior to admission.

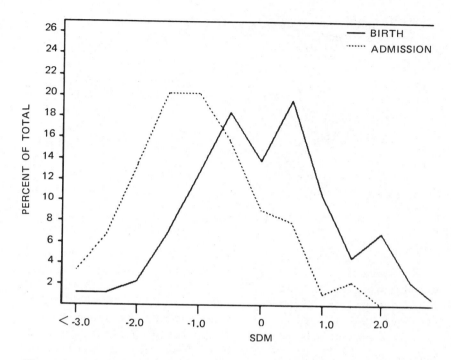

**Figure 1**   The scale used is based on the normal population from the NCHS files. Zero is the mean of the normal population, +1 and +2 are the standard deviations above the mean, –1, –2, –3 are the standard deviations below the mean.

The AMI mothers were somewhat younger than the non-AMI mothers. The AMI patients were products of mothers with a greater number of pregnancies and a lower weight gain during pregnancy. The mean weight gain was 10.2 ± 4.0 kg for the AMI mothers and 15.1 ± 5.8 kg for the non-AMI mothers. The average weight for the AMI mothers at the time of admission of the infants also was lower. Only 66% of the AMI mothers received prenatal care regularly. Eleven percent of the AMI mothers received prenatal care occasionally and 22% of the AMI mothers received no prenatal care. Fifty percent of the AMI mothers had anemia during pregnancy. Forty percent of the AMI mothers consumed some alcohol during their pregnancy.

**Table 3**  Anthropometric Comparison of AMI Versus Non-AMI ($\overline{X} \pm$ SD)

|  | Wt/Ht Z score[a] | Ht/age Z score | Wt/age Z score |
|---|---|---|---|
| **Birth** | | | |
| AMI | −1.11 ± 0 | −0.78 ± 0.35 | −0.57 ± 0.66 |
| Non-AMI | −0.50 ± 1.004 | −0.02 ± 1.11 | −0.18 ± 1.18 |
| **Admission** | | | |
| AMI | −1.60 ± 0.96 | −1.06 ± 1.07 | −1.84 ± 0.83 |
| Non-AMI | −0.93 ± 0.99 | −0.79 ± 1.19 | −1.24 ± 0.99 |
| **Discharge** | | | |
| AMI | −0.70 ± 1.06 | −1.63 ± 0.91 | −1.65 ± 0.76 |
| Non-AMI | −0.79 ± 0.51 | −1.16 ± 1.46 | −1.05 ± 0.85 |

[a]Mean Z scores and standard deviations (−0.57 is ½ SD below the mean).

The AMI infants failed to gain appropriate weight after birth. The mean weight gain per day from birth for the AMI infants was −5.50 ± 11.4 and 1.01 ± 26.7 for the non-AMI infants. In order to more effectively illustrate the nutritional insult suffered by these infants from birth to the time of admission, the weight/age standard deviations from the NCHS standard mean or Z scores were utilized (5,6). At birth 44% of all the infants were at the mean or above, whereas 25% of the AMI infants were at the mean or above. At admission, only 11% of all the patients were at the mean or above. Eighty-nine percent of all the infants and all of the AMI patients were below the mean (Fig. 1).

At birth, the infants were slightly below the mean for weight and height. At the time of admission, the nutritional deficit suffered by the AMI children is evidenced by a reduction in weight/height, height/age, and weight/age (Table 3). The deficits are consistently greater for the infants with acquired monosaccharide intolerance than for the non-AMI infants. At discharge the weight/height has improved, the height for age has worsened, and the weight for age has improved slightly. The deficits in height are greater for all of the infants in the study at the time of admission and continue to worsen through the time of discharge because more time is required to recover height.

Malnutrition at the time of admission in the AMI group was evident by the arm/FOC ratio (circumference of the upper arm at the midpoint divided by the circumference of the head) (7) (Fig. 2). In this study the correlation

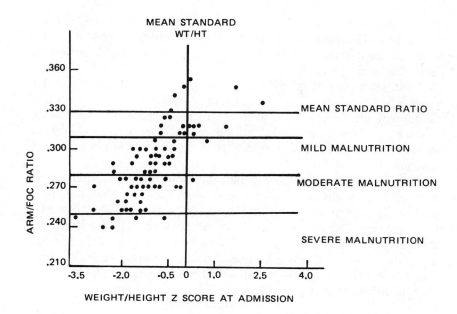

**Figure 2**    The arm/FOC ratio is obtained by estimating the midportion of the upper arm, measuring the circumference at this location, and measuring the head circumference. The midarm circumference divided by the head circumference (arm/FOC ratio) has been described as a general index of nutritional status (7). The normal mean standard is 0.33, a mild degree of malnutrition exists when the ratio is less than 0.31, 0.279 to 0.25 indicates moderate malnutrition, and severe malnutrition is present when the ratio is below 0.25.

between the ·weight/height Z score and the arm/FOC ratio for the total population was 0.72 and was highly significant. Half of the AMI patients were distributed in the mild degree of malnutrition and half were moderately malnourished. In contrast, 11% of the non-AMI patients were above the mean standard ratio, 37% were mildly malnourished, 43% were moderately malnourished, and 9% were severely malnourished.

The AMI infants were younger than the non-AMI diarrheal patients. Forty-four percent of the AMI patients were 23 days or less. The mean age in days at admission was 27.5 ± 14.0 for the AMI patients and 37.9 ± 22.6 for the non-AMI patients. Thus the deficit in growth of the AMI infants which occurred between birth and admission occurred faster and was more severe than in the other patients.

Seventy-two percent of all patients in the study and 78% of the AMI patients had a history of diarrhea prior to admission of 7 days or less. One patient with diarrhea and none of the AMI patients presented with a history of more than 38 days of diarrhea prior to hospitalization. It is unlikely that such a short illness could account for the stunting of height observed at admission.

There were feeding problems in the population studied as reflected by at least one formula change that occurred between birth and admission in 43% of all study patients and in 45% of the AMI patients. Twenty-six percent of all patients and 22% of the AMI patients had experienced two or more formula changes. Fifty percent of the AMI patients and 41% of the non-AMI infants had been fed foods other than formula. However, the feeding problems of the AMI patients did not appear to be different from those of other patients with diarrhea.

## Summary

This study began in October 1980 and will continue until October 1982. The most recent analysis of data indicated that 90 subjects with diarrhea (10 of whom had acquired monosaccharide intolerance) had been enrolled in the study. All of the AMI infants enrolled were more malnourished than expected. The nutritional insult had occurred between birth and a mean age of 37 days. The duration of diarrhea prior to admission was not related to the degree of malnutrition. A significant number of formula changes and the early introduction of solids for such young infants indicates feeding problems. The AMI mothers were younger, had more pregnancies, lower weight gain, and more anemia during the pregnancies. AMI infants as a group were more malnourished than the non-AMI group; however, AMI did not occur in all malnourished infants with diarrhea. AMI did not appear to be related to any specific feeding pattern or diet. AMI was not related to any specific etiological agent of diarrheal disease.

## Acknowledgments

This work is a publication of the USDA/ARS, Children's Nutrition Research Center at the Department of Pediatrics, Baylor College of Medicine and Texas Children's Hospital. The author thanks B. L. Nichols, G. S. Gopalakrishna, K. Evans, F. Jalili, K. Fraley, J. Stuff, and E. O. Smith for the collection and management of the data and H. L. DuPont, University of Texas Medical School, Houston, Texas for bacterial and viral studies of the stool specimens.

## References

1. Lifshitz, F., Coello-Ramirez, P., Gutierrez-Topete, G., and Contreras-Gutierrez, M. L. (1970). Monosaccharide intolerance and hypoglycemia in infants with diarrhea. I. Clinical course of 23 infants. *J. Pediatr. 77*: 595–603.
2. Lifshitz, F., Coello-Ramirez, P., and Contreras-Gutierrez, M. L. (1971). Response of infants to carbohydrate oral loads after recovery from diarrhea. *J. Pediatr. 79*:612–617.
3. Jalili, F., Smith, E. O., Nichols, V. N., Mintz, A. A., and Nichols, B. L. (1982). A comparison of acquired monosaccharide intolerance and acute diarrheal syndrome. *Pediatr. Gastroenterol. Nutr.,* in press.
4. Klish, W. J., Udall, J. N., Rodriguez, J. T., Singer, D. B., and Nichols, B. L. (1978). Intestinal surface area in infants with acquired monosaccharide intolerance. *J. Pediatr. 92*:566–571.
5. Waterlow, J. C., Buzina, R., Keller, W., Lane, J. M., Nichaman, M. Z., and Tanner, J. M. (1977). The presentation and use of height and weight data for comparing the nutritional status of groups of children under the age of 10 years. *Bull. WHO 55*:489–498.
6. Graitcer, P. L., Gentry, E. M., Nichaman, M. Z., and Lane, J. M. (1981). Anthropometric indicators of nutrition status and morbidity. *J. Trop. Pediatr. 27*:292–298.
7. Kanawati, A. A., and McLaren, D. S. (1970). Assessment of marginal malnutrition. *Nature 228*:573–575.

# 3

# BREATH HYDROGEN TESTING IN INFANTS WITH DIARRHEA

CARLOS H. LIFSCHITZ
*Baylor College of Medicine*
*and Texas Children's Hospital, Houston, Texas*

Dietary carbohydrate (CHO) is a common cause of formula intolerance in infants recovering from diarrhea (Chapter 1). Signs of severe intolerance include abdominal distention, watery stools with or without fecal reducing substances, and/or acidic pH (lower than 5.5). Clinical CHO intolerance is not an "all-or-nothing" phenomenon, but marks the end of a covert range of diminished CHO absorption ability. In milder instances of intolerance there may be diarrhea without excretion of carbohydrates in feces and without acid stools.

When CHO is absorbed incompletely by the small intestine and reaches the colon, it is exposed to the enzymatic action of bacteria and $H_2$ is produced (1). In normal men approximately 84–90% of the $H_2$ that is produced by bacterial action upon CHO is eliminated with flatus. The rest

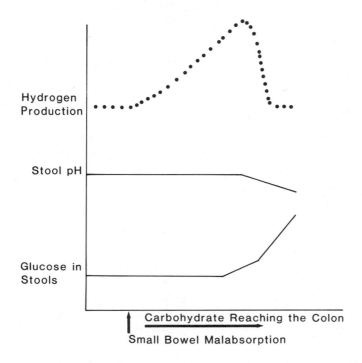

**Figure 1**  Correlation between $H_2$ production and amount of CHO reaching the colon. When no small bowel malabsorption occurs, no $H_2$ is produced, fecal pH is $> 5.5$ and no glucose is present in the stools. The vertical arrow indicates the point where progressively greater amounts of CHO are malabsorbed by the small bowel and reach the colon (horizontal arrow). This is accompanied by a progressive increase in BHL to a point where the accumulation of acid in the colon inhibits bacterial fermentation, the $H_2$ production falls, glucose is found in stools, and fecal pH is $< 5.5$.

diffuses into the bloodstream and is eliminated in breath. Therefore, the determination of $H_2$ concentration in breath constitutes a semiquantitative method for the evaluation of CHO malabsorption which may be more sensitive than the measurement of sugar excretion by semiquantitative methods (2). Moreover, the breath hydrogen test (BHT) has the advantage of being a noninvasive technique that requires no blood samples.

Solomons and co-workers, however, presented data showing that pulmonary excretion of $H_2$ was significantly lower in children with acute gastroenteritis and diarrhea when compared to nondiarrhea controls (3). They suggested that this test was not useful in diagnosing CHO intolerance in children with acute gastroenteritis. This finding can be explained by investigations which showed that when the pH of the milieu where the fermentation reaction occurs is acidic, the bacterial enzymes are inhibited and less $H_2$ is produced (4). Excess CHO reaching the large bowel, as occurs in diarrhea, can result in accumulation of fermentation products and a fall in the colonic pH (Fig. 1). Our experience (5) and that of other authors (6) confirm that there is a lower $H_2$ production in patients with acute gastroenteritis, but most children with ongoing diarrhea exhibit a substantial rise in breath $H_2$ when CHO is malabsorbed by the small bowel.

Here we report our experience with the BHT in infants with diarrhea while being fed different carbohydrate-containing formulas. This test was found useful to diagnose and monitor the carbohydrate malabsorption which frequently complicates diarrheal disease in infancy (2). The breath hydrogen levels (BHL) were more sensitive for the diagnosis of CHO malabsorption than the detection of sugar and acidic feces. The $H_2$ production by colonic bacteria during recovery from diarrhea was correlated with the amounts, types, and manner of formula feedings.

### The Breath Hydrogen Test in Infants with Diarrhea

We have utilized the BHT to study CHO absorption by infants with diarrhea. We tested hospitalized infants under 3 months of age who required admission because of their diarrhea. These infants had been sick approximately 8 days prior to admission. Once admitted, all received intravenous fluids for approximately 12 hr followed by a trial of an oral hydrating solution and, if well tolerated, were begun on a commercial formula combining soy protein and either glucose or corn syrup solids (glucose polymers) as the CHO source. A small number of patients received sucrose-containing formulas. CHO concentration in the formula was increased as tolerated until full-strength ($\sim$ 7% CHO) was reached at approximately 48 hr after admission. If a patient responded to a dietary CHO load with frequent and looser stools and/or with low pH ( $<$ 5.5) and/or the presence of glucose, the amount of CHO was decreased.

Patients were fed exclusively the above-indicated infant formulas every 2–4 hr and most were tested for the first time within 96 hr of admission. They were not fasted for the study. Two to four breath samples were collected between feeds. Prior to the test, patients had been given the formula that was used as a challenge for at least four feedings. Patients who were started on antibiotics on admission and produced very small amounts of $H_2$ were not included for the analysis of the results. None of the patients had received antibiotics before admission.

To collect breath samples a plastic face mask was used, such as that commonly used for oxygen administration (7), to which a sampling tube had been inserted. The tube was connected to a 20-ml plastic syringe through a stopcock. By observing the respiratory movements, 2 or 3 ml of air could be collected at each expiration until a total of 20 ml had been obtained. By collecting breath samples every 30–60 min over a 2- or 3-hr period, it is possible to estimate the quantity of $H_2$ produced in the intestine (8). The samples can be analyzed immediately or may be stored in gas-tight syringes or bags for several hours. The breath sample is injected into a gas chromatograph for analysis. The area of the $H_2$ peak is expressed as parts per million and normalized to alveolar concentration using the breath $CO_2$ as an internal standard (9). This compensates for variables that arise from collection, storage, or dilution by ambient air.

### Results and Interpretation of BHL

High breath hydrogen levels were a constant feature in infants with diarrhea. Although it is difficult to compare the peak BHL of one patient with that of another because of the differences in CHO received, bacterial flora and transit time tests on the same individual on different days are reproducible and give useful information.

The BHL were highest within 96 hr of admission even when the amount of CHO intake per kilogram of body weight was the lowest (Fig. 2). As the patients improved, greater amounts of CHO intake yielded comparably less $H_2$, as an indication that more CHO was being absorbed more efficiently by the bowel. At the time of discharge the BHL were 80% lower than those when first tested. When the amount of CHO per kilogram of body weight was increased, generally a small and transient rise in BHL was observed. In these situations the CHO increase in the diet was clinically well-tolerated.

However, when an increase in the CHO content of the formula was accompanied by a considerable fall in BHL, this was a sign of poor clinical tolerance and was followed by acidic stools which sometimes contained glucose. Conversely, when the amount of dietary CHO was decreased, the BHL increased and acidic and loose stools resolved. The sudden decrease of BHL may be seen in patients when the amount of CHO reaching the

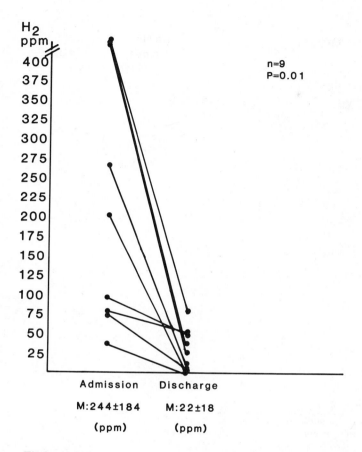

**Figure 2** BHL within 96 hr of admission and at discharge from hospital. Discharge BHL are 80% lower than those determined on admission.

colon exceeds tolerance and great amounts of acid are produced by bacterial fermentation, the colonic BH decreases, and less $H_2$ is produced because of the resulting bacterial enzyme inhibition (Chapter 10). This is followed by acid stools.

By comparing the BHL produced on admission, two groups of infants were identified: one group produced low levels ($<$ 55 ppm) and the other produced much higher levels with large interindividual variability (Fig. 3).

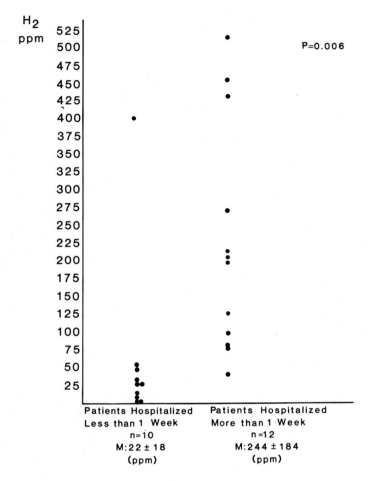

**Figure 3** Comparison of BHL within 96 hr of admission of patients who required less than 1 week of hospitalization (left) with those who required more than 1 week (right). Breath samples were obtained within 96 hr of admission when the infants were receiving at least 0.3 g/kg of carbohydrate per feeding. Discharge breath tests were done within 96 hr before the patients were sent home or to an intermediate care facility to recover from malnutrition.

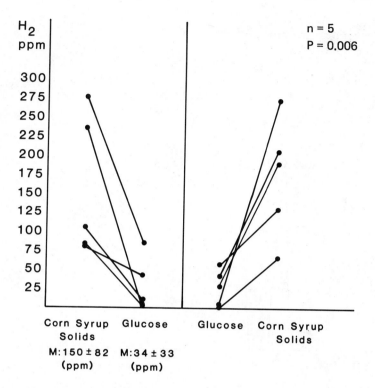

**Figure 4** Effect of CHO substitution on BHL in children with diarrhea. When glucose was substituted for corn syrup solids, BHL fell considerably (left). Conversely, the substitution of corn syrup solids for glucose produced a marked elevation of BHL, indicating that glucose polymers reach the colon in a greater proportion than glucose monomers.

The significantly higher BHL determined at the time of admission occurred in patients who required hospitalizations longer than 1 week; in contrast, those patients who required shorter hospital stays had lower BHL. This would suggest that the degree of CHO malabsorption by the small bowel (i.e., mucosal lesion) was already established at the time of admission to the hospital. Clinical improvement of the patients that remained in the hospital for more than 1 week was accompanied by a fall in BHL of greater than 80%.

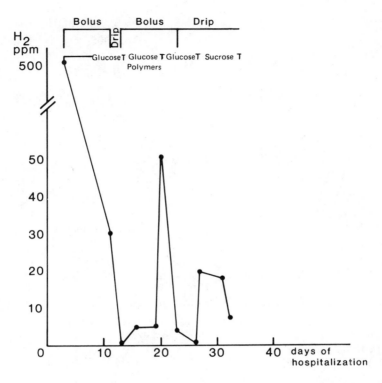

**Figure 5**  Effect of milk drip on BHL in a child with diarrhea. Drip feeding was accompanied by a substantial fall in BHL. When sucrose was substituted for glucose, an elevation of BHL was observed although levels attained were lower than those resulting from formula given as a bolus.

The effect of CHO substitution also was studied. When the same amount of corn syrup solids was substituted for glucose as the CHO source in the formulas, the patients produced significantly greater amounts of $H_2$ (Fig. 4). This may indicate that more CHO reaches the colon when glucose polymers are fed. Despite the higher BHL, however, most patients tolerated formulas containing glucose polymers very well and the majority were discharged on such formulas. The reason for the high amount of $H_2$ produced when corn syrup solids were used as a CHO source may be that glucoamylase and other brush-border enzymes that digest glucose polymers before absorption may not be as well preserved in these patients as described (10). When sucrose was substituted for corn syrup solids or glucose, greater amounts of $H_2$ were produced, confirming the knowledge that secondary sucrose intolerance occurs frequently in children with severe diarrhea (2) (Chapter 6), and that small bowel sucrose digestion and absorption are lower than those of glucose or glucose polymers.

The manner in which the formula was administered was studied as well. Continuous feeding of the formula by means of a nasogastric tube was implemented in those infants who were unable to tolerate bolus feedings, as manifested by watery stools, sometimes with glucose and/or low pH. Each time a formula drip was substituted for bolus feedings, a fall in the BHL was observed (Fig. 5). The fall in BHL suggests an improvement of small bowel CHO absorption when continuous feeding of the formula by means of a nasogastric tube was implemented. This confirms reports that this method of nutrient administration is beneficial in patients with severe diarrhea (11).

### Discussion of Interpretation of BHT and Carbohydrate Intolerance

CHO long has been recognized as a frequent cause of formula intolerances in infants recovering from diarrhea (2). In the past, dietary CHO was considered to be well-tolerated when a patient's stools were neither too frequent nor too loose and did not have reducing substances and/or a pH below 5.5. Whenever any of the above fecal characteristics were present, the formula CHO was changed or its concentration reduced because of intolerance.

No information concerning the colonic fate of malabsorbed CHO was available before the clinical signs of intolerance became evident because a noninvasive method to study carbohydrate malabsorption did not exist. Today the BHT permits the semiquantitative study of CHO malabsorption by the small bowel before severe intolerance occurs. However, certain considerations have to be kept in mind when interpreting results of the BHT: (a) $H_2$ is a by-product of a fermentation reaction of colonic anaerobic bacteria acting upon CHO; (b) when the same amount of CHO reaches the colon, the BHL may differ from one patient to another but are reproducible in the same individual under the same conditions; (c) the use of antibiotics, very rapid transit time, and colonic acid pH produce a lower BHL than would be expected; (d) the presence of anaerobic bacteria in the small bowel can give a falsely positive BHT; and (e) the absence of adequate $H_2$-producing colonic flora can give a falsely negative BHT.

Patients should have received the formula for a few feedings prior to the test. It is not unusual to find good clinical tolerance and very low BHL when the formula is given for the first time to a child with diarrhea.

The fact that elevated BHL were found constantly in every $H_2$-producing patient is evidence that small bowel CHO malabsorption is a frequent event duing recovery from diarrhea. In contrast, the presence of CHO in stool is uncommon; even patients with severe lactose malabsorption may produce large numbers of stools without carbohydrate or acid pH (2). Therefore, intermediate mechanisms must exist to recover the malabsorbed CHO that has reached the large bowel. Studies in animals (12) and in humans (13) indicate that CHO is fermented by bacteria and transformed into volatile fatty acids (VFA) (acetic, propionic, butyric, etc.) which subsequently are absorbed by the colon in exchange for bicarbonate. When colonic bacteria fail to ferment the CHO, little or no $H_2$ or VFA are produced and CHO can be detected in stool. This change in colonic function can occur when the amount of sugar reaching the colon is so great that bacteria are unable to ferment the entire amount or if the transit time is so short that there is not enough time for the enzymatic reactions to take place. It also can occur when the amount of colonic bacteria is decreased or the flora is inadequate (i.e., use of antibiotics) (Chapter 10).

When CHO is effectively fermented and transformed into VFA the colon is unable to absorb them if there are large amounts produced. However, rapid transit time, or other unknown mechanisms could impair absorption. The VFA remain in the intestinal lumen, the pH falls, $H_2$ production falls, and stools have a pH below 5.5. As discussed previously, CHO reaching the colon is transformed into acids which are exchanged for bicarbonate. Therefore, this may create an important loss of bicarbonate in some patients with diarrhea and may contribute to the frequently observed metabolic acidosis.

### Conclusion

By means of the BHT, we have been able to prove that small bowel CHO malabsorption is a common phenomenon during recovery from diarrhea. In the presence of adequate bacterial flora in the colon, CHO is fermented into metabolic products, some of which can be absorbed in exchange for bicarbonate. By this mechanism, the organic osmolar load of the colonic content is decreased and less water is secreted into the feces. If the colon is able to absorb the VFA produced, stools will not be acidic. If the bacterial flora are able to ferment the CHO, no glucose will appear in the stools. The colon plays a major role in the metabolism of CHO malabsorbed by the small bowel in recovery from diarrhea. The nature of the failure of colonic CHO absorption and the metabolic consequences of colonic failure are under active investigation by our laboratory.

## Acknowledgments

This work is a publication of the USDA/ARS, Children's Nutrition Research Center in the Department of Pediatrics at Baylor College of Medicine and Texas Children's Hospital. The author wishes to thank Drs. A. A. Mintz and G. S. Gopalakrishna for permitting the study of their patients at the Ben Taub General Hospital in Houston, Texas. Data collection was facilitated by K. Evans and Dr. C. S. Irving provided the stimulus for the approach to data interpretation.

## References

1. Levitt, M. D. (1969). Production and excretion of hydrogen gas in man. *N. Engl. J. Med. 281*:122–127.
2. Lifshitz, F., Coello-Ramirez, P., Gutierrez-Topete, G., and Cornado-Cornet, M. C. (1971). Carbohydrate malabsorption in infants with diarrhea. *J. Pediatr. 79*:760–767.
3. Solomons, N. W., Garcia, R., Schneider, R., Viteri, F. E., and Argueta Von Kaenel, V. (1979). $H_2$ Breath test during diarrhea. *Acta Paediatr. Scand. 68*:171–172.
4. Perman, J. A., Modler, S., and Olson, A. C. (1981). Role of pH in production of hydrogen from carbohydrates by colonic bacterial flora. *J. Clin. Invest. 67*:643–650.
5. Lifschitz, C. H., and Nichols, B. L. (1982). Clinical applications of breath hydrogen testing. In *Clinical Disorders in Pediatric Nutrition*, F. Lifshitz (Ed.), Marcel Dekker, New York, in press.
6. Robb, T. A., and Davidson, G. P. (1980). Letter to the editor. *Acta Paediatr. 69*:687–688.
7. Watkins, J. B. (1980) Personal communication.
8. Solomons, N. W., Viteri, F., and Rosenberg, I. H. (1978). Development of an interval sampling hydrogen breath test for carbohydrate malabsorption in children: Evidence for a circadian pattern of breath $H_2$ concentrations. *Pediatr. Res. 12*:816–823.

9. Niu, H.-C., Schoeller, D. A., and Klein, P. D. (1979). Improved gas chromatographic quantitation of breath hydrogen by normalization to respiratory carbon dioxide. *J. Lab. Clin. Med. 94*:755–763.

10. Lebenthal, E., and Lee, P. C. (1980). Glucoamylase and disaccharidase activities in normal subjects and in patients with mucosal injury of the small intestine. *J. Pediatr. 97*:389–393.

11. Parker, P., Stroop, F., and Greene, H. (1981). Controlled comparison of continuous versus intermittent feeding in the treatment of infants with intestinal disease. *J. Pediatr. 99*:360–364.

12. Imoto, S., and Namioka, S. (1978). VFA metabolism in the pig. *J. Anim. Sci. 47*:479–487.

13. McNeil, N. I., Cummings, J. H., and James, W. P. T. (1978). Short chain fatty acid absorption by the human large intestine. *Gut 19*:819–822.

# 4

# CORRELATION BETWEEN LACTASE DEFICIENCY AND LACTOSE MALABSORPTION TO LACTOSE INTOLERANCE

EMANUEL LEBENTHAL and THOMAS M. ROSSI
*State University of New York at Buffalo
and The Children's Hospital at Buffalo, New York*

The subject of lactase deficiency has remained a controversial issue for several decades. Primarily, confusion persists concerning terminology. Frequently, the terms "lactase deficiency," "lactose malabsorption," and "lactose intolerance" are used interchangeably in the literature. This has arisen in part because different methods have been used to establish the diagnosis of lactase deficiency. Comparing the results of indirect methods of assessing lactase activity, that is, Lactose Tolerance Test (LTT), Lactose Breath Hydrogen Test (LBHT), stool pH, and reducing substances to the direct measurement of intestinal enzyme activity has been difficult. Each test has its own inherent limitations (1). Further difficulties arise in correlating the entity of lactose intolerance to milk intolerance, hindering precise recommendations regarding the desirability of milk consumption in various ages, ethnic groups, and disease states. In addition, numerous reports have appeared implicating lactase deficiency in the etiology of many common disease entities.

It is the purpose of this chapter to first outline some of the facts regarding the enzyme and its deficiency. Controversial clinical issues and especially the correlation to laboratory tests are discussed later.

## Criteria for Diagnosis

For purpose of clarity, lactase deficiency (hypolactasia) is defined as the state in which a subnormal concentration of lactase activity is found in a small intestinal mucosal biopsy specimen. Lactase deficiency may occur either secondary to disease entities which cause injury to the small intestinal mature epithelial cell brush-border area, or as a primary isolated entity. Lactose malabsorption refers to the state in which dietary lactose remains unhydrolyzed and subsequently unabsorbed from the gastrointestinal tract. Symptoms may or may not result from lactose malabsorption. Lactose intolerance, on the other hand, describes the condition in which symptoms such as bloating, abdominal pain, and diarrhea ensue following ingestion of dietary lactose.

In general, the LTT and LBHT offer good screening tests for the diagnosis of lactose malabsorption. Both require the ingestion of 2 g/kg oral aqueous lactose load with serial measurements of blood glucose and expired hydrogen, respectively. These two tests, along with measurement of stool for pH and reducing substances, provide indirect measurement for intestinal lactase activity. The most sensitive definitive test is the direct assay of the intestinal enzyme activity by use of peroral intestinal biopsy procedure (1,2).

## Classification of Hypolactasia

In defining hypolactasia, one must remember that varying degrees of enzyme activity may exist. The enzyme activity may be completely absent or depressed to a variable degree below the considered normal level. In addition, lactase deficiency may be classified as either primary or secondary. Primary deficiency is related to either congenital lactase deficiency, developmental lactase deficiency, or adult-type lactase deficiency. Secondary lactase deficiency occurs as a nonspecific finding accompanying injury to the brush-border area by diverse etiologies (Chapter 6).

## Congenital Lactase Deficiency

The diagnosis of this entity requires a normal small intestinal histology, depressed or absent lactase activity, and a normal complement of the α-glucosidases (sucrase and maltase). Most patients reported in the past as having congenital deficiency did not fulfill the foregoing criteria. Diagnoses were based on the LTT which, unfortunately, cannot distinguish between primary or secondary lactase deficiency. The LTT, as well as other indirect measurements of lactase deficiency, such as the LBHT and the presence of acidic stools containing reducing substances, corroborate the malabsorption of lactose, but do not describe the state of integrity of the small intestinal mucosal architecture.

Congenital lactase deficiency is considered extremely rare, if it exists at all (Chapter 6). Of 1500 peroral small intestinal biopsies performed because of chronic diarrhea at the Children's Hospital of Buffalo, only one case of congenital lactase deficiency has been suspected. Congenital lactase deficiency, when suspected, must be distinguished from glucose-galactose malabsorption which may present with similar clinical findings (development of diarrhea, vomiting, distention, and irritability after the first few feedings). Congenital lactase deficiency must also be differentiated from "developmental lactose intolerance" (3). A transient lactase deficiency is seen in premature infants resulting from delay in the development of full-term newborn levels of activity (Chapter 5).

## Development of Lactase Activity

In the human, lactase activity is detected from the third month of gestation (3). By 26–34 weeks and 35–38 weeks, activity increased from 30 to 70%, respectively, of that found at term (Fig. 1). In contrast, the α-glucosidases, sucrase, and maltase, reach 70% of the newborn level by 26–34 weeks of gestation. This indicates that preterm infants may hydrolyze the α-glucosidases more efficiently than lactose.

At birth and in the neonatal period, virtually all mammals have high lactase activity. The activity declines after the weaning period, usually less than one-tenth of the peak activity. Humans, however, deviate from this concept.

## Adult-Type Lactase Deficiency

In humans, lactase activity may be low in adults (4,5) or may persist at levels comparable to those of the newborn period (5,6). The behavior of the enzymatic state appears to vary with the ethnic group studied. The relative

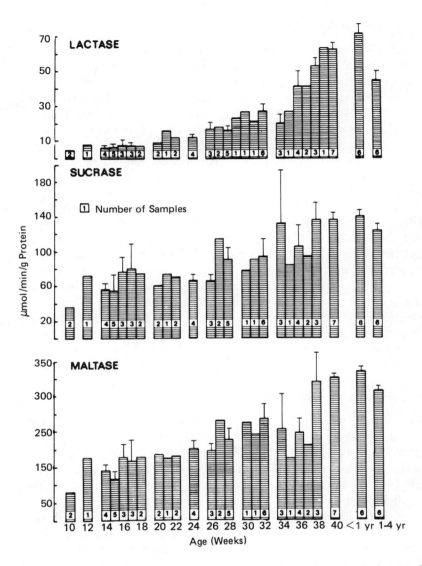

**Figure 1** Developmental pattern of disaccharidase activities in human fetal midjejunum between the 10th and 40th week of gestation. Each column is a mean ± SEM of numbers of samples given on the columns. (From Ref. 3.)

**Table 1** Human Small Intestine Disaccharidase Activities and Ratios at Different Ages

| Age | No. of biopsies | Lactase | Sucrase | Maltase | Palatinase | Ratios Sucrase/lactase | Maltase/lactase | Correlation of coefficient sucrase and maltase |
|---|---|---|---|---|---|---|---|---|
| | | ($\mu$mol disaccharide hydrolized/g protein/min) | | | | | | |
| 6 wk-1 yr | 31 | 32.1 ± 10.1 | 52.1 ± 16.9 | 179.1 ± 48.7 | 14.2 ± 3.9 | 1.7 ± 0.5 | 5.8 ± 1.5 | 0.77 |
| 1-2 yr | 38 | 35.1 ± 12.1 | 56.1 ± 16.3 | 185.3 ± 4.3 | 14.2 ± 4.3 | 1.7 ± 0.5 | 5.7 ± 1.9 | 0.93 |
| 2-3 yr | 22 | 30.3 ± 9.7 | 63.7 ± 15.8 | 210.9 ± 66.0 | 18.2 ± 6.0 | 2.1 ± 0.6 | 7.1 ± 1.8 | 0.83 |
| 3-5 yr | 16 | 33.9 ± 18.0 | 51.7 ± 17.6 | 185.9 ± 55.9 | 14.8 ± 4.6 | 1.9 ± 0.9 | 7.2 ± 4.1 | 0.87 |
| 5-9 yr | 32 | 22.6 ± 14.3a | 51.9 ± 18.3 | 185.4 ± 52.6 | 15.3 ± 4.4 | 3.5 ± 2.5 | 12.7 ± 9.0 | 0.96 |
| 9-20 yr | 21 | 24.3 ± 17.0 | 64.2 ± 35.1 | 200.0 ± 87.3 | 17.2 ± 7.8 | 8.5 ± 13.0 | 25.7 ± 38.4 | 0.90 |
| 20-50 yr | 12 | 25.1 ± 24.2 | 55.1 ± 32.3 | 188.3 ± 86.2 | 15.6 ± 7.3 | 26.8 ± 53.2 | 91.9 ± 181.8 | 0.99 |

aP < 0.01 of lactase activity as compared with the groups from 6 weeks to 5 years of age. Each value represents the mean ± SD.
*Source*: Ref. 10.

frequency of the two phenotypes, lactase deficiency or lactase persistence, vary from one part of the world to another. The persistence of lactase activity appears to be the exception rather than the rule. The conclusion reached regarding the variations of enzyme activity in the different ethnic groups have been made primarily on the basis of the LTT rather than by direct measurement of the intestinal mucosa for the specific activity of lactase. Thus, evidence of lactase activity has been indirectly estimated. The data suggests that only in Northern Europeans and in members of two nomadic tribes in Africa (4,7,8) does lactase activity persist in 80–90% of the population. The majority of the world population, on the other hand, demonstrates lactase deficiency. It has been suggested that the inheritance of lactase activity is controlled by a single autosomal recessive gene (9).

The age at which lactase activity declines has been investigated in the population of New England (10) (Chapter 6) from a retrospective analysis of peroral small intestinal biopsy specimens. From 1077 jejunal biopsies from patients with failure to thrive or irritable colon syndrome and their parents and siblings, 172 morphologically normal biopsies were selected and assayed for the activities of lactase, sucrase, maltase, and palatinase. The mucosal lactase activity and sucrase-to-lactase ratio were plotted against age (Table 1). Ages of patients ranged from 6 weeks to 50 years.

In the first 3 years, the mean lactase activity was 32.1 ± 10.1. $\mu$mol/g protein per minute, and the sucrase-to-lactase ratio was 1.7 ± 0.5 with no change from year to year. Between 3 and 5 years, there was a significant difference in the standard deviation of lactase activity compared with the standard deviation of previous years. From the 5th year through adulthood, a significant shift developed in the mean and standard deviation of lactase activity compared with previous years. A similar pattern was revealed by the sucrase-to-lactase ratio. After the 5th year, two distinct groups emerged. One with a range of sucrase-to-lactase of 1.0–4.0, and the second with low lactase activity exhibiting a ratio of 4:7. Until the age of 5 years, all biopsy specimens had high lactase activity, whereas after 5 years most biopsy specimens had low lactase activity.

The major finding in these data was the absence of low lactase activity before 5 years of age in the heterogenous Caucasian population of New England. This result correlates with studies evaluating the development of lactose intolerance in different populations around the world. In one study, evaluation of a group of African, Asian, and Latin American children living in New York City showed all children under the age of 5 years to be tolerant of lactose (11). Similarly, lactose intolerance in Finland and India appears by 5 and 3 years of age, respectively (12,13).

Although lactase deficiency may manifest itself after 5 years of age, the actual age at which activity declines will vary in different populations. In the Thai and Bantu populations, hypolactasia is evident by 4 years (14). In black Americans (15), however, the proportion of hypolactasia increased up to age 14 years, and in Finland (12), hypolactasia may be expressed as late as 15–20 years. These differences may reflect different alleles of a regulatory gene in the different populations, or they may reflect environmental influences.

## Hypothesis for the Persistence of Lactase Activity in Adulthood

Most of the world exhibits a high proportion of hypolactasic individuals (6, 16). High activity seems to be associated with those societies which traditionally have herded domesticated animals. The most notable examples are the populations of Central and Northern Europe and their overseas descendants. In addition, the pastoral, nomadic Hamitic tribes of central Africa, which depend on dairy herds, are in this group in contrast to the Bantu of the same region who exhibit lactase deficiency. In cultures which have existed without domesticated dairy animals, for example, the Chinese, Koreans, Japanese, American Indians, and Eskimos, the prevalence of adult lactase deficiency approaches 70–100% (17–19). In contrast, the prevalence of lactase deficiency in Caucasians in the United States, England, Germany, and Switzerland is estimated to be less than 20%. In Denmark, 2.6–6.6% prevalence is reported, whereas in Sweden and Finland, less than 1% and 17%, respectively, have been reported (20).

It is postulated that milk being available to all age groups in societies with domesticated and herded dairy animals exerted selective pressures for the acquisition and spread of a unique genetic based trait, that is, persistent lactase activity. It is estimated that this event took approximately 10,000 years. Persistent lactase activity served a definite advantage to the populations mentioned, permitting them to utilize a plentiful food resource without experiencing the adverse effects of lactose intolerance (1).

A second postulate for the persistence of lactase activity suggests individual adaptation to lactose in the diet. Earlier experiments show that the mere presence of lactose-containing foods in the diet may stimulate lactase activity in the lactase-deficient individual (21,22). Small but statistically significant increments in lactase activity have been seen in adult rats fed a high lactose diet for 5–10 weeks (23). On the other hand, prolonged nursing of rat pups past the weaning period did not prevent the normal postweaning decline in lactase activity. However, the animals did experience a delay in this usual

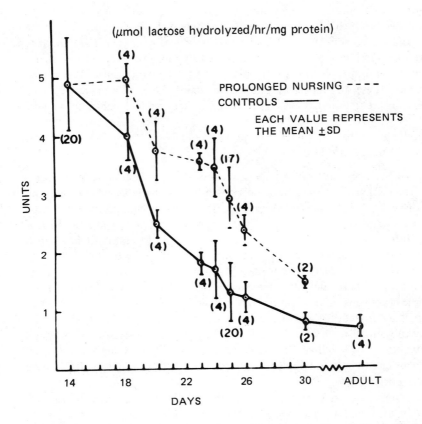

**Figure 2** The effect of prolonged nursing on lactase activity in the rat. (From Ref. 24.)

pattern of decline in lactase activity. Specific activities of the enzyme were slightly greater than control animals for the weaning period (24) (Fig. 2). Additionally, in humans, the total removal of lactose from the diet for up to 2 months did not decrease lactase activities in adults, and the feeding of diets containing 150 g of lactose per day did not change their lactase level (6,25). At present, it is generally accepted that lactose in the diet will not induce the synthesis of the enzyme lactase.

In the evolution of the persistence of lactase activity, two genetic possibilities exist. First, the synthesis of a new enzyme which is distinct from the fetal enzyme may occur. Second, a "regulatory gene" may be altered to an extent that it fails to "shut off" (depress) lactase synthesis at the program-med time (26). To distinguish between the two possibilities, the biochemical properties of neutral lactase from infants and adults with or without hypolac-tasia were compared. The enzymes, irrespective of the source, have the same chromatographic properties, substrate affinities, pH preference, and electro-phorectic mobility (27). These data suggest that the persistence of high lac-tase activity in adults results possibly from a regulatory gene mutation such that a reduction of lactase activity is delayed to a later age or completely eliminated (26).

### Relationship of Lactase Deficiency to Disease States

Given the current knowledge that adult-type lactase deficiency is genetically predetermined, it is difficult to ascribe this phenomenon to the etiologies of disease entities unless in the given disease, two alleles are affected at the same time. Nevertheless, preliminary studies which looked at the entity, tried to link lactase deficiency with such entities as duodenal ulcer disease, irritable colon syndrome, ulcerative colitis, and even viral hepatitis, diabetes mellitus, and cystic fibrosis (28–34). With further investigations, the associations turned out to be more apparent than real. In all of the above reports, no critical evaluation of the racial-ethnic origins and ages were included.

In a recent observation (35), we found that patients with cystic fibrosis have lactase deficiency in association with the ethnically related adult lactase deficiency and not secondary to cystic fibrosis itself. Lactase deficiency was not found in those patients with normal intestinal histology who were less than 5 years of age. The acquired causes of specific lactase deficiency and/or generalized oligodisaccharidase deficiencies associated with intestinal injury, diarrhea, and carbohydrate intolerance are reviewed elsewhere (see Chapter 1) (36,37).

### Recurrent Abdominal Pain (RAP) and Lactase Deficiency

A related matter of special interest and concern, and not yet entirely re-solved, is the controversy regarding the association of lactase deficiency with the entity of recurrent abdominal pain of childhood. The problem of RAP has plagued parents, pediatricians, and children for years. Children with this entity suffer reduction of regular activities, loss of school days, and extensive medical evaluation. The entity is not a disease, but rather a poorly defined syndrome. No clear definition exists and, therefore, the diagnosis is difficult. The list of differential diagnoses is endless and after extensive evaluation, only a small number of children are found to have an organic problem. The hope that such a complex entity could be resolved by the simple elimination of milk from the diet is an enticing proposition. The hope has been kindled by recent reports (38–41). In 1979, Barr, et al. (40), studied lactose malabsorption using the LBHT in 32 of 80 (40%) patients with RAP. Of 32 patients, 28 were then placed on a 6-week, nonblinded trial consisting of 2 weeks of lactose-free diet, 2 weeks of lactose-containing diet, followed by another 2-week period of lactose-free diet. Pain episodes were recorded, but lactose comsumption was not measured. An increase in pain frequency was noted when malabsorbers were placed on lactose-containing diets as compared to lactose-free periods. The authors concluded that lactose malabsorption may play a significant contributory role in the syndrome of recurrent abdominal pain in childhood.

Similarly, Liebman, 1979 (41) identified 11 of 38 patients with recurrent abdominal pain to be lactose intolerant by the LTT method. Elimination of lactose from the diet for 4 weeks relieved the pain in 10 of the 11 patients. Thus, the author felt lactose intolerance to play an etiological role for the entity of recurrent abdominal pain.

In the support of the hypothesis that RAP of childhood may be caused by lactase deficiency, the literature lacked controlled double-blinded studies. In addition, in the studies quoted, no critical evaluation of the prevalence of lactase deficiency in a general population with a similar age and ethnic background as a group of children with RAP was given.

In an attempt to address these important aspects, we evaluated the prevalence of intestinal lactase deficiency in patients with RAP and in a group of age and ethnically matched control subjects. In addition, a double-blind study of milk tolerance was undertaken using children with RAP in whom LTT had been performed. A 12-month follow-up was also conducted to evaluate the effect of various diets on the outcome of RAP (42). Results published in detail elsewhere (42) indicate that the prevalence of lactase deficiency is equivalent in RAP and control populations (31 versus 26.4%); symptoms occur in a large percentage of malabsorbers following LTT (71 versus 20% in absorbers), and following a 6-week period of high lactose diet (48 versus 24% in absorbers); however, long-term (12 months) lactose elimination from a regular diet made little difference in the resolution of pain in absorbers or in patients of unknown lactose absorptive capacity, as described below.

Of 95 patients with RAP, 69 underwent LTT and 27 intestinal biopsies with determination of lactase activity. This group was contrasted with a group of 61 control patients of similar age and ethnic origin to the RAP population who underwent small intestinal biopsy as a diagnostic procedure for reasons other than abdominal pain. The results published in detail elsewhere (42) indicate that the prevalence of lactase deficiency in intestinal mucosal biopsy specimens is equivalent in the population with RAP compared to age and ethnically matched control subjects (31 versus 26.4%, respectively). In addition, an abnormal LTT was found in 21 of 69 (30.4%) patients. Of these 21 patients, 15 (71%) reported symptoms compared to 8 of 41 (20%) of patients with normal LTT. The finding of increased symptoms in lactose malabsorbers after lactose loading is not surprising. Others (43–45) have reported the incidence of symptoms in malabsorbers to be 70–92% following testing.

The study also included two diet trials, three successive 6-week double-blinded diet trials, and a 12-month diet trial (42). The three 6-week diet trials consisted of permitting patients either (a) normal dietary habits with or without milk, (b) chocolate-flavored cow's milk-based lactose-containing formula (400 ml/day), or (c) chocolate-flavored soy-based nonlactose-containing formula (400 ml/day). The parents were asked to document in a diary the occurrence of all episodes of abdominal pain, irrespective of severity, experienced by their children. The frequency of abdominal pain was considered increased if the number of episodes per week were 20% or more than the frequency during period (a). During the period in which 400 ml of milk was consumed daily, 10 of 21 (47.6%) of lactose malabsorbers reported a significant increase of pain frequency, whereas 4 of 17 (23.5%) lactose absorbers reported an increase in symptoms. Following soy challenge, 7 of 21 (33.3%) malabsorbers versus 4 of 17 (23.5%) lactose absorbers reported an increase in pain frequency. Thus, it appears that giving a high lactose load, either by testing (LTT) or by high dietary intake to malabsorbers, is likely to produce symptoms.

During a 12-month milk elimination diet, symptoms of abdominal pain resolved in 6 of 15 (40%) of lactose malabsorbers compared with 5 of 13 (38.4%) lactose absorbers. These values also correlate with finding that 5 of 12 (41.7%) patients who were lactose absorbers receiving a regular diet were free from symptoms in 1 year. Similarly, in another group of 41 patients with RAP in whom no evaluation of lactose absorption was made, symptoms resolved in 6 of 17 (35.5%) of those who had milk elimination and 8 of 24 (33%) of those who received a regular diet for the 12 months.

The results of the long-term elimination diet study, therefore, exonerates lactose in the pathogenesis of RAP. Elimination of symptoms after a 1-year lactose-free diet occurred with similar frequency in patients who were absorbers or malabsorbers and those in whom no determination of lactose absorption was made. It, therefore, appears that lactose loading, either by testing or by lactose diet, can produce symptoms in lactose-intolerant patients. It seems possible that lactose elimination from those malabsorbers who are injudiciously receiving a lactose load should alleviate the symptoms related to its ingestion, but not necessarily the RAP these children are experiencing. Lactose intolerance and RAP appear to be two separate entities.

The cause of RAP most probably centers around a complex interplay of many psychological as well as organic factors. For the practitioner, however, it is worthwhile considering lactose intolerance as an aggravating factor of the symptom if the age and ethnic background of the child are risk factors.

### Clinical Correlation of Lactase Deficiency, Lactose Malabsorption, and Milk Intolerance

Statements regarding the desirability of milk consumption in different age and ethnic groups have been tenous. Several factors need to be considered in order to understand the uncertainties more clearly. In general, there is lack of correlation between lactase deficiency, lactose malabsorption, and milk intolerance for several reasons. First, clinical symptoms such as bloating, gaseousness, abdominal pain, and cramps are difficult to assess objectively, especially in evaluating infants and children. Second, other concerns include the quantity of milk or lactose that is needed to produce symptoms in children who are lactase deficient. The standard dose of lactose (2 g/kg) given in an aqueous solution is considered unphysiological. For example, a 10-year-old child weighing 32 kg would have to ingest 1000 ml of milk at one sitting in order to approximate the amount of lactose administered in the LTT. The only individuals for which a 2 g/kg lactose load would represent a physiological dose would be young infants weighing less than 5 kg. Another factor to consider in the production of symptoms is the vehicle used for lactose delivery. This may affect a gastric emptying time and intestinal motility in general. A slow rate of delivery of lactose could theoretically result in more effective hydrolysis. Also, a slower rate of entry of a substance of high osmolarity could lead to a less abrupt secretory response in the small intestine. Thus, the aqueous solution of oral lactose as administered in the diagnostic tests may empty more rapidly than meals also containing fats and proteins, and thereby, produce symptoms more readily (46).

Relationship Between Dose and Symptoms

Several studies have tried to examine the dose-response relationship of oral lactose administration. However, the articles dealing with the significance of milk intolerance secondary to lactose malabsorption are conflicting. They do not completely identify the etiological relationship. In one study, Mitchell et al. (47) compared the effects of separate feedings of 8 oz of milk to 12 g of aqueous lactose (amount of lactose in 8 oz of milk) in 13 lactose-intolerant but healthy teenagers. The symptoms developed by the patients were as follows: seven of 13 (54%) developed abdominal bloating and /or cramps after drinking 8 oz of milk. None had diarrhea. Eight of 13 (59%) were symptomatic with the equivalent amount of lactose (12.5 g). Symptoms produced were much less severe than with the standard 50 g oral lactose load, suggesting a dose-response relationship.

Similarly, Garza and Scrimshaw (48) observed the response to gradual amounts of lactose (12, 18, and 24 g) contained in peanut butter and jelly sandwich fed over successive days. Clinical symptoms developed in 10% with the 12-g lactose feeding, 30% in those fed 18 g, and 40% in those given the 24-g dosage. Six- to 9-year-old subjects in this study were not intolerant to 240 ml of milk, but 21% of malabsorber subjects reported symptoms after 1½ glasses and 40% after 2 glasses of whole milk.

In contrast to the above studies, Stephenson and Latham (49) found that most of the lactose malabsorber subjects were able to consume moderate amounts of milk without experiencing any serious symptoms. All intolerant subjects consumed at least 15 g of lactose in water and as milk; most could consume 30 g with no or only milk symptoms, indicating an extremely wide range of subjective symptoms of tolerance among lactose malabsorbers.

Reporting similar findings, Haverberg and Scrimshaw (50) administered lactose-free or lactose-containing (4.5%) dairy drinks to 110 teenagers on four consecutive mornings under double-blinded conditions. Neither absorbers nor malabsorbers reported significantly different gastrointestinal symptoms after 240 ml of lactose-containing compared with 240 ml of lactose-free formula. Seventeen absorbers and 21 malabsorbers reported symptoms inconsistent with intolerance due to lactose. That is, these individuals developed symptoms after lactose-free milk or after small dosages of lactose-containing milk (after 240 ml). In contrast, no symptoms occurred after ingestion of 480 ml of lactose-containing milk. The results indicated that most of the individuals who reported symptoms did so for reasons other than the lactose content.

We can conclude that even though a patient may be diagnosed to have lactase deficiency or lactose malabsorption, the potential for intolerance symptoms will be less if lactose is given in a low dosage, and as part of a meal rather than during the artificial setting of an aqueous solution. Double-blinded studies utilizing isocaloric meals with and without lactose are needed to further clarify the issue.

## Awareness of Milk Intolerance

The influence of an awareness of lactose intolerance on one's milk-drinking habits is an important clinical issue. Excluding the possible adverse effects milk may have on the very young lactose-intolerant patient, the symptoms of lactose intolerance may not necessitate an avoidance of milk by older individuals. Lactose-intolerant teenagers (47) indicated that they would accept milk even though symptoms might occur. In another study, Lisker and Aguilar (51) noted that future milk aversion was expressed by 80% of those patients developing severe symptoms of intolerance, whereas 97% of those with mild symptoms stated that they would not avoid the offending agent. Thus, it appears that the type and severity of the symptoms will determine consumption.

To further elucidate the scope of the problem of lactase deficiency, authors have commented on the milk-drinking habits of people who were unaware of their intolerance. Paige et al. (52) supported the view that milk consumption is directly influenced by the lactose tolerance-intolerance of the child. Among 300 black elementary school children, 20% failed to drink at least one-half of an 8-oz carton of milk at lunchtime. The authors further indicated that milk rejectors had a higher incidence of malabsorption (75%) than milk acceptors (35%). Similarly (10), of 106 subjects interviewed with documented high intestinal lactase activity, more than 90% admitted to ingestion of over 1 qt of milk per day. In 12 families with lactase deficiency, milk consumption was less than 250 ml per day. This further corroborates the hypothesis of milk aversion by the lactase-deficient patients.

Other authors (11,13) have not upheld this view. Garza and Scrimshaw (48) found no significant difference between the milk intakes of black lactose-tolerant and black lactose-intolerant children. Also no difference of milk intake was found between 5- to 7-year-old black and white children from Boston.

## Conclusion

It appears that lactase deficiency is common among the populations of the world after the age of 3-5 years. Lactase-deficient individuals need not necessarily develop symptoms upon the ingestion of lactose- or milk-containing substances. The development of symptoms will depend to a certain extent on (a) total enzyme content of the small intestine, (b) dose of lactose (milk) ingested, (c) vehicle in which lactose is presented, (d) variabilities in gastric emptying time and intestinal transit, (e) intestinal secretion after exposure to an osmotic challenge, and (f) bacterial flora (see Chapter 1).

In the past, many disease entities have been linked to lactase deficiency. However, knowledge of the genetics of lactase deficiency and results of more recent investigations indicate that these associations were more apparent than real. Lactase deficiency and the different disease entities appear to be separate issues. Since the dosage of lactose is one factor inducing abdominal pain in malabsorber with or without RAP, it is wise to exclude lactose from those malabsorbers who are unaware of their intolerance.

## References

1. Lebenthal, E., and Rossi, T. M. (1981). Lactose malabsorption and intolerance. In *Textbook of Gastroenterology and Nutrition in Infancy.* E. Lebenthal (Ed.), Raven Press, New York, pp. 673–688.
2. Lebenthal, E. (1978). Lactose intolerance. In *Digestive Diseases in Children,* E. Lebenthal (Ed.), Grune and Stratton, New York, pp. 367–388.
3. Antonowicz, I., and Lebenthal, E. (1977). Developmental pattern of small intestinal enterokinase and disaccharidase activities in the human fetus. *Gastroenterology 72*:1299–1303.
4. Bayless, T. M., and Rosensweig, N. S. (1962). Racial difference in the incidence of lactase deficiency. *J. Am. Med. Assoc. 197*:968–972.
5. Huang, S. S., and Bayless, T. M. (1966). Milk and lactose intolerance in healthy orientals. *Science 160*:83–84.
6. Cuatrecasas, P. D., Lockwood, D. H., and Caldwell, J. R. (1965). Lactase deficiency in the adult. *Lancet 1*:14–18.
7. Cook, G. C., and Kajubi, S. K. (1966). Tribal incidence of lactase deficiency in Uganda. *Lancet 1*:725–729.
8. Kretchmer, N., Hurwitz, R., Ransome-Kuti, O., Dungy, C., and Alkija, W. (1971). Intestinal absorption of lactose in Nigerian ethnic groups. *Lancet 2*:392–395.

9.  Sahi, T. M., Isokoski, M., Jussila, J., Launiala, K., and Pyorala, K. (1973). Recessive inheritance of adults-type lactose malabsorption. *Lancet 2*:823–826.

10. Lebenthal, E., Antonowicz, I., and Schwachman, H. (1975). Correlation of lactase activity, lactose tolerance and milk consumption in different age groups. *Am. J. Clin. Nutr. 28*:595–600.

11. Jones, N. V., and Latham, M. L. (1973). Lactose intolerance in young children and their parents. *Am. J. Clin. Nutr. 26*:XXVII (Abstr.).

12. Sahi, T. M., Isokoski, M., Jussila, J., and Launiala, K. (1972). Lactose malabsorption in Finnish children of school age. *Acta Pediatr. Scand. 61*:11–16.

13. Reddy, V., and Pershad, J. (1972). Lactase deficiency in Indians. *Am. J. Clin. Nutr. 25*:114–119.

14. Cook, G. C. (1967). Lactase activity in newborn and infant Baganda. *Br. Med. J. 1*:527–530.

15. Huang, S. S., and Bayless, T. M. (1967). Lactose intolerance in healthy children. *N. Engl. J. Med. 276*:1283–1287.

16. Auricchio, S., Rubino, A., and Landolt, M. (1963). Isolated intestinal lactase deficiency in the adult. *Lancet 1*:324–326.

17. Gray, G. M. (1978). Intestinal disaccharidase deficiencies and glucose-galactose malabsorption. In *Metabolic Basis of Inherited Diseases,* 4th ed., J. B. Stanbury, J. B. Wyngaarden, and D. S. Fredrickson (Eds.), McGraw-Hill, New York, pp. 1526–1536.

18. Simoons, F. J. (1970). Primary adult lactose intolerance and the milking habit: A problem in biologic and cultural interrelations. II. A culture historical hypothesis. *Am. J. Dig. Dis. 15*:695–710.

19. Simoons, F. J. (1973). Progress report: New light on ethnic differences in adult lactose intolerance. *Am. J. Dig. Dis. 18*:595–611.

20. Sahi, T. (1974). The inheritance of selective adult type lactose malabsorption. *Scand. J. Gastroenterol. 30*(Suppl. 9):1–73.

21. Bolin, T. D., and Davis, A. E. (1969). Asian lactose intolerance and its relation to intake of lactose. *Nature 222*:382.

22. Bolin, T. D., and Davis, A. E. (1970). Lactose intolerance in Australian born Chinese. *Aust. Ann. Med. 19*:40–41.

23. Fischer, J. E. (1957). Effects of feeding diet containing lactose upon Beta-d-galactosidase activity and organ development in the rat digestive tract. *Am. J. Physiol. 188*:49–53.

24. Lebenthal, E., Sunshine, P., and Kretchmer, N. (1974). Effect of prolonged nursing on lactase activity in the rat. *Gastroenterology 64*:863.

25. Knudsen, K. B., Welsch, J. D., and Kronenberg, R. S. (1968). Effect of a non-lactose diet on human intestinal disaccharidase activity. *Am. J. Dig. Dis. 13*:593.

26. Paigen, K. (1980). Temporal genes and other developmental regulators

in mammals. In *Molecular Genetics of Development,* W. Loomis and T. Leighton (Eds.), Academic Press, New York, pp. 27–31.

27. Lebenthal, E., Tsuboi, K., and Kretchmer, N. (1973). Characterization of human intestinal lactase and hetero beta-galactosidase in infants and adults. *Gastroenterology 67*:1107–1113.

28. Anderson, A. R. (1942). Ulcerative colitis an allergic phenomenon. *Am. J. Dig. Dis. 9*:91.

29. Antonowicz, I., Reddy, V., Khan, K. T., and Schwachman, H. (1968). Lactase deficiency in patients with cystic fibrosis. *Pediatrics 42*:492.

30. Jones, R. H. T. (1964). Disaccharide intolerance and mucoviscidosis. *Lancet 2*:120.

31. Auricchio, S., Rubino, A., Landolt, M., Semenza, G., and Prader, A. (1963). Isolated intestinal lactase deficiency in the adult. *Lancet 2*: 324.

32. Weser, E., Rubin, W., Ross, L., and Sleisenger, M. A. (1965). Lactase deficiency in patients with the "irritable bowel syndrome." *N. Engl. J. Med. 273*:1070.

33. Chalfin, D., and Holt, P. R. (1965). Lactase deficiency in ulcerative colitis, regional enteritis and viral hepatitis. *Lancet 2*:81–83.

34. Nordio, S., Lamedica, G. M., Berlo, A., and Vignolo, L. (1966). Disaccharidase activities of duodenal mucosa of children. *Ann. Paediatr. 206*:287.

35. Antonowicz, I., Lebenthal, E., and Schwachman, H. (1978). Disaccharidase activities in small intestinal mucosa in patients with cystic fibrosis. *J. Pediatr. 92*:214–219.

36. Lifshitz, F. (1981). Carbohydrate malabsorption. In *Clinical Disorders in Pediatric Gastroenterology and Nutrition,* F. Lifshitz (Ed.), Marcel Dekker, New York, pp. 229–248.

37. Lifshitz, F. (1981). Secondary carbohydrate intolerance in infancy. In *Clinical Disorders in Pediatric Gastroenterology and Nutrition,* F. Lifshitz (Ed.), Marcel Dekker, New York, pp. 327–340.

38. Bayless, T. M., and Huang, S. S. (1972). Recurrent abdominal pain due to milk and lactose intolerance in school age children. *Pediatrics 47*: 1029.

39. Barr, R. G., Becker, M. C., Hegmann, R. W., and Watkins, J. D. (1978). Lactose malabsorption, abdominal pain and lactose ingestion in a multiethnic school population. *Gastroenterology 74*:1006.

40. Barr, R. G., Levine, M. D., and Watkins, J. B. (1979). Recurrent abdominal pain of childhood due to lactose intolerance: a prospective study. *N. Engl. J. Med. 300*:1449–1452.

41. Liebman, W. M. (1979). Recurrent abdominal pain in children: lactose and sucrose intolerance, a prospective study. *Pediatrics 64*:43–45.

42. Lebenthal, E., Rossi, T. M., Nord, K. S., and Branski, D. (1981). Recur-

rent abdominal pain and lactose absorption in children. *Pediatrics 67*: 828–832.

43. Lisker, R., Aguilar, L., and Zavala, E. (1978). Intestinal lactase deficiency and milk drinking capacity in the adult. *Am. J. Clin. Nutr. 31*: 1499.

44. Johnson, J. D., Simoons, F. J., Hurwitz, R., Grange, A., Mitchell, C. H., Sinatra, F. R., Sunshine, P., Robertson, W. V., Bennett, P. H., and Kretchmer, N. (1977). Lactose malabsorption among Pima Indians of Arizona. *Gastroenterology 72*:1299–1304.

45. Newcomer, A. D., McGill, D. B., Thomas, P. J., and Hofman, A. F. (1978). Tolerance to lactose among lactase deficient American Indians. *Gastroenterology 74*:44–47.

46. Torun, B., Solomons, N. W., and Viteri, F. E. (1979). Lactose malabsorption and lactose intolerance implications for general milk consumption. *Arch. Lat. Am. Nutr. 29*:445–494.

47. Mitchell, K. G., Bayless, T. M., Paige, D. M., Goodgame, R. W., and Huang, S. S. (1975). Intolerance of eight ounces of milk in healthy lactose intolerant teenagers. *Pediatrics 56*:718–721.

48. Garza, C., and Scrimshaw, N. S. (1976). Relationship of lactose intolerance to milk intolerance in young children. *Am. J. Clin. Nutr. 29*: 192–196.

49. Stephenson, C. S., and Latham, M. L. (1974). Lactose intolerance and milk consumption, the relation of tolerance to symptoms. *Am. J. Clin. Nutr. 27*:296–303.

50. Haverberg, L., Kwon, P., and Scrimshaw, N. S. (1980). Comparative tolerance of adolescents of different ethnic backgrounds to lactose-containing and lactose-free dairy drinks. I. Initial experience with a double blind procedure. *Am. J. Clin. Nutr. 33*:17–21.

51. Lisker, R., and Aguilar, L. (1978). Double blind study of milk lactose intolerance. *Gastroenterology 74*:1283–1285.

52. Paige, D. M., Bayless, T. M., Ferry, G. D., and Graham, G. G. (1971). Lactose malabsorption and milk rejection in Negro children. *Johns Hopkins Med. J. 129*:163.

# 5

# DEVELOPMENTAL ASPECTS OF CARBOHYDRATE MALABSORPTION IN THE PREMATURE INFANT

JOHN B. WATKINS
*University of Pennsylvania School of Medicine
and The Children's Hospital of Philadelphia, Pennsylvania*

The infant born prematurely presents a unique challenge and opportunity for learning for the physician, nutritionist, and biologist about certain patterns of development and function of the gastrointestinal tract (1–3). In early gestation, characteristic morphological features of the gastrointestinal organ appear but with little evidence for actual functioning. By mid-to-late gestation, the functional components have developed (e.g., enzymes, disaccharidases), but are not integrated into functional units. During the perinatal period in the term infant, cooperative gastrointestinal function at last comes to the fore. Fat digestion, for example, proceeds by utilizing a series of exogenous and endogenous lipases, and biliary lipid secretion quantitatively increases, as do intraluminal bile acid concentrations (4). Lastly, in the mucosal phase of fat digestion, there are changes in the physicochemical

characteristics of the enterocyte-lipids (5) which, combined with an enlarge-
ment of the functional surface area of the small intestine and a maturation
of the enterocyte's enzymatic and transport functions, serve to achieve a
remarkably efficient absorptive unit (6,7).

This chapter focuses on the digestion and utilization of various carbohydrates available to the preterm infant. Particular attention is paid to the
observations that the premature and full-term infant may actually present a
paradigm for the child or adult who has low levels or amounts of intestinal
lactase activity. Thus, attention is also paid to the adaptive mechanisms which
may exist or develop to cope with incomplete small intestinal digestion and
absorption of lactose.

### Carbohydrate Absorption in Premature Infants

In almost every mammal studied, the specific activity of intestinal lactase is
greatest in the perinatal period and then decreases rapidly at the termination
of suckling or weaning. Various reviews have detailed the hormonal depend-
ence and environmental factors which influence this process (8,9) (Chapter
4). In the human, the disaccharidases are detected early in gestation and increase rapidly after the 20th week of gestation; and except for lactase, they
reach adult levels of activity by the 27th to 28th week of gestation. As seen
in Figure 1, the activity of lactase tends to lag behind that of sucrase and
does not reach "normal" or term levels until 36 weeks of gestation. Auricchio
et al. (10) have estimated from the intestinal lactase specific activity, and the
respective lengths of small intestine obtained from infants of differing gestational ages, that only a small percentage of the lactose ingested by the small
preterm infant would be effectively hydrolyzed, assuming complete transport of the constituent monosaccharides. These estimates are illustrated in
Table 1, and since a maximum rate is assumed, may actually be an overesti-
mation of the amount absorbed. For purposes of comparison, body weights
and a constant intake have also been estimated. Based on these supposi-
tions, it would be anticipated that an infant in the 1300–1400 g range might
be expected to have nearly 55–70% of the lactose ingested passing into the
colon; and even an infant near term may not effectively hydrolyze substantial
quantities of lactose.

A detailed analysis of the factors which would influence the net small intestinal absorption of carbohydrate must also include evidence that monosaccharide transport (e.g., glucose), which is known to proceed by an energy-
dependent sodium–requiring specific transport system, is present in the small

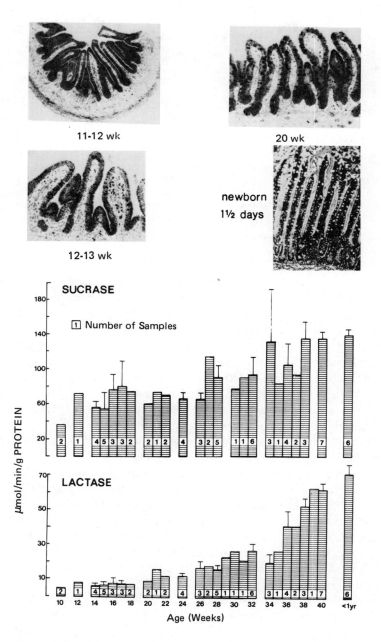

**Figure 1** Development of human intestinal villi and disaccharidases during gestation. Upper panel depicts the evolution of intestinal villus during fetal life. Lower panel illustrates the activity of intestinal sucrase and lactase at different gestational ages. Individual numbers refer to the number of fetal intestinal samples analyzed. (Adapted from Ref. 2.)

**Table 1**  Calculated Maximal In Vitro Hydrolysis of Lactose by the Entire Neonatal Small Intestine

| Gestational age (lunar months) | N | Lactose hydrolysis[a] (g/24 hr) Minimum | Maximum | Mean[b] wt. (g) | Lactose intake at 120 kcal/kg/day (g) | Estimated percentage malabsorbed |
|---|---|---|---|---|---|---|
| 6 | 1 | 0.3 | — | 875 | 10.8 | 97 |
| 7–8 | 6 | 3.8 | 6.4 | 1375 | 16.9 | 62–78 |
| 8–9 | 8 | 5.8 | 23.4 | 2100 | 25.8 | 9–72 |

[a]Ref. 10.

[b]Based on intrauterine growth curve.

intestine of the developing infant. Isolated cell preparations (11) and flux-chamber studies would suggest that net transport is diminished (12) and that quantitatively, it may be less than that observed in the adult intestine. Perfusion studies in normal small intestine provide estimates that the maximum rate of glucose absorption is about 1.3 mmol/min per 25 cm of jejunum or approximately 50 g/hr in the upper small intestine (13). The capacity of the ileum to absorb glucose is decreased as compared to the jejunum. In the infant, the number of perfusion studies are limited, but the data do demonstrate that rates of absorption at low glucose concentrations appear to be approximately 20% below the adult maximum (14,15).

Recent studies also suggest that the rates of absorption may differ markedly in the young versus old intestine due to unstirred layer effects alone (5). The presence of an unstirred layer which overlays the enterocytes, and thus separates them from the bulk intestinal contents (16) is important for the rate of diffusion of carbohydrates as well as lipids and proteins through intestinal cells. Accordingly, a consideration of the aqueous solubility and the diffusion properties of differing nutrients through a theoretical unstirred layer of varying thicknesses must be considered in the analysis of all the factors which combine to impact upon effective utilization of lactose as the principal carbohydrate source for the infant.

It appears then that lactose intake exceeds the ability of the small intestine to hydrolyze and absorb the sugar in the infant. Even though this seems unreasonable at first glance, considerable evidence is available to support this contention. For example, significant amounts (0.5–2%) of glucose, galactose,

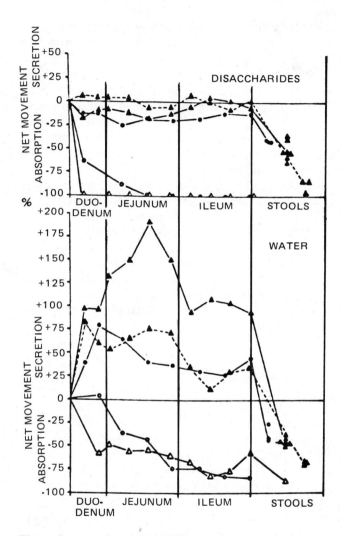

**Figure 2**   Net movement of water and disaccharides in the intestinal tract of patients with congenital lactose malabsorption. Disaccharide absorption studies were done by a classic perfusion system. Solid symbols, lactose; open symbols, sucrose; broken line indicates an investigation in patient MJ after the 3-week ingestion of a lactose-containing diet. (Adapted from Ref. 18.)

and even lactose are routinely detected in the stools of normal breast-fed infants or those fed modified cow's milk formula (17), even in the infant with an entirely normal growth curve and clinical course. An insight into the pathophysiological mechanisms which result from this degree of carbohydrate malabsorption are available from the early studies of infants with normal intestinal morphology and a congenital lactase deficiency (18). As can be seen in Figure 2, there was virtually no absorption of the lactose from the small intestine. Evidence for normal transport processes for substances other than lactose existed. There was a normal absorption of the constituent monosaccharides, glucose and galactose, and a normal alanine transport. As can be seen, in order to maintain isotonicity when lactose is perfused, a large amount of water enters the small intestine and then the colon. Interestingly, in the colon, net water absorption occurs and considerably less carbohydrate is excreted in the feces than enters the colon. In this study, nearly 55% of the malabsorbed lactose is converted to lactate or other nonsugar components. This reduces the osmolality and permits water reabsorption in the colon. Prior lactose feeding to the children with congenital lactose malabsorption (dotted line, Fig. 2) seems to facilitate this process. Thus, clearly one must balance out the diminished absorption in the small intestine with the compensatory capacity of the colon.

**Colonic Metabolism of Malabsorbed Carbohydrate**

Experimental Methods

The mechanism(s) responsible for the metabolism and utilization of carbohydrate in the colon and other carbohydrate-containing glycoproteins have recently been evaluated by Bond, Levitt (19), and Perman (20) (Chapter 10). In their studies, the fate of the nonabsorbed glucose was investigated by measuring breath $^{14}CO_2$ and fecal $^{14}CO_2$ after direct instillation of $^{14}C$ U-labeled glucose, lactate and acetate in the cecum. The appearance of $^{14}CO_2$ in breath was as rapid after the intracecal as after intragastric instillation. The conversion of $^{14}$glucose to $^{14}CO_2$ in the colon was dependent upon the presence of bacterial flora and did not occur after similar experiments in germ-free rats. In contrast, acetate and lactate were converted to $^{14}CO_2$ under both conditions, suggesting that this process does not require bacterial fermentation. Estimations of colonic blood flow and the amount of oxygen available determined that aerobic oxidation of glucose is unlikely to occur in the colon. Accordingly, the major products of the anaerobic metabolism of glucose are short-chain fatty acids, which may be absorbed and oxidized by the host. For the remaining $^{14}C$ recovered in the stool after cecal instillation (less than 20%), only 3% was in a dialyzable form, confirming that very little of the glucose reaching the colon appears in the feces in an osmotically active form. Thus, the colonic flora benefits the infant by reducing the osmotic load of nonabsorbed carbohydrate, and by facilitating the salvage of a large percentage of the carbohydrate calories not absorbed in the small bowel through the anerobic conversion to soluble metabolizable intermediates.

Investigation of the factors which influence the intestinal microbial ecosystems are now being studied in greater detail with the recognition that significant interrelations between diet and the colonic microbial community are significant for human health (21). A detailed examination of the bacterial metabolic pathways is available in several excellent reviews (22). Products of the large intestine fermentation are similar to those of the rumen. Acetate, proprionate, and butyrate are formed along with $CH_4$, $H_2$, and $CO_2$; estimates of the amount of hexose required to support the biomass of intestinal bacteria (approximately $1 \times 10^{11}$ cell per gram feces) indicate that far more volatile fatty acids (VFA) are produced than can be accounted for in the excreted feces. VFA have been demonstrated to be absorbed across the colonic wall, accompanied by absorption of $HCO_3^-$ in the colon (23). In the rabbit, VFA production can supply up to 30–40% of its energy requirement, and in the porcupine this is estimated to be in the range of 16–20%. The fate of the glucose products, $H_2$ and $CH_4$, produced in the large bowel is that they are absorbed into the blood and removed in the lungs, and exhaled or expelled as flatus.

The limits of the ability of the flora to metabolize sugar have not been extensively studied, although the diarrhea usually observed after ingestion of 50 g lactose in lactase-deficient subjects indicate that the metabolism to and absorption of short-chain fatty acids in the colon are insufficiently rapid to prevent diarrhea completely after such loads, although bacterial action may ameliorate the volume of diarrhea. Interesting, studies by Perman demonstrate that prolonged administration of a nonabsorbed carbohydrate reduces the fecal pH and the rate of breath $H_2$ production in vivo or from in vitro fecal incubations (20). Thus, multiple factors including diet may contribute to influence metabolism and perhaps the types of bacteria within the human colonic ecosystem (Chapter 10).

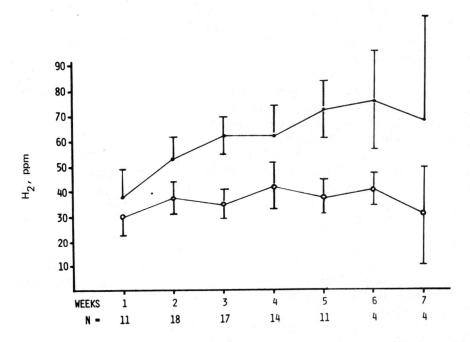

**Figure 3** Mean (0) and peak (•) hydrogen concentrations in prematures during a 7-week period of study. N = number of studies during each week. (Adapted from MacLean, W. C., and Fink, B. B. (1981). In *Lactose Digestion: Clinical and Nutritional Implications,* Johns Hopkins Univ. Press, Baltimore, p. 207.)

## Clinical Studies

In the newborn infant, the colon is virtually sterile at birth, but rapidly becomes colonized in the first few days of life. In a recent study in our laboratory, substantial quantities of hydrogen could be demonstrated in the breath of full-term infants delivered by cesarean section by 7 days of age (24). Peak hydrogen values were 55 ± 15 ppm (mean ± SEM) while the infants were consuming lactose loads of 1.8 ± 0.2 g/kg at each feeding. Breath hydrogen values in this range are considered indicative of substantial lactose malabsorption in older children and adults (25). Furthermore, the onset of $H_2$ excretion at a lactose load of 2 g/kg could be shown to correlate with the appearance of sufficient numbers of $H_2$-producing bacteria in the feces when

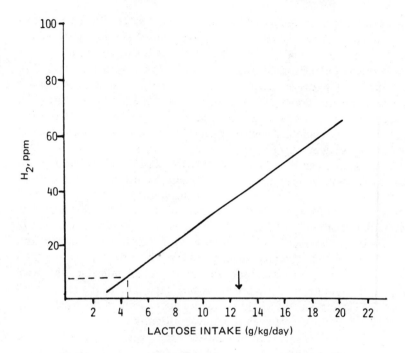

**Figure 4**  Regression curve of 5-hr mean $H_2$ concentration of lactose intake per day. (From Ref. 26.)

they were isolated and altered in vitro using lactose as the sole carbohydrate source. MacLean and Fink (26), using a similar technique, studied a larger group of premature infants ranging from 29 to 38 weeks of gestation. Seventy-five percent of the infants were found to excrete more than 8 ppm hydrogen by 2 weeks of age, and all were excreting larger amounts as total energy as lactose intake increased (see Fig. 3). No systematic study has yet been carried out to investigate the influence of antibiotic therapy and diet on the type of bacteria which colonize the fecal flora, or the osmolarity of the feces at a constant intake of carbohydrate. Several investigators have noted loose diarrheal stools after antibiotics and that coincident with the appearance of $H_2$ in breath, the fecal-reducing substances and water decrease, resuming a normal stool pattern (27).

Several approaches can be used to quantify the magnitude of lactose malabsorption in these infants and in lactase-deficient adults. Levitt has determined the amount of lactose reaching the ileal cecal valve, directly by a perfusion technique, and compared this to the amount of $H_2$ produced and excreted in breath (28). Similarly, comparison to the hydrogen produced after a known dose of a nonabsorbed sugar such as lactulose may also be used (20). Total volumes of hydrogen excreted may also be estimated by a method utilized by Solomons, assuming a given tidal volume and respiratory rate (29). Using such assumptions, MacLean estimated an average of 8.3–13.9 g lactose/kg per day were metabolized by the premature infants whose mean lactose intake was 12.5 g/kg per day (26).

Similar estimates can be achieved directly (see Fig. 4) where mean breath hydrogen excretion was compared to the daily lactose intake (26). From these studies in premature infants, little or no hydrogen is produced until daily lactose intake exceeds 4.5 g/kg per day. It increases directly thereafter so that at the usual intake of 12.5 g/kg per day, one may estimate that nearly 64% of the lactose ingested, or 8.0 g/kg per day, are available for metabolism by the colonic bacteria. Despite the magnitude of the carbohydrate and total energy intake which escapes absorption in the small intestine, the fecal losses of carbohydrate in these infants is not large, but in the range maximally of 4.9 kcal or 3.1 kcal/2 kg per day, or about 2.5% of the total energy intake. Similar findings have been reported by Kien, who performed careful balance studies and estimates of total fecal and urine energy loss in two groups of growing premature infants fed formulas of similar caloric density but differing carbohydrate composition (30).

### Final Considerations

Since both premature and full-term infants appear to malabsorb differing but significant amounts of lactose for up to at least 5-6 months of age (31), is there any potential benefit to the infant of this physiological malabsorption? Does lactose in the diet serve to conserve a large intestinal flora of predominately lactose fermenters as opposed to putrefactive bacteria or others potentially more pathogenic to the infant? Since lactose is uniquely present in milk and has been shown to facilitate the absorption of calcium in experimental animals (32) and perhaps in the human as well (33), careful consideration should be given to the complete removal of lactose from the diet, particularly in infants without symptoms who are growing well. One might anticipate from these preliminary studies that considerable attention will now be paid to colonic absorptive functions, the colonization of the ileum and large intestine by bacteria, and the physical state of various nutritionally significant compounds in the colon. Thus, the concept of lactose absorption might logically be expanded to include both absorption in the component monosaccharides, glucose and galactose, as well as the absorption and utilization of the products of colonic bacterial fermentation. Thus, the overall loss of energy to the infant may be far less than assumed from the data which estimates small bowel absorption alone.

Similarly, the possible adverse effects of metabolism of intralumenal carbohydrates by colonic flora should be considered (Chapter 10). Metabolic acidosis has been described in premature infants following a lactose oral load (34), and at times transient lactose intolerance may occur in these infants (35).

## Acknowledgments

Thanks to Catherine Chiles, Ron Barr, and Jay Perman for their contributions and to D. Hicklin-Blackshear for secretarial assistance.

Supported in part by grants HD-13932 and HD-13913 from The National Institutes of Health; grant G034 2 from The Cystic Fibrosis Foundation; and The Wolbach Fund, Children's Hospital Medical Center, Boston, Massachusetts.

## References

1. Henning, S. J. (1981). Postnatal development: coordination of feeding, digestion, and metabolism. *Am. J. Physiol. 241*:G199–214.
2. Grand, R. J., Watkins, J. B., and Troti, F. M. (1976). Development of the human gastro-intestinal tract: a review. *Gastroenterology 70*:790–81.
3. Koldovsky, O. (1979). Development of sucrase activity: effect of maternal hormonal status and fetal programming of jejuno-ileal differences. In *Development of Mammalian Absorptive Processes*, Excerpta Medica, New York, pp. 147–168.
4. Watkins, J. B. (1974). Bile acid metabolism and fat absorption in newborn infants. *Pediatr. Clin. North Am. 21*:501–512.
5. Thompson, A. B. R. (1979). Unstirred water layer and age-dependent changes in rabbit jejunal D-glucose transport. *Am. J. Physiol. 236*: E685–691.

6.  Holtzapple, P. G., Starr, C. M., and Morck, T. (1980). Phosphatidyl-choline synthesis in the developing small intestine. *Biochem. J. 186*: 399–403.
7.  Berendsen, P. B., and Blanchette-Mackie, E. J. (1979). Milk lipid absorption and chylomicron production in the suckling rat. *Anat. Rec. 195*:397–414.
8.  Boyle, J. T., and Koldovsky, O. (1980). Critical role of adrenal glands in precocious increase in jejunal sucrase activity following premature weaning in rats: negligible effect of food intake. *J. Nutr. 110*:169–177.
9.  Kendall, K., Jumawan, J., and Koldovsky, O. (1979). Development of jejunoileal differences of activity of lactase, sucrase and acid B-galactosidase in isografts of fetal rat intestine. *Biol. Neonate 36*:206–214.
10. Auricchio, S., Rubino, A., and Murset, G. (1965). Intestinal glycosidase activities in the human embryo, fetus, and newborn. *Pediatrics 35*: 944–954.
11. Gall, D. G., and Chapman, D. (1976). Sodium ion transport in isolated intestinal epithelial cells: comparison of the effect of actively transported sugars on sodium ion efflux in cells isolated from jejunum and ileum. *Biochim. Biophys. Acta 419*:314–319.
12. Shepherd, R. W., Hamilton, J. R., and Gall, D. G. (1980). The postnatal development of sodium transport in the proximal small intestine of the rabbit. *Pediatr. Res. 14*:250–253.
13. Modigliani, R., and Bernier, J. J. (1971). Absorption of glucose, sodium and water by the human jejunum studied by intestinal perfusion with a proximal occluding balloon at variable flow rates. *Gut 12*:184–193.
14. Torres-Pinedo, R., Rivera, C. E., and Fernandez, S. (1966). Studies on infant diarrhea. II. Absorption of glucose and net fluxes of water and sodium chloride in a segment of jejunum. *J. Clin. Invest. 45*:1916–1922.
15. Rey, F., Drillet, F., Schmitz, J., and Rey, J. (1974). Influence of flow rate on the kinetics of the intestinal absorption of glucose and lysine in children. *Gastroenterology 66*:79–85.
16. Thompson, A. B. R. (1979). Limitations of Michaelis-Menten kinetics in presence of intestinal unstirred layers. *Am. J. Physiol. 236*:E701–709.
17. Davidson, A. G. F., and Mullinger, M. (1970). Reducing substances in neonatal stools detected by clinitest. *Pediatrics 46*:632–635.
18. Launiala, K. (1968). The mechanism of diarrhoea in congenital disaccharide malabsorption. *Acta Paediatr. Scand. 57*:425–432.
19. Bond, J. H., and Levitt, M. D. (1976). Fate of soluble carbohydrate in the colon of rats and man. *J. Clin. Invest. 57*:1158–1164.
20. Perman, J. A., Modler, S., and Olson, A. C. (1981). Role of pH in production of hydrogen from carbohydrate by colonic bacterial flora. Studies in vivo and in vitro. *J. Clin. Invest. 67*:643–650.

21. Wolin, M. J. (1981). Fermentation in the rumen and human large intestine. *Science 213*:1463–1468.
22. Wolin, M. J. (1979). In *Advances in Microbial Ecology*, Vol. 3, M. Alexander (Ed.), Plenum, New York, pp. 49–77.
23. McNeil, N. I., Cummings, J. H., and James, W. P. T. (1978). Short chain fatty acid absorption by the human large intestine. *Gut 19*:819–822.
24. Chiles, C., Watkins, J. B., and Barr, R. G. (1979). Lactose utilization in the newborn: role of colonic flora. *Pediatr. Res. 13*:365.
25. Barr, R. G., Watkins, J. B., and Perman, J. A. (1981). Mucosal function and breath hydrogen excretion: Comparative studies in the clinical evaluation of children with nonspecific abdominal complaints. *Pediatrics 68*: 526–533.
26. MacLean, W. C., Jr., and Fink, B. B. (1980). Lactose malabsorption by premature infants: magnitude and clinical significance. *J. Pediatr. 97*: 383–388.
27. MacLean, W. C., Jr., and Fink, B. B., Chiles, C., Barr, R. G., and Watkins, J. B. Personal communication, 1982.
28. Bond, J. H., Currier, B., Buchwald, H., and Levitt, M. D. (1980). Colonic conservation of malabsorbed carbohydrate. *Gastroenterology 78*:444–447.
29. Solomons, N. W., Viteri, F. E., and Hamilton, L. H. (1977). Application of a simple gas chromatographic technique for measuring breath hydrogen. *J. Lab. Clin. Med. 90*:856–862.
30. Kien, C. L., Sumners, J. E., Stetina, J. S., et al. (1981). Carbohydrate energy absorption in premature infants. (Unpublished abstract) XII International Congress of Nutrition, August, 1981.
31. Douwes, A. C., Oosterkamp, R. F., Fernandes, J., Los, T., and Jongbloed, A. A. (1980). Sugar malabsorption in healthy neonates estimated by breath hydrogen. *Arch. Dis. Child. 55*:512–515.
32. Leichter, J., and Tolensky, A. F. (1975). Effect of dietary lactose on the absorption of protein fat and calcium in the post weaning rat. *Am. J. Clin. Nutr. 28*:238–241.
33. Ziegler, E. E., and Forman, S. J. (1980). Lactose and mineral absorption in infancy. *Pediatr. Res. 14*:513a.
34. Lifshitz, F., Diaz-Bensussen, S., Martinez-Garza, V., Abdo-Bassols, F., and Diaz del Castillo, E. (1971). Influence of disaccharides on the development of systemic acidosis in the premature infant. *Pediatr. Res. 5*: 213–225.
35. Abdo-Bassols, F., Lifshitz, F., Del Castillo, E. D., and Martinez-Garza, Y. (1971). Transient lactose intolerance in premature infants. *Pediatrics 48*:816–821.

# 6

# INTESTINAL DISACCHARIDASES
## structure, function, and deficiency

ROBERT K. MONTGOMERY, MAUREEN M. JONAS, and RICHARD J. GRAND
*Harvard Medical School
and The Children's Hospital Medical Center, Boston, Massachusetts*

Final cleavage of dietary disaccharides to their constituent monosaccharides occurs in the small intestine. With a few specific exceptions (such as the absence of lactase in the pinnipeds) mammals, including humans, have five disaccharidases in their intestinal mucosa: sucrase, maltase, lactase, isomaltase, and trehalase. Data on the occurrence and function of the disaccharidases have been ably reviewed by Semenza (1) and more recently by Gray (2).

## Disaccharidase Structure and Function

The controversy over the site of action of the disaccharidases has been resolved in favor of localization on the luminal surface membrane of the enterocyte. Thus, disaccharide digestion is clearly a surface phenomenon; the disaccharidases are not secreted (3). Purification studies indicate that the disaccharidases are high molecular weight glycoproteins, with molecular weights ranging from approximately 200,000 up to 500,000 and containing up to 40% carbohydrate by weight. Sucrase, isomaltase, maltase, and trehalase are $\alpha$-glucosidases; lactase is a $\beta$-galactosidase. Current data on sucrase, lactase, and maltases are reviewed below and in Chapter 4. Since there is little data on trehalase, and trehalose is not a significant dietary component, trehalase is not discussed.

## Sucrase-Isomaltase

Sucrase-isomaltase is the most thoroughly studied of the disaccharidases, although a great deal remains to be elucidated about its structure, synthesis, and processing. The enzyme has been purified to homogeneity from rabbit (4,5), rat (6), and human small intestine (7). Initially it was found that sucrase (sucrose $\alpha$-glucohydrolase, EC 3.2.1.48) and isomaltase (dextrin 6-$\alpha$-glucanohydrolase, EC 3.2.1.10) co-purified as a single high molecular weight species identified by nondenaturing polyacrylamide gel electrophoresis, gel chromatography, and ultracentrifugation. The enzyme from rabbit intestine has been most critically examined. By sodium dodecyl sulfate polyacrylamide gel electrophoresis (SDS-PAGE), apparent molecular weights of 140,000 and 160,000 for sucrase and isomaltase and a total complex weight of 300,000 were obtained (8). Detailed ultracentrifugation analysis gave molecular weight estimates of 270,000 and 280,000 for sucrase-isomaltase in two different detergent solutions (9). The latter is more accurate, as SDS-PAGE is well known to overestimate the molecular weight of glycoproteins.

Kinetic and inhibition studies of sucrase and isomaltase activities indicate that the two activities are independent of one another (10). Cogoli et al. (5) partially denatured the rabbit enzyme by alkaline treatment, leaving isomaltase activity unaffected. By acylation with citraconic anhydride, Braun et al. (11) separated the purified rabbit enzyme into two independent subunits having either sucrase or isomaltase activity. Conklin et al. (7) separated active human sucrase and isomaltase subunits by $\beta$-mercaptoethanol/urea treatment, thus demonstrating that both human and rabbit enzymes consisted of a dimer, whose two subunits each carried an independent enzymatic site. Similarly, the rat enzyme can be separated into two subunits by SDS/mercaptoethanol treatment (12,13), although enzyme activities cannot be evaluated after this procedure.

Maestracci (14) quantitatively removed sucrase, maltase, and lactase from the microvillus membrane by proteolytic cleavage using papain or elastase. Sucrase-isomaltase can be removed from the membrane and purified either by protease digestion or detergent solubilization. Sigrist et al. (15) purified sucrase-isomaltase from rabbit intestine solubilized with Triton X-100 and found that the enzyme aggregated readily in the absence of detergent, suggesting a greater hydrophobicity in the detergent-solubilized enzyme, although chemical composition and molecular weight of the two forms were nearly identical. The electrophoretic mobility of isomaltase from proteolytic and detergent-solubilized enzyme differs in both rabbit (16) and rat (13), although that of sucrase does not. This difference in mobility represents the molecular weight of a very hydrophobic anchor sequence which is cleaved off the isomaltase subunit by proteases. Frank et al. (17) sequenced this anchor segment from rabbit sucrase-isomaltase and showed that it represents the N-terminal end of the isomaltase. In addition, Brunner et al. (16) demonstrated that detergent-solubilized sucrase-isomaltase would reinsert into artificial lipid bilayers, demonstrating that the hydrophobic tail does indeed function as an anchor for the enzyme.

In the last few years, data have begun to accumulate on the intracellular synthesis of sucrase-isomaltase. Using a labeled terminal sugar precursor ([$^3$H] fucose), Hauri et al. (18) demonstrated that a purified rat enterocyte Golgi fraction contained only a single, high molecular weight form of rapidly labeled, immunoprecipitable sucrase-isomaltase. Since the label appeared in both brush-border subunits at later times and the high molecular weight form could be cleaved by elastase into two subunits, comigrating with those from brush border, these data indicate that sucrase-isomaltase is synthesized as a single high molecular weight polypeptide, as suggested by Semenza (19). This conclusion is supported by the demonstration of a single large sucrase-isomaltase protein in pancreatic duct ligated pig microvillus membranes (20) and in transplanted fetal rat intestine lacking normal luminal factors (12,13).

Evidence for an even earlier form has recently been presented by Grand and Ryan (21), Cezard et al. (22), and Montgomery et al. (13). Using cell fractionation techniques, the former investigators identified a microsomal, high molecule weight form of sucrase-isomaltase, which by labeling characteristics appeared to be a synthetic precursor of the microvillous membrane form of the enzyme. In contrast, Cezard et al. (22) reported that the early labeled form of sucrase-isomaltase consisted of soluble cytosol monomers

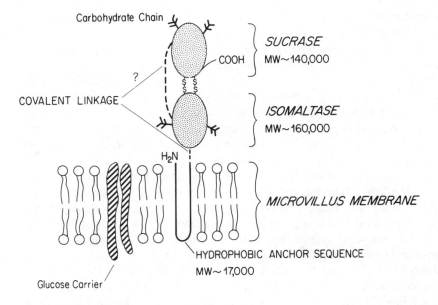

Figure 1   Schematic representation of intestinal sucrase-isomaltase and its insertion into the microvillous membrane of the enterocyte.

of sucrase and isomaltase. Danielsen et al. (23,24) have found two high molecular weight forms of pig sucrase-isomaltase in a cell fraction which includes endoplasmic reticulum. One of these appears to be an early precursor which has not yet undergone the initial glycosylation step occurring concurrent with or just subsequent to the synthesis of the protein. Human sucrase-isomaltase was reported by Kelly and Alpers (25) to contain 40% carbohydrate by weight, while the rat enzyme contains 20%. Herscovics et al. (26) found that the carbohydrate portion of rat sucrase-isomaltase contained a large proportion of asparagine-linked oligosaccharides of the complex type and a small amount of high manose oligosaccharides.

From electron microscopic examination of Triton X-100-solubilized rabbit sucrase-isomaltase, Nishi and Takesue (27) concluded that the enzyme complex is an elongated oval, with the long axis perpendicular to the membrane, consisting of two smaller, similar sized ovals, roughly 45 × 65 Å. From the location of precipitates of anti-sucrase and anti-isomaltase antibodies, Nishi et al. (28) determined that the sucrase subunit was distal to the membrane, while the isomaltase was proximal to it. The dimer projected about 150 Å from the membrane surface, apparently with a gap of about 20 Å between the isomaltase and lipid layer. This is consistent with the presence of a single peptide chain attaching the protein to the membrane, and consistent in other respects with the biochemical data presented above. This information is summarized in Figure 1.

## Lactase-Phlorizin Hydrolase

Lactase is the disaccharidase of greatest clinical significance, but, until recently, few data on its structure or mechanism of synthesis were available. There are three separate β-galactosidase activities in the intestinal mucosa, but only one microvillus membrane lactase (29,30). Lactase has been purified from rat (29,31) and human (29,30) small intestine. Purification of rat lactase results in copurification of lactase (β-D-galactoside galactohydrolase, EC 3.2.1.23) and phlorizin hydrolase (glycosyl-N-acylsphingosine glycohydrolase, EC 3.2.1.62) activities, strongly indicating that the two are associated (31). It is not yet known if the two enzyme activities are on separate subunits or separate but on the same subunit.

The structure of the enzyme remains unclear. Gray and Santiago (30) estimated the molecular weight of human lactase at 280,000 by ultracentrifugation. Birkenmeier and Alpers (32) found five protein bands by electrophoresis of rat lactase under nonreducing, nondenaturing conditions, with a major protein band having a molecular weight of 132,000. Green and Hauri (33) described an electrophoretically distinct lactase present only in the distal small intestine of rats. Cousineau and Green (34) demonstrated that sialic acid residues susceptible to removal by neuraminidase accounted for the difference in electrophoretic mobility between the proximal and distal forms. However, Green and Hauri (33) solubilized rat microvillus membranes with detergent and found single proximal and distal protein bands on electrophoresis. Using the same system, but papain-solubilized lactase, Cousineau and Green (34) found two protein bands in both proximal and distal lactase. The human enzyme has recently been examined by Skovbjerg et al. (35). These authors found a single protein band with detergent-solubilized jejunal lactase run under reducing, denaturing conditions. This protein had a molecular weight of 160,000. Their data also indicate a high molecular weight form incorporating two subunits of similar molecular weight, which they suggest may represent a precursor form. The amphiphilic form had a molecular weight of 320,000, while the papain-solubilized form had a molecular weight of 280,000 the difference possibly representing an anchor sequence. In contrast, data from the same laboratory (24) on pig lactase suggests that the endoplasmic reticulum contains an unglycosylated precursor form which by SDS-PAGE analysis is slightly smaller than the single subunit of 160,000 molecular weight found on the microvillus membrane. The discrepancy between these two findings remains to be resolved. Further examination of the intracellular processing of the enzyme is needed to elucidate this question and provide a foundation for understanding the biochemical mechanisms involved in lactase deficiency.

## Maltase-Glucoamylase

Much less biochemical information is available for maltase-glucoamylase (EC 3.2.1.20 and 3.2.1.3, respectively). Sucrase-isomaltase has maltase activity, but electrophoretic studies of human (36) and rat (37) microvillus membranes have clearly demonstrated the presence of a distinct enzyme which has maltase and glucoamylase activities. Maltase is the largest of the disaccharidases, with a molecular weight for the human enzyme estimated at 440,000 (36) and the rat enzyme at 500,000. Kelly and Alpers (25) purified human glucoamylase almost to homogeneity, as judged by polyacrylamide gel electrophoresis. They found that the enzyme consisted of at least two isozymes, contained 32–38% carbohydrate by weight, and had a molecular weight estimated at 210,000 by equilibrium sedimentation. Their kinetic data suggested a single catalytic site, but they did not rule out the possibility that the enzyme might consist of two subunits. The purified rat enzyme appears to consist of two subunits which form stable aggregates of three different sizes under several conditions, including boiling in 1% SDS and 1% mercaptoethanol. The native form is a multimer, but because of difficulty in assessing molecular weight accurately for these glycoproteins, it is not clear what the subunit structure is (38). Maroux and Louvard (39) concluded that the pig maltase was attached to the membrane by an anchor segment. However, Flanagan and Forstner (38) found that the detergent- and protease-solubilized forms of rat maltase were very similar, both forms having the same N-terminal amino acids. Although maltase is solubilized from microvillus membrane by both elastase and papain (14), these data suggest that there is not an anchor sequence analagous to that of sucrase-isomaltase. Danielsen et al. (23) have recently reported data indicating that pig maltase-glucoamylase is initially synthesized as a single high molecular weight precursor. Although the biochemistry of maltase-glucoamylase is only beginning to be elucidated, it appears to be generally similar in structure and biosynthesis to the other disaccharidases.

### Primary Sucrase-Isomaltase Deficiency

Congenital sucrase-isomaltase deficiency is inherited as an autosomal recessive trait (40). It occurs in approximately 0.8% of North Americans (40) and in up to 10% of the Eskimos of Greenland (41). The disorder may be initially recognized in infants, children, or adults; this suggests that the deficiency of the enzyme is a lifelong condition. Obligate heterozygotes can be shown to have intermediate enzyme activity (40). The histology of the small intestine is normal in primary sucrase-isomaltase deficiency.

The molecular basis for the enzyme deficiency is not known. In 1973, Dubs et al. (42), using indirect immunofluorescence with an antibody to rabbit sucrase-isomaltase, demonstrated material in the intestine of functionally deficient humans that cross-reacted with the antibody. This suggested the presence of an inactive protein as the basis for the disorder. However, there have been two studies to the contrary. Preiser et al. (43) found that there was absence of the previously determined sucrase-isomaltase bands when brush-border proteins from patients with sucrose intolerance were separated by gel electrophoresis. In addition, there was no evidence for a structurally altered enzyme with a different electrophoretic mobility. In agreement with these results was the study by Gray et al. (44) in 1976. They demonstrated that, in normal subjects, values for sucrase-isomaltase in brush-border preparations were the same by hydrolytic assay and radioimmunoassay, while in patients with sucrase-isomaltase deficiency, there was no enzyme detected by either method. Also, their radioimmunoassay technique disclosed no cross-reacting protein anywhere in the enterocytes when the antibody was tested against intestinal homogenates. These results suggest total absence of the enzyme in deficient patients. Thus, the nature of the molecular defect may be total repression of the structural gene controlling the synthesis of sucrase-isomaltase, a major alteration in the structural gene producing an unrecognizable or unstable protein, or the production of an abnormal messenger RNA with resultant absence of synthesis of the protein.

Sucrase-isomaltase deficiency may present in infancy, when sucrose is introduced into the diet, with severe diarrhea, secondary malabsorption, and failure to thrive (45). In young children, it may be detected during evaluation of chronic diarrhea without growth retardation (46,47). Alternatively, it may not be manifest until adulthood when patients complain of intermittent abdominal distention, cramps, flatulence, and diarrhea: symptoms which closely mimic those of the "irritable bowel syndrome."

Until recently, the diagnosis of sucrase-isomaltase deficiency was made either by direct assay of the enzyme activity in intestinal biopsy specimens, or the cumbersome sucrose tolerance test which involved serial measurements of serum glucose after an oral sucrose load. The advent of the interval breath hydrogen test has made possible the simple noninvasive diagnosis of this disorder in patients of all ages (48).

Since symptoms occur only in the presence of orally ingested sucrose, therapy consists simply of removing sucrose from the diet. As sucrose-isomaltase–deficient children mature, they are often able to tolerate increasing amounts of dietary sucrose and starch, although it has been shown that there is no concomitant increase in enzyme specific activity (49). This tolerance is felt to result from the normal growth and increasing surface area of the intestine, as well as a subconsciously self-imposed diet which is low in sucrose. There have been reports (50,51) of induction of sucrase-isomaltase activity in experimental animals and in normal human subjects by altering dietary carbohydrate sources, but only one report (52) in which a single sucrase-isomaltase-deficient patient was noted to exhibit increased sucrase-isomaltase activity after being given a diet very high in fructose. The mechanism for this response is unclear, but since the highest value for sucrase-isomaltase activity attained was only 15% of normal levels, it is doubtful that this phenomenon would be of clinical significance.

## Secondary Sucrase-Isomaltase Deficiency

Since sucrase-isomaltase is a constituent of the microvillus membrane of villus enterocytes, any process that causes villus injury or damages the intestinal epithelium causes a secondary decrease in sucrase-isomaltase activity. Examples of these processes are infectious enteritis, gluten-sensitive enteropathy, radiation enteritis, drug-induced (such as chemotherapeutic agents) enteritis, and Giardiasis. However, under these conditions, lactase, which is originally present in much smaller amounts in the microvillus membrane, is usually more severely affected, and lactose malabsorption is more clinically significant. Also, in secondary sucrase-isomaltase deficiency, the enzyme activity does not reach the extremely low levels encountered in primary sucrase-isomaltase deficiency, and thus patients are able to tolerate some dietary sucrose during their illness. The small intestinal histopathology is always abnormal in secondary sucrase-isomaltase deficiency, reflecting the primary cause of the enteritis, and specific therapy is directed toward the underlying illness (Chapter 1).

## Congenital Lactase Deficiency

In 1959, Holzel et al. (53) described two siblings who exhibited marked lactose intolerance and malnutrition, attributed to congenital absence of lactase. The strict criteria for congenital deficiency of the enzyme are (a) absence of enzyme activity from birth which is persistent throughout life, (b) absence of other disaccharide or monosaccharide intolerance, and (c) normal small bowel mucosal morphology. As is true for other inborn errors of metabolism, this condition is quite rare; there have been few cases described which fulfill all of these criteria (Chapter 4). The defect is felt by some to be due to an alteration in the structural gene encoding lactase synthesis. The tiny amount of apparent residual lactase activity in these patients has been attributed to lysosomal acid $\beta$-galactosidase demonstrated to be present in normal amounts (54). Other workers have found no difference in electrophoretic banding patterns of lactase from patients with congenital and those with later onset deficiencies and propose a similar regulatory defect in both disorders (55). Diagnosis of this condition is made by demonstrating normal small bowel mucosal histology, absence of lactase activity, and presence of other disaccharidase activities in normal amounts. Treatment is simply a lactose-free diet and correction of the secondary nutritional disturbances.

## Genetic "Late-Onset" Lactase Deficiency

The most common form of lactase deficiency worldwide is that which occurs on a genetic basis after early childhood (Chapter 4). The global epidemiology of this entity has been the subject of many studies, and has disclosed the highest incidence in African blacks and Orientals, moderate incidences in Western blacks, Native Americans, and Caucasians of Mediterranean descent, and lowest incidences in Caucasians of Scandinavian and Anglo-Saxon descent. This pattern has suggested that persistence of lactase into adulthood represents an adaptive mutation in those parts of the world where dairy

**Table 1**  Prevalence of Genetic Late-Onset Lactose Malabsorption Among Ethnic or Racial Groups

| Group | No. of persons in study | Ages of persons | No. of persons with LM | Prevalence of LM (%) |
|---|---|---|---|---|
| Alaskan Eskimos | 36 | Adults | 34 | 94 |
| Oklahoma Native Americans | 20 | Adults | 19 | 95 |
| Children in Ghana | 100 | 2–6 | 73 | 73 |
| Bantu | 52 | Adults | 51 | 95 |
| Orientals in the United States | 11 | Adults | 11 | 100 |
| Danes | 670 | Adults | 16 | 2 |
| "Anglo-American" whites | 142 | Adults | 21 | 15 |
| American whites | 25 | 4–5 | 6 | 24 |
| American blacks | 98 | Adults | 79 | 81 |
| Mexican Americans | 75 | 10–14 | 42 | 56 |
| Indians in Bombay | 100 | Adults | 64 | 64 |

LM, lactose malabsorption.
*Source*: Adapted from Ref. 56, p. 24.

farming and lifelong milk drinking have been common for centuries. Recently, Simoons has documented evidence for this hypothesis in an extensive review of the epidemiological literature (56). Examples from his accumulated data are given in Table 1. Documentation of lactose malabsorption varied widely among studies.

Genetic "late-onset" lactase deficiency is also age-dependent. Reduction in levels of the enzyme begins at 5 years of age in white children and 3 years of age in black children (57). Lactose intolerance in children under these ages is always abnormal, and an underlying mucosal lesion should be actively delineated.

In late-onset lactase deficiency there is rarely complete absence of enzyme activity; usually 5–10% of control activity persists. The enzymological properties, such as chromatographic mobility, Km and pH activity curve of this persistent lactase are identical to those of lactase from control subjects (54). For these reasons, late-onset deficiency is believed to represent an alteration in a regulatory gene which encodes for a delayed "turn-off" in the synthesis of the enzyme.

Since this entity represents a specific enzyme defect, the morphology of the small intestinal mucosa in affected individuals is normal. There has been some controversy about whether lactose ingestion in this setting causes secondary deficiencies (Chapter 1). Although the lactose malabsorption may result in considerable symptoms and promote a significant osmotic diarrhea, most authors agree that neither histopathological damage nor clinically significant secondary malabsorption of other nutrients occurs (58).

Clinical symptoms of lactose intolerance range from mild abdominal discomfort to the full-blown syndrome of diffuse abdominal cramps, bloating, flatulence, and watery diarrhea. The amount of lactose necessary to elicit symptoms varies from person to person. Recently lactose intolerance has been proposed as a cause of irritable bowel syndrome in adults and recurrent abdominal pain in children (59,60) (Chapter 4). Early studies showed an increased incidence of abnormalities in functional lactose tolerance testing in these groups, but follow-up studies examining the association of symptoms with dietary lactose have questioned lactose intolerance as an etiological factor.

Diagnosis of late-onset lactase deficiency involves demonstration of an abnormal functional test of lactase absorption, that is, a lactose tolerance test or a lactose breath hydrogen test, or a low level of lactase activity in small bowel mucosa, in the presence of normal activities of other disaccharidases and normal morphology. Causes of secondary lactase deficiency, as described below, must be excluded. Treatment is simply avoidance of dietary lactose.

## Secondary Lactase Deficiency

Any insult to the small intestinal mucosa with injury to the epithelium results in reductions in the levels of disaccharidases (Chapter 1). Secondary lactose intolerance is common in this setting, and may be seen with acute infectious enteritis, chronic enteritis, Giardiasis, gluten-sensitive enteropathy, inflammatory bowel disease, radiation enteritis, injury to the bowel due to antineoplastic drugs, etc. In these conditions, the small intestinal mucosal histology is abnormal (with the exception of some cases of Giardiasis) in either a specific or a nonspecific pattern. Recent work has localized lactase to a distal site on the villus, and the authors postulate that this is the reason it is most severely affected by villus injury (61). The degree of deficiency is correlated with the extent of villus damage. Return of lactase depends upon treatment of the primary disorder, but enzyme activity often lags behind return of normal morphology. Recovery of lactose tolerance may take several months from the time healing begins. This pattern seems to be unique to lactase and is as yet unexplained. In this situation, secondary lactase deficiency may be noted with a near-normal or minimally abnormal small bowel biopsy. Diagnosis, then, is by measurement of enzyme activity in mucosal tissue, a traditional lactose tolerance test, or the simpler lactose breath hydrogen test (Chapter 3). Treatment consists of a lactose-free diet until return of lactose tolerance is demonstrated.

### Glucoamylase

Glucoamylase is a brush-border enzyme which acts on starch and dextrins by removing successive glucose units from the nonreducing ends of the molecule (25). It can be distinguished from pancreatic amylase by its different pH optimum, its heat stability, its lack of requirement for chloride or calcium, and its inhibition by 1 M glycerol. The main role for glucoamylase is the hydrolysis of short chain glucose polymers and starches. This is of greatest significance in infants up to 4 months of age, who have reduced pancreatic amylase in duodenal fluid (62). During these first few months, glucoamylase may be the primary enzyme involved in starch digestion if starch is presented in the diet.

Congenital glucoamylase deficiency has not been described. A recent study of children with small intestinal mucosal injury demonstrated that mucosal levels of the enzyme decreased with increasing severity of the lesion (63). Glucoamylase activity was not as severely affected as were disaccharidase activities. Perhaps this relative resistance is responsible for the minimal clinical importance thus far attributed to secondary glucoamylase deficiency.

### Clinical Assessment of Disaccharide Intolerance

The most direct method for the diagnosis of a disaccharidase deficiency is the measurement of the enzyme activity in biopsy specimens of the small intestinal mucosa. This procedure is expensive, time-consuming, of some small risk to the patient, and requires technical expertise. There are several alternate methods for preliminary screening and then specific diagnosis of these deficiencies.

Malabsorption of disaccharides in the small intestine allows them to reach the colon. They are then metabolized by colonic flora, with the resultant production of $H_2$, $CO_2$, and organic acids, especially lactic acid (Chapters 3 and 10). This can be identified by a change in stool pH to less than 6. Undigested lactose can be detected in a stool sample by examining for reducing substances. Sucrose is not a reducing sugar; the stool must be acid hydrolyzed in order to detect reducing substances in a patient with sucrose malabsorption.

Classic sugar tolerance tests involve oral ingestion or intraduodenal instillation of the disaccharide, and measurement of serum glucose levels at fixed intervals thereafter. Patients with malabsorption of the sugar will have a blunted rise in serum glucose. In order to minimize the error due to peripheral tissue utilization of glucose, capillary blood samples may be used. In a study comparing various indirect methods of detecting lactase deficiency, the oral lactose tolerance test had a 24% (6/25) false-negative rate and a 4% (1/25) false-positive rate (64).

The recent advent of $H_2$ breath tests has made testing for disaccharidase deficiencies simple and noninvasive (Chapter 3). As stated above, colonic flora metabolize unabsorbed lactose or sucrose to $H_2$ and $CO_2$. These bacteria are the only source of $H_2$ gas in the intestinal tract and a constant proportion of this $H_2$ is excreted via the lungs (65) (Chapter 10). The test is accomplished by administering a standardized dose of the test sugar and sampling end-expiratory breath at fixed intervals. A rise in $H_2$ greater than 10 ppm over baseline is considered indicative of malabsorption. There is an estimated false-negative rate of 2% due to absence of $H_2$-producing bacteria in some patients, which may occur sporadically or secondary to antibiotic therapy (66). This phenomenon may be documented by lack of increased breath $H_2$ excretion following ingestion of a nonabsorbable substrate such as lactulose. False-positive results may be seen in the circumstance of small intestinal bacterial overgrowth (65). Correlation of breath test results, disaccharidase activities in biopsy specimens, and symptomatology has varied somewhat from study to study, but in general this test has become a useful tool in many clinical settings.

## Acknowledgments

This work was supported in part by USPHS Research Grants HD-14498 and AM-14523, and by Pediatric Gastroenterology Research Training Grant AM-07333.

The authors are indebted to Mrs. Marianna Sybicki, Ms. Ann Forcier, and Mr. Arthur Perez for expert technical assistance, and to Ms. Shirley Lerner for preparation of the manuscript.

## References

1. Semenza, G. (1968). Intestinal oligosaccharidases and disaccharidases. In *Handbook of Physiology*, C. F. Code (Ed.), sec. 6, vol. V, American Physiological Society, Washington, D.C., pp. 2543–2566.

2. Gray, G. M. (1981). Carbohydrate absorption and malabsorption. In *Physiology of the Gastrointestinal Tract*, L. R. Johnson (Ed.), vol. 2, Raven, New York, pp. 1063–1072.

3. Ugolev, A. M., DeLaey, P., Iezuitova, N. N., Rakhimov, K. R., Timofeeva, N. M., and Stepanova, A. T. (1979). Membrane digestion and nutrient assimilation in early development. In *Development of Mammalian Absorptive Processes*, CIBA Symp. vol. 70, Excerpta Medica, New York, pp. 221–246.

4. Kolinska, J., and Semenza, G. (1967). Studies on intestinal sucrase and on intestinal sugar transport. V. Isolation and properties of sucrase-isomaltase from rabbit small intestine. *Biochim. Biophys. Acta 146*: 181–195.

5. Cogoli, A., Eberle, A., Sigrist, H., Joss, C., Robinson, E., Mosimann, H., and Semenza, G. (1973). Subunits of the small-intestinal sucrase-isomaltase complex and separation of its enzymatically active isomaltase moiety. *Eur. J. Biochem. 33*:40–48.

6. Kolinska, J., and Kraml, J. (1972). Separation and characterization of sucrase-isomaltase and of glucoamylase of rat intestine. *Biochim. Biophys. Acta 284*:235–247.

7. Conklin, K. A., Yamashiro, K. M., and Gray, G. M. (1975). Human intestinal sucrase-isomaltase: Identification of free sucrase and isomaltase and cleavage of the hybrid into active distinct subunits. *J. Biol. Chem. 250*:5735–5741.

8. Brunner, J., Hauser, H., Braun, H., Wilson, K. J., Wacker, H., O'Neill, B., and Semenza, G. (1979). The mode of association of the enzyme complex sucrase-isomaltase with the intestinal brush border membrane. *J. Biol. Chem. 254*:1821–1828.

9. Spiess, M., Hauser, H., Rosenbusch, J. P., and Semenza, G. (1981). Hydrodynamic properties of phospholipid vesicles and sucrase isomaltase-phospholipid vesicles. *J. Biol. Chem. 256*:8977–8982.

10. Dahlqvist, A., Auricchio, S., Semenza, G., and Prader, A. (1963). Human intestinal disaccharidases and hereditary disaccharide intolerance. The hydrolysis of sucrose, isomaltose, palatinose (isomaltulose), and a 1,6-α-oligosaccharide (isomalto-oligosaccharide) preparation. *J. Clin. Invest. 42*:556–562.

11. Braun, H., Cogoli, A., and Semenza, G. (1975). Dissociation of small-intestinal sucrase-isomaltase complex into enzymatically active subunits. *Eur. J. Biochem. 52*:475–480.

12. Hauri, H. P., Quaroni, A., and Isselbacher, K. J. (1980). Monoclonal antibodies to sucrase/isomaltase: Probes for study of postnatal development and biogenesis of the intestinal microvillus membrane. *Proc. Natl. Acad. Sci. USA 77*:6629–6633.

13. Montgomery, R. K., Sybicki, M. A., Forcier, A. G., and Grand, R. J. (1981). Rat intestinal microvillus membrane sucrase-isomaltase is a single high molecular weight protein and fully active enzyme in the absence of luminal factors. *Biochim. Biophys. Acta 661*:346–349.

14. Maestracci, D. (1976). Enzymic solubilization of the human intestinal brush border membrane enzymes. *Biochim. Biophys. Acta 433*:469–418.

15. Sigrist, H., Ronner, P., and Semenza, G. (1975). A hydrophobic form of the small-intestinal sucrase-isomaltase complex. *Biochim. Biophys. Acta 406*:433–446.

16. Brunner, J., Hauser, H., and Semenza, G. (1978). Single bilayer lipid-protein vesicles formed from phosphatidylcholine and small intestinal sucrase-isomaltase. *J. Biol. Chem. 253*:7538–7546.

17. Frank, G., Brunner, J., Hauser, H., Wacker, H., Semenza, G., and Zuber, H. (1978). The hydrophobic anchor of small-intestinal sucrase-isomaltase. *FEBS Letters 96*:183–188.

18. Hauri, H. P., Quaroni, A., and Isselbacher, K. J. (1979). Biogenesis of intestinal plasma membrane: Posttranslational route and cleavage of sucrase-isomaltase. *Proc. Natl. Acad. Sci. USA 76*:5183–5186.

19. Semenza, G. (1979). Mode of insertion of the sucrase-isomaltase complex in the intestinal brush border membrane: Implications for the biosynthesis of this stalked intrinsic membrane protein. In *Developments of Mammalian Absorptive Processes*, CIBA Symp. vol. 70, Excerpta Medica, New York, pp. 133–146.

20. Sjostrom, H., Noren, O., Christiansen, L., Wacker, H., and Semenza, G. (1980). A fully active, two-active-site, single-chain sucrase-isomaltase from pig small intestine. *J. Biol. Chem. 255*:11332–11338.

21. Grand, R. J., and Ryan, S. J. (1979). Intracellular processing of jejunal sucrase. *Gastroenterology 74*:1126A.

22. Cezard, J. P., Conklin, K. A., Das, B. C., and Gray, G. M. (1979). Incomplete intracellular forms of intestinal surface membrane sucrase-isomaltase. *J. Biol. Chem. 254*:8969–8975.

23. Danielsen, E. M., Sjostrom, H., and Noren, O. (1981). Biosynthesis of intestinal microvillar proteins. *FEBS Letters 127*:129–132.

24. Danielsen, E. M., Skovbjerg, H., Noren, O., and Sjostrom, H. (1981). Biosynthesis of intestinal microvillar proteins. *FEBS Letters 132*:197–200.

25. Kelly, J. J., and Alpers, D. H. (1973). Properties of human intestinal glucoamylase. *Biochim. Biophys. Acta 315*:113–120.

26. Herscovics, A., Quaroni, A., Bugge, B., and Kirsch, K. (1981). Partial characterization of the carbohydrate units of rat intestinal sucrase-isomaltase. *Biochem. J. 197*:511–514.
27. Nishi, Y., and Takesue, Y. (1978). Localization of intestinal sucrase-isomaltase complex on the microvillus membrane by electron micro-scopy using nonlabeled antibodies. *J. Cell. Biol. 79*:516–525.
28. Nishi, Y., Tamura, R., and Takesue, Y. (1980). Intestinal sucrase-isomaltase complex: Morphological identification of the subunit directly bound to the microvillar membrane. *J. Ultrastruct. Res. 73*:331–335.
29. Alpers, D. H. (1969). Separation and isolation of rat and human intestinal β-galactosidases. *J. Biol. Chem. 244*:1238–1246.
30. Gray, G. M., and Santiago, N. A. (1969). Intestinal β-galactosidases. Sep-aration and characterization of three enzymes in normal human intestine. *J. Clin. Invest. 48*:716–728.
31. Schlegel-Haueter, S., Hore, P., Kerry, K. R., and Semenza, G. (1972). The preparation of lactase and glucoamylase of rat small intestine. *Biochim. Biophys. Acta 258*:506–519.
32. Birkenmeier, E., and Alpers, D. H. (1973). Enzymatic properties of rat lactase-phlorizin hydrol. *Biochim. Biophys. Acta 350*:100–112.
33. Green, J. R., and Hauri, H. P. (1977). Lactase enzymes in the intestinal brush border membrane of the suckling rat. *FEBS Letters 84*:233–235.
34. Cousineau, J., and Green, J. R. (1980). Isolation and characterization of the proximal and distal forms of lactase-phlorizin hydrolase from the small intestine of the suckling rat. *Biochim. Biophys. Acta 615*:147–157.
35. Skovbjerg, H., Sjostrom, H., and Noren, O. (1981). Purification and characterisation of amphiphilic lactase/phlorizin hydrolase from human small intestine. *Eur. J. Biochem. 114*:653–661.
36. Maestracci, D., Preiser, H., Hedges, M., Schmitz, J., and Crane, R. K. (1975). Enzymes of the human intestinal brush border membrane. Identification after gel electrophoretic separation. *Biochim. Biophys. Acta 382*:147–156.
37. Galand, G., and Forstner, G. G. (1974). Isolation of microvillus plasma membranes from suckling-rat intestine. *Biochem. J. 144*:293–302.
38. Flanagan, P. R., and Forstner, G. G. (1978). Purification of rat intestinal maltase-glucoamylase and its anomalous dissociation either by heat or by low pH. *Biochem. J. 173*:553–563.
39. Maroux, S., and Louvard, D. (1976). On the hydrophobic part of amino-peptidase and maltases which bind the enzyme to the intestinal brush border membrane. *Biochim. Biophys. Acta 419*:189–195.
40. Kerry, K. R., and Townley, R. R. W. (1965). Genetic aspects of intestinal sucrase-isomaltase deficiency. *Aust. Paediatr. J. 1*:223.

41. McNair, A., Gudmand-Høver, E., Jarnum, S., and Orrild, L. (1972). Sucrose malabsorption in Greenland. *Br. Med. J. 2*:19–21.

42. Dubs, R., Steinman, B., and Gitzelmann, R. (1973). Demonstration of an inactive enzyme antigen in sucrase-isomaltase deficiency. *Helv. Paediatr. Acta 28*:187–198.

43. Preiser, H., Menard, D., Crane, R. K., and Cerda, J. J. (1974). Deletion of enzyme protein from the brush border membrane in sucrase-isomaltase deficiency. *Biochim. Biophys. Acta 363*:279–282.

44. Gray, G. M., Conklin, K. A., and Townley, R. R. W. (1976). Sucrase-isomaltase deficiency. Absence of an inactive enzyme variant. *N. Engl. J. Med. 294*:750–753.

45. Antonowicz, I., Lloyd-Still, J. D., Khaw, K. T., and Shwachman, H. (1972). Congenital sucrase-isomaltase deficiency. Observations over a period of 6 years. *Pediatrics 49*:847–853.

46. Ament, M. E., Perera, D. R., and Esther, L. J. (1973). Sucrase-isomaltase deficiency—a frequently misdiagnosed disease. *J. Pediatr. 83*:721–727.

47. Gudmand-Höyer, E., and Krasilnikoff, P. A. (1977). The effect of sucrose malabsorption on the growth pattern in children. *Scand. J. Gastroenterol. 12*:103–107.

48. Perman, J. A., Barr, R. G., and Watkins, J. B. (1978). Sucrose malabsorption in children: Noninvasive diagnosis by interval breath hydrogen determination. *J. Pediatr. 93*:17–22.

49. Prader, A., Semenza, G., and Auricchio, S. (1963). Intestinal absorption and malabsorption of disaccharides. *Schweiz. Med. Wschenschr. 93*: 1272–1279.

50. Lebenthal, E., Kretchmer, K., and Sunshine, P. (1971). Nutritional adaptation: Effect of dietary carbohydrates on intestinal disaccharidase activity in the infant rat. Presented for the Society of Pediatric Research, Atlantic City, N.J., April, 1971, p. 79 (Abstr.).

51. Rosensweig, N. S., and Herman, R. H. (1968). Control of jejunal sucrase and maltase activity by dietary sucrose or fructose in man. *J. Clin. Invest. 47*:2253–2262.

52. Greene, H. L., Stifel, F. B., and Herman, R. H. (1972). Dietary stimulation of sucrase in a patient with sucrase-isomaltase deficiency. *Biochem. Med. 6*(No. 5):409–418.

53. Holzel, A., et al. (1959). Defective lactose absorption causing malnutrition in infancy. *Lancet i*:1126.

54. Lifshitz, F. (1982). Disaccharide intolerance. In *Food Intolerance*, R. K. Chandra (Ed.), Elsevier-North Holland, Amsterdam, in press.

55. Freiburghaus, A. U., Schmitz, J., Schindler, M., Rogthauwe, H. W., Kuitunen, P., Launiala, K., and Hadorn, B. (1976). Protein patterns of brush-

border fragments in congenital lactose malabsorption and in specific hypolactasia of the adult. *N. Engl. J. Med. 294*:1030–1032.

56. Simoons, F. J. (1978). The geographic hypothesis and lactose malabsorption. *Am. J. Dig. Dis. 23*:963.

57. Hyams, J. S., Stafford, R. J., Grand, R. J., and Watkins, J. B. (1980). Correlation of lactose breath hydrogen test, intestinal morphology and lactase activity in young children. *J. Pediatr. 97*:609–612.

58. Debongnie, J. C., Newcomer, A. D., McGill, D. B., and Phillips, S. F. (1979). Absorption of nutrients in lactase deficiency. *Dig. Dis. Sci. 24*: 225–231.

59. Barr, R. G., Levine, M. D., and Watkins, J. B. (1979). Recurrent abdominal pain of childhood due to lactose intolerance. *N. Engl. J. Med. 300*: 1449–1452.

60. Liebman, W. M. (1979). Recurrent abdominal pain in children: lactose and sucrose intolerance. A prospective study. *Pediatrics 64*:43–45.

61. Boyle, J. T., Celano, P., and Koldovsky, O. (1980). Demonstration of a difference in expression of maximal lactase and sucrase activity along the villus in the adult rat jejunum. *Gastroenterology 79*:503–507.

62. Lebenthal, E. (1978). Pancreatic function and disease in infancy and childhood. *Adv. Pediatr. 25*:223.

63. Lebenthal, E., and Lee, P. C. (1980). Glucoamylase and disaccharidase activities in normal subjects and in patients with mucosal injury of the small intestine. *J. Pediatr. 97*:389–393.

64. Newcomer, A. D., McGill, D. B., Thomas, P. J., and Hofmann, A. F. (1975). Prospective comparison of indirect methods for detecting lactase deficiency. *N. Engl. J. Med. 293*:1232–1236.

65. Levitt, M. D. (1969). Production and excretion of hydrogen gas in man. *N. Engl. J. Med. 281*:122–127.

66. Bond, J. H., and Levitt, M. D. (1977). Use of breath hydrogen ($H_2$) in the study of carbohydrate absorption. *Am. J. Dig. Dis. 22*:379–382.

# PATHOPHYSIOLOGY
# OF CARBOHYDRATE INTOLERANCE

# 7

# ROTAVIRUS AND LACTASE

IAN H. HOLMES
*University of Melbourne, Parkville, Victoria, Australia*

It may seem remarkable that one of the most ubiquitous viruses, capable of causing serious disease in infants, was the last to be recognized, but such appears to be the case. Both in developed and in developing countries, rotaviruses are reported to be the single most important agents identified in infants and young children with acute gastroenteritis requiring medical attention (1). Although they are then much less serious, infections in older children and in adults also seem to be common and in this way it appears that numerous strains of rotavirus persist in populations (2-4).

## Rotavirus

Rotavirus in humans were not found until 1973 because they were not readily isolated, and did not produce cytopathic effects in cell lines and

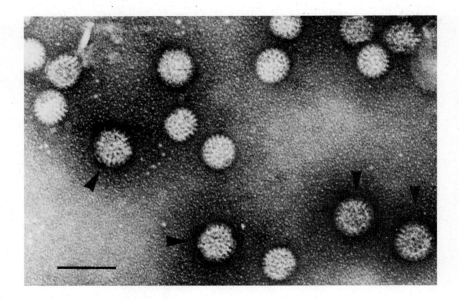

**Figure 1**   Human rotavirus from a fecal specimen, negatively stained with ammonium molybdate. Intact particles are indicated by arrowheads. The remainder have lost their outer capsid layer and their subunit structure is clearer. Bar indicates 100 nm.

under routine conditions of cultivation which were successful for most other viruses. It is very probable that human rotaviruses were successfully propagated in calves in 1942, but this work was too unconventional for general acceptance and was largely unrecognized for nearly 30 years (5,6). More recent rotavirus research owes a great deal to the studies of Kraft and Mebus on epizootic diarrhea of infant mice (EDIM) and Nebraska calf scours, which we now recognize as infections due to murine and bovine rotaviruses, respectively (3,7,8).

Human rotaviruses were discovered by electron microscopy (9-11) and it was immediately obvious that they must belong to a known family of viruses, the Reoviridae. Further morphological and biochemical studies confirmed this, and rotaviruses are now classified as a genus in this family (12-15). Rotavirus particles consist of two concentric icosahedral protein capsids enclosing 11 segments of genomic double-stranded RNA. Each RNA segment is

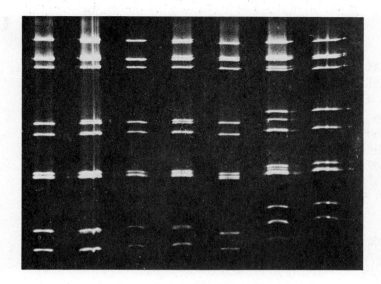

**Figure 2** Genomic double-stranded RNA from various human rotavirus samples analyzed by electrophoresis in 10% polyacrylamide gel as described by Rodger et al. (14). Samples were electrophoresed from top to bottom, and in track 5 all 11 genome segments are resolved. Tracks 2, 4, and 6 from the left contain mixtures of the samples run alone on either side of them, and demonstrate differences in mobility of certain RNA segments, indicating strain differences.

one gene, that is, it encodes one virus-specific protein (16). Probably five proteins make up the inner capsid of the rotavirus particle, and three more including a major glycoprotein form the approximately spherical outer capsid (17,18) (Fig. 1).

The basic studies originally undertaken for purposes of classification had an unanticipated practical application, when it was found that the patterns of bands produced when the viral RNA was analyzed by gel electrophoresis varied from one isolate to another. Currently this is the most powerful technique available for distinguishing between strains of rotaviruses and is being applied to epidemiological studies (4,19) (Fig. 2). The predominant strains present in communities often vary from year to year but in at least one instance a strain has persisted within a hospital for 4 years (4).

## Infectivity and Trypsin

The contrast between the large numbers of rotavirus particles excreted by infected infants and the difficulties encountered in growing the human strains in cell culture is striking (20). It is not so surprising, however, if we reflect that in vivo rotaviruses are restricted to growth in the gastrointestinal tract and do not cause systemic infections, so there must be factors responsible for limiting their spread. One such factor has been discovered—infectivity of rotaviruses depends on the presence of trypsin on or around the cells in which they grow (21,22).

The mechanism of trypsin activation of rotavirus infectivity has been worked out in some detail. The polypeptide encoded by genome segment 4 is assembled as part of the outer capsid of the virus particle, but such particles are not infectious until this polypeptide is cleaved at a specific site by trypsin, which would normally occur in the gut whenever particles are released by breakdown of an infected cell (23). Particles with uncleaved polypeptide 4 apparently adsorb normally to the next cell to be infected, but are blocked at the uncoating stage of replication (24). Many rotaviruses of animal origin can now be routinely isolated and cultivated provided that trypsin is added to the cell culture medium, and very recently successful isolations of human strains have been reported (25–27). Nevertheless, rotaviruses still grow best in their natural habitat.

## Lactase Hypothesis

In 1976 a "lactase hypothesis" was proposed in an attempt to explain the high degree of cell specificity of rotaviruses and the fact that infections are most notable in infants or other very young animals (28). It had been observed in experimental rotavirus infections of mice, calves, and piglets, using fluorescent antibodies to identify infected cells, that only the differentiated columnar epithelial cells found towards the ends of the villi were susceptible to rotavirus (29–31). The same cells in their replicating, undifferentiated form in the crypts and lower parts of the villi were not infected. During recovery from the acute infection which results in loss of much of the mature epithelium, the villi are repopulated with enzymatically immature cuboidal epithelial cells which appear insusceptible to infection, and in fact this may be one of the factors which normally limits the duration of rotavirus infections (30). The extensive loss of differentiated enterocytes and their partial

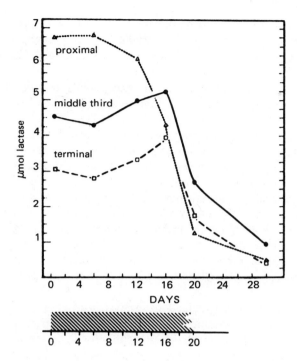

**Figure 3**  Coincidence in timing of the decrease in susceptibility to symptomatic murine rotavirus infection and decrease of lactase levels in the small intestine of mice. (Data from Refs. 32 and 47.)

replacement by enzymatically immature precursors results in transient malabsorption of disaccharides (Chapter 1).

Although it is now known that rotaviruses can infect humans or animals of all ages (3), symptomatic infections are most common in the young, and it was noted that in mice, susceptibility appeared to decrease sharply when the sucklings approached the age of weaning (29,31). Two recent studies have confirmed these findings (33,34).

Thus it was suggested that one of the molecules which appear as components of the brush-border membrane during differentiation of the enterocytes might also act as a receptor for rotaviruses. Few animal virus receptors have been definitively identified, but in bacterial systems receptors for several bacteriophages have turned out to be membrane proteins with particular metabolic functions, for example, the receptor for phage lambda in *Escherichia coli* is involved in uptake of maltose from the medium (35). The distribution of rotavirus receptors and the timing of their decrease in mice, which would account for the decrease in their susceptibility to infection around their 18th day of age, suggested that the receptor could be lactase (28) (Fig. 3).

A second reason for the choice of lactase was that it was believed to be involved in the uncoating of rotavirus particles in the early stages of the multiplication cycle, but this is now known to be incorrect. It has been shown very elegantly by Cohen and his colleagues (36) that uncoating of rotaviruses depends on removal of calcium ions which bind the outer capsid proteins to the inner. In vitro this can readily be accomplished by chelating agents, which must explain the original observations of uncoating with lactase preparations, and in vivo uncoating would be expected to occur automatically as soon as the adsorbed rotavirus particle traversed the cell membrane, because of the very low concentration of free calcium ions present in the cytosol (37).

In a recent further study of rotavirus infections in mice, Wolf et al. (34) showed that they could accelerate intestinal maturation by administration of corticosteroids, and the period of maximum susceptibility to infection was shortened. By the time the steroid-treated mice had become rotavirus resistant, small intestinal maltase activity had increased but lactase activity had apparently not yet decreased. A more direct test of the "lactase-as-receptor" hypothesis is still awaited. The question has recently been taken up once again in our laboratory, and the receptor has been shown to be a glycoprotein with essential sialic acid groups (38,39). Whether it will turn out to be lactase or one of the other functional brush-border glycoproteins remains to be seen, but at least the field is narrowed down a little.

### Final Considerations

Severe rotaviral diarrhea most typically occurs in infants in the 6–18 month age group, whereas infections in neonates tend to be much milder, and less virus is excreted (40–42). Serum antibodies against rotavirus do not appear to prevent infection (1), so the antirotaviral immunoglobulin G (IgG) transferred across the placenta seems unlikely to explain this partial disease resistance of the neonate. On the other hand, mothers who breast feed their infants generally supply both secretory antibodies (IgA) to rotavirus and trypsin inhibitors in their colostrum and milk, and both can be protective if their levels are sufficiently high (42,43).

The high frequency of occurrence of infantile gastroenteritis in all parts of the world, and the fact that diarrheal disease in malnourished children is often lethal, has led to the development of a major Diarrheal Diseases Control Programme by the World Health Organization. Much of the activity to date has centered on formulation and testing of an effective glucose-electrolyte mixture for oral rehydration, and current efforts are designed to greatly extend its availability and use in primary health care (44). Inclusion of a research component on viral diarrheas has followed recognition of the importance of rotaviruses as human pathogens (45). At present there is a great deal of interest in the possibility of producing a vaccine to control the disease, since the virus does not seem a likely candidate for eradication and has demonstrated its ability to spread even under conditions of good hygiene (1,46). It is hoped that further studies on receptors and possible inhibitors of adsorption, and especially on the stimulation and extension of the duration of mucosal immunity in the intestine, will contribute to the eventual control of rotaviral disease.

## References

1. Kapikian, A. Z., Wyatt, R. G., Greenberg, H. B., Kalica, A. R., Kim, H. W., Brandt, C. D., Rodriguez, W. J., Parrott, R. H., and Chanock, R. M. (1980). Approaches to immunization of infants and young children against gastroenteritis due to rotaviruses. *Rev. Infect. Dis. 2*:459–469.
2. Sack, D. A., Gilman, R. H., Kapikian, A. Z., and Aziz, K. M. S. (1980). Seroepidemiology of rotavirus infection in rural Bangladesh. *J. Clin. Microbiol. 11*:530–532.
3. Holmes, I. H. (1979). Viral gastroenteritis. *Progr. Med. Virol. 25*:1–36.
4. Rodger, S. M., Bishop, R. F., Birch, C., McLean, B., and Holmes, I. H. (1981). Molecular epidemiology of human rotaviruses in Melbourne, Australia, from 1973 to 1979, as determined by electrophoresis of genome ribonucleic acid. *J. Clin. Microbiol. 13*:272–278.
5. Light, J. S., and Hodes, H. L. (1943). Studies on epidemic diarrhea of the newborn: isolation of a filtrable agent causing diarrhea in calves. *Am. J. Public Health 33*:1451–1454.
6. Hodes, H. L. (1976). American Pediatric Society Presidential Address. *Pediatr. Res. 10*:201–204.

7. Kraft, L. M. (1958). Observations on the control and natural history of epidemic diarrhea of infant mice (EDIM). *Yale J. Biol. Med. 31*:121–137.
8. Mebus, C. A., Underdahl, N. R., Rhodes, M. B., and Twiehaus, M. J. (1969). Calf diarrhea (scours) reproduced with a virus from a field outbreak. *Univ. Nebr. Agric. Exp. Sta. Res. Bull. 233*:1–16.
9. Bishop, R. F., Davidson, G. P., Holmes, I. H., and Ruck, B. J. (1973). Virus particles in epithelial cells of duodenal mucosa from children with acute non-bacterial gastroenteritis. *Lancet 2*:1281–1283.
10. Flewett, T. H., Bryden, A. S., and Davies, H. (1973). Virus particles in gastroenteritis. *Lancet 2*:1497.
11. Middleton, P. J., Szymanski, M. T., Abbott, G. D., Bortolussi, R., and Hamilton, J. R. (1974). Orbivirus acute gastroenteritis of infancy. *Lancet 1*:1241–1244.
12. Flewett, T. H., and Woode, G. N. (1978). The rotaviruses. *Arch. Virol. 57*:1–23.
13. Holmes, I. H., Ruck, B. J., Bishop, R. F., and Davidson, G. P. (1975). Infantile enteritis virus:morphogenesis and morphology. *J. Virol. 16*:937–943.
14. Rodger, S. M., Schnagl, R. D., and Holmes, I. H. (1975). Biochemical and biophysical characteristics of diarrhea viruses of human and calf origin. *J. Virol. 16*:1229–1235.
15. Matthews, R. E. F. (1979). Classification and nomenclature of viruses. *Intervirology 12*:132–296.
16. Smith, M. L., Lazdins, I., and Holmes, I. H. (1980). Coding assignments of dsRNA segments of SA11 rotavirus established by *in vitro* translation. *J. Virol. 33*:976–982.
17. Rodger, S. M., Schnagl, R. D., and Holmes, I. H. (1977). Further biochemical characterization, including the detection of surface glycoproteins, of human, calf and simian rotaviruses. *J. Virol. 24*:91–98.
18. McCrae, M. A., and Faulkner-Valle, G. P. (1981). Molecular biology of rotaviruses. I. Characterization of basic growth parameters and pattern of macromolecular synthesis. *J. Virol. 39*:490–496.
19. Kalica, A. R., Sereno, M. M., Wyatt, R. G., Mebus, C. A., Chanock, R. M., and Kapikian, A. Z. (1978). Comparison of human and animal rotavirus strains by gel electrophoresis of viral RNA. *Virology 87*:247–255.
20. Flewett, T. H. (1976). Implications of recent virological researches. In *Acute Diarrhoea in Childhood*, CIBA Foundation Symposium, vol. 42, Elsevier-Excerpta Medica–North Holland, Amsterdam, pp. 237–250.
21. Babiuk, L. A., Mohammed, K., Spence, L., Fauvel, M., and Petro, R. (1977). Rotavirus isolation and cultivation in the presence of trypsin. *J. Clin. Microbiol. 6*:610–617.

22. Matsuno, S., Inouye, S., and Kono, R. (1977). Plaque assay of neonatal calf diarrhea virus and the neutralizing antibody in human sera. *J. Clin. Microbiol.* 5:1–4.

23. Espejo, R. T., Lopez, S., and Arias, C. (1981). Structural polypeptides of simian rotavirus SA11 and the effect of trypsin. *J. Virol.* 37:156–160.

24. Clark, S. M., Roth, J. R., Clark, M. L., Barnett, B. B., and Spendlove, R. S. (1981). Trypsin enhancement of rotavirus infectivity: mechanism of enhancement. *J. Virol.* 39:816–822.

25. Wyatt, R. G., James, W. D., Bohl, E. H., Theil, K. W., Saif, L. J., Kalica, A. R., Greenberg, H. B., Kapikian, A. Z., and Chanock, R. M. (1980). Human rotavirus type 2: cultivation *in vitro*. *Science* 207:189–191.

26. Sato, K., Inaba, Y., Shinozuka, T., and Matsumoto, M. (1981). Isolation of human rotavirus in cell culture. *Arch. Virol.* 69:155–160.

27. Urasawa, T., Urasawa, S., and Taniguchi, K. (1981). Sequential passages of human rotavirus in MA-104 cells. *Microbiol. Immunol.* 25:1025–1035.

28. Holmes, I. H., Rodger, S. M., Schnagl, R. D., Ruck, B. J., Gust, I. D., Bishop, R. F., and Barnes, G. L. (1976). Is lactase the receptor and uncoating enzyme for infantile enteritis (rota) viruses? *Lancet* 1:1387–1389.

29. Wilsnack, R. E., Blackwell, J. H., and Parker, J. C. (1969). Identification of an agent of epizootic diarrhea of infant mice by immunofluorescent and complement fixation tests. *Am. J. Vet. Res.* 30:1195–1209.

30. Mebus, C. A., Stair, E. L., Underdahl, N. R., and Twiehaus, M. J. (1971). Pathology of neonatal calf diarrhea induced by a reo-like virus. *Vet. Pathol.* 8:490–505.

31. Hall, G. A., Bridger, J. C., Chandler, R. L., and Woode, G. N. (1976). Gnotobiotic piglets experimentally inoculated with neonatal calf diarrhoea reovirus-like agent (rotavirus). *Vet. Pathol.* 13:197–210.

32. Cheever, F. S., and Mueller, J. H. (1947). Epidemic diarrheal disease of suckling mice. *J. Exp. Med.* 85:405–416.

33. Little, L. M., and Shadduck, J. A. (1981). Pathogenesis of rotavirus infection in mice. *Abstr. 5th Int. Congr. Virol.* :195.

34. Wolf, J. L., Cukor, G., Blacklow, N. R., Dambrauskas, R., and Trier, J. S. (1981). Susceptibility of mice to rotavirus infection: Effects of age and administration of corticosteroids. *Infect. Immunol.* 33:565–574.

35. Szmelcman, S., and Hofnung, M. (1975). Maltose transport in *Escherichia coli* K12: involvement of the bacteriophage lambda receptor. *J. Bacteriol.* 124:112–118.

36. Cohen, J., Laporte, J., Charpilienne, A., and Scherrer, R. (1979). Activation of rotavirus RNA polymerase by calcium chelation. *Arch. Virol.* 60:177–186.

37. Carafoli, E., and Cromptom, M. (1978). The regulation of intracellular calcium. In *Current Topics in Membranes and Transport*, vol. 10, F. Bronner and A. Kleinzeller (Eds.), Academic Press, New York, pp. 151–216.

38. Bastardo, J. W., and Holmes, I. H. (1980). Attachment of SA-11 rotavirus to erythrocyte receptors. *Infect. Immunol. 29*:1134–1140.

39. Raghu, G. Personal communication.

40. Banatvala, J. E., Chrystie, I. L., and Totterdell, B. M. (1978). Rotavirus infections in human neonates. *J. Am. Vet. Med. Assoc. 173*:527–530.

41. Bishop, R. F., Cameron, D. J. S., Veenstra, A. A., and Barnes, G. L. (1979). Diarrhea and rotavirus infection associated with differing regimens for postnatal care of newborn babies. *J. Clin. Microbiol. 9*:525–529.

42. McLean, B. S., and Holmes, I. H. (1981). Effects of antibodies, trypsin and trypsin inhibitors on susceptibility of neonates to rotavirus infection. *J. Clin. Microbiol. 13*:22–29.

43. McLean, B., and Holmes, I. H. (1980). Transfer of antirotaviral antibodies from mothers to their infants. *J. Clin. Microbiol. 12*:320–325.

44. Pierce, N. F., and Hirschhorn, N. (1977). Oral fluid: a simple weapon against dehydration in diarrhoea. *WHO Chron. 31*:87–93.

45. WHO Scientific Working Group (1980). Rotavirus and other viral diarrheas. *Bull. WHO 58*:183–198.

46. Ryder, R. W., McGowan, J. E., Jr., Hatch, M. H., and Palmer, E. L. (1977). Reovirus-like agent as cause of nosocomial diarrhea. *J. Pediatr. 90*:698–702.

47. Moog, F., Denes, A. E., and Powell, P. M. (1973). Disaccharidases in the small intestine of the mouse: normal development and influence of cortisone, Actinomycin D, and cycloheximide. *Dev. Biol. 35*:143–159.

# 8

# PATHOGENESIS OF GLUCOSE MALABSORPTION IN ACQUIRED MONOSACCHARIDE INTOLERANCE

BUFORD L. NICHOLS, JR.
*Baylor College of Medicine*
*and Texas Children's Hospital, Houston, Texas*

The clinical features of acquired monosaccharide intolerance (AMI) consist of chronic diarrhea with failure to thrive in the first few months of life (1,2). The clinical presentation most frequently follows acute gastroenteritis, although it may present after surgery or severe systemic infections during this early period. The nature of the diarrhea is diagnostic. The diarrhea abates when the child has fasted and recurs when carbohydrate feedings are resumed. There is a threshold to the carbohydrate intolerance indicating that it is not an idiosyncratic reaction. The diarrhea resulting from carbohydrate feeding in excess of tolerance is not diagnostic in appearance, but has glucose present, a lower pH, and a low sodium concentration. Such fecal changes can be a transient phenomenon in recovery from acute gastroenteritis; however, they are recurrent in the child with AMI.

**Table 1** Histological Findings in Mucosal Diseases[a]

| | AMI[b] | GSE[c] | P |
|---|---|---|---|
| Mitotic index (% mitotic cells in crypts) | 3.7 ± 1.0 | 7.5 ± 4.0 | < 0.01 |
| Mitotic migration (fractional migration from crypt base) | 0.5 ± 0.1 | 0.8 ± 0.1 | < 0.01 |
| Interepithelial lymphocytes (% of epithelial cells) | 12.0 ± 2.0 | 45.0 ± 26.0 | < 0.001 |

[a]No differences found in mucosal thickness, villus height, crypt depth, and villus to crypt ratio. (Unpublished data of G. Daoud.)

[b]AMI, acquired monosaccharide intolerance.

[c]GSE, gluten-sensitive enteropathy.

Jejunal mucosal atrophy has been present in all infants with AMI studied thus far (3). In severe cases there was total absence of villus structure and a thinning of the remaining mucosa (4) (Table 1). The enterocytes tend to be better ordered and have less infiltration with round cells than in gluten-sensitive enteropathy. The number of mitotic figures and their distribution along the crypts usually is reduced. The mucosal enzymes usually are at the lower range of normal when expressed on a per unit of protein basis (5)

**Table 2** Disaccharidase Activities in Mucosal Diseases: Geometric $\overline{M}$ (units/g Protein)

| | Normal range (n) | Normal mean | AMI[a] | GSE[b] |
|---|---|---|---|---|
| Disaccharidase | | (48) | (10) | (3) |
| Lactase | 11– 92 | 32.4 | 7.7 | 5.9 |
| Sucrase | 26–191 | 75.7 | 20.9 | 11.6 |
| Maltase | 93–681 | 265.5 | 128.5 | 33.7 |
| Villus: crypt ratio | | 1:2:8 | 1:3:16 | 1:2:6 |
| | | > 4 | < 1 | < 1 |

[a]AMI, acquired monosaccharide intolerance.

[b]GSE, gluten-sensitive enteropathy based upon clinical response. (Unpublished data of R. Calvin.)

(n) = number of observations.

(Table 2). The response of the mucosal atrophy to nutritional rehabilitation is slow. Most children recover sufficient mucosal surface area to tolerate their caloric needs from carbohydrate in approximately 2 weeks.

In this chapter the clinical features and the pathophysiology which may underline the clinical course of the patients is discussed. It is important to understand the possible factors which may be implicated in the etiopathogenesis of this entity to carry out the treatment and prevention of this complication of gastroenteritis in infancy.

### Clinical Features of AMI

At the clinical level, these patients have severe carbohydrate intolerance which is characterized by the recurrence of diarrhea with the presence of glucose in the stool and usually with a reduction of fecal pH to less than 5.5. They present generalized disaccharide intolerance and despite substitution of sucrose for lactose, there is no relief of the symptoms. The intolerance of sucrose is not overcome by feeding glucose or glucose oligosaccharides (Polycose) (Fig. 1). The physical findings of patients with AMI are those of marasmus or marasmic kwashiorkor. The most universal sign is atrophy of the filiform papillae of the tongue. Easy pluckability of the hair is very common, but often is difficult to detect because the infants are shaved for scalp vein intravenous therapy during initial rehydration. The body weight usually is less than birth weight and the arm/head circumference ratio is reduced to between 0.28 and 0.24, reflecting mild-to-moderate malnutrition. The physical findings of kwashiorkor often occur after prolonged intravenous therapy with glucose solutions. The host defenses are compromised during the period of most severe illness, and in the absence of prompt nutritional rehabilitation, septicemia, meningitis, and localized visceral infections complicate management and account for the high mortality of these infants (1). All of these physical findings and host defense defects are correctable with nutritional recovery.

The typical clinical course of an infant with AMI is as follows: the infant presents at approximately 30 days of age with diarrhea and dehydration of greater than 5% of rehydrated weight. The diarrhea responds to the fasting associated with intravenous hydration; within 12 hr the infant is rehydrated and by 24 hr has begun to reveal a desire to feed. The initial feeding of an oral hydrating solution (5% glucose and electrolyte mix) may be well-tolerated and thus by 24 hr after admission the infant is receiving adequate

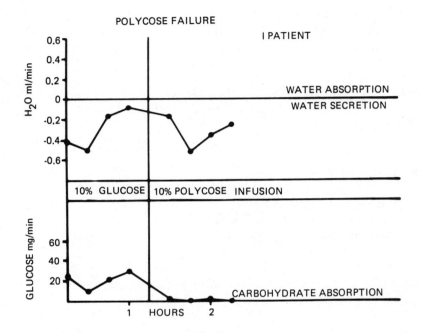

**Figure 1** Effect of osmolar load by glucose and undigested glucose polymers on water flux and glucose uptake from the jejunum (30 cm). A perfusion technique which compared absorption and secretion to an unabsorbed polyethylene glycol marker was used. Water secretion usually becomes positive when the polymer is substituted for glucose, but in this case secretion persisted, and the hydrolysis and absorption of glucose from the polymer were zero. (From W. J. Klish, unpublished data.)

volumes of solution to allow a trial on formula (Table 3). A nonlactose-containing formula usually is chosen because of the frequency of transient lactose intolerance in the postdiarrheal period. The infant seems to tolerate a feeding of half-strength and full-strength nonlactose formula; however, after several days, the patient develops a profound watery diarrhea associated with glucose and acid in the stools. Rehydration by intravenous fluids often is required to compensate for the fecal response to full-strength feeding. Following recovery of water balance, the infant again is started on an oral hydrating solution. At this point, diarrhea recurs with the return of glucose and acid in the stool. A half-strength oral hydrating solution is tried

Table 3  Relationship Between Diet and Fecal Characteristics at Admission for Acute Diarrhea (M ± SD (n))

| Dietary regimen | Fasted | Clear liquids | Half-strength formula | Full-strength formula |
|---|---|---|---|---|
| Diet | | | | |
| AMI[a] | 100% | Pedialyte 100% | ProSobee 80%<br>Pregestimil 20% | ProSobee 75%<br>Pregestimil 25% |
| Non-AMI[b] | 100% | Pedialyte 85%<br>Other 15% | ProSobee 65%<br>Lactose formula 28%<br>Other 7% | ProSobee 64%<br>Lactose formula 27%<br>Other 9% |
| Duration (hr) | | | | |
| AMI | 11.6 ± 6.8 ( 7) | 9.1 ± 7.1 ( 7) | 17.8 ± 7.7 (10) | 22.4 ± 4.2 ( 8) |
| Non-AMI | 13.3 ± 6.7 (38) | 9.6 ± 5.6 (40) | 18.8 ± 6.8 (61) | 19.3 ± 6.9 (56) |
| Fecal weight (g/kg/hr) | | | | |
| AMI | 2.9 ± 1.7 | 3.9 ± 4.1 | 2.8 ± 1.8 | 2.1 ± 2.5 |
| Non-AMI | 2.8 ± 1.8 | 4.3 ± 3.8 | 3.9 ± 3.0 | 4.1 ± 5.1 |
| Number of stools (total) | | | | |
| AMI | 3.1 ± 2.9 | 2.9 ± 2.0 | 3.8 ± 2.3 | 4.3 ± 2.3 |
| Non-AMI | 2.9 ± 3.2 | 2.3 ± 2.1 | 4.5 ± 2.8 | 5.0 ± 2.9 |

Table 3 (continued)

| Dietary regimen | Fasted | Clear liquids | Half-strength formula | Full-strength formula |
|---|---|---|---|---|
| Glucose in stools | | | | |
| 1–2 + AMI | ( 1) | ( 1) | ( 1) | ( 1) |
| 1–2 + Non-AMI | ( 8) | (12) | (15) | (16) |
| 3–4 + AMI | ( 1) | ( 0) | ( 0) | ( 0) |
| 3–4 + Non-AMI | ( 2) | ( 4) | ( 8) | ( 1) |
| pH < 5.5 | | | | |
| AMI | ( 4) | (0) | ( 2) | ( 2) |
| Non-AMI | ( 7) | (9) | (12) | (11) |
| Guiac + | | | | |
| AMI | ( 4) | (0) | ( 0) | ( 0) |
| Non-AMI | (10) | (8) | (13) | (11) |

aAMI, acquired monosaccharide intolerance subjects.

bNon-AMI, subjects not developing AMI.

M ± SD (n) = Mean ± standard deviation.

(n) = number of observations.

**Table 4**  Proposed Pathophysiological Mechanisms
Leading to Small Bowel Mucosal Atrophy

Insults

Specific dietary factors such as carbohydrates,
soy lectins, or gluten

Immunological, including allergic

Gastrointestinal infections

again the following day with the same response. Because of the inability to tolerate a 2.5% glucose solution by mouth, a central line is placed and total parenteral nutrition (TPN) is begun. After prolonged fasting and nutritional rehabilitation, the glucose intolerance improves. At this point, the infant is started on a modular formula with 2.5 or 3.0% glucose. At one time we recommended that AMI subjects be treated by substituting a honey mixture of glucose and fructose for disaccharides (6). Our subsequent clinical experience has indicated that infants with AMI are not benefited by the substitution of equal concentrations of fructose for glucose. Over a period of several days glucose concentration in this formula is increased to 5%. When 5% glucose formula is tolerated in a formula providing 0.66 kcal/ml, the TPN is discontinued. After 2 weeks of satisfactory recovery on the 5% glucose modular formula, the sucrose formula is substituted and the infant is followed in a nutritional recovery ward for an additional 2 weeks. After at least 1 month of good growth on the sucrose formula, a lactose formula is given. The child subsequently continues to gain weight on regular cow's milk formula. In a subset of these infants the feeding of adequate carbohydrate calories is associated with persistent acidosis which may be relieved by fasting or by central or peripheral intravenous nutrition. In these rare cases, recovery is limited by the metabolic acidosis present in the children unless large amounts of neutralizing base are given.

### Pathophysiology

What are the underlying mechanisms of this clinical course? The mucosal atrophy seen in biopsy is correlated with a reduction in the glucose absorption rates in intestinal perfusion studies (3). A linear correlation exists between the quantitative surface area and the rate of glucose transport. The substitution of glucose oligosaccharides for glucose results in a reduced secretion of water and salt from the mucosa into the luminal bowel (7). This observation suggests that small bowel diarrhea is not a secretory process according to the cholera model, but is an osmotic phenomenon associated with reduced rates of absorption of osmoles from the lumen (Chapter 9). The substitution of glucose polymers reduces the osmolar load within the lumen. With improvement of symptoms in rare individual patients, the hydrolysis of the glucose oligosaccharides is defective and the oligosaccharides remain undigested and unabsorbed in the lumen of the small bowel (8). The results of perfusion studies in one such patient are indicated in Figure 1. The sub-

improvement in mucosal function. It has long been known that AMI is more frequent among infants with diarrhea who have lactose intolerance and continue to receive lactose-containing milk formulas (16). Many of these infants develop progressive mucosal atrophy while fed soy-based formulas. This suggests that there may be factors in the soy formula that have a toxic effect on the intestinal mucosa. An investigation of an older group of patients has shown that soy formulas are associated with alterations in mucosal function (17) (Chapter 13). This form of mucosal damage appears to be mediated by the presence of lectin activity in the soy proteins which react with specific receptor sites on the enterocytes. These interactions can be demonstrated in vitro and presumably take place in vivo. It is not known whether such mechanisms can contribute to the progressive damage to the mucosa in AMI subjects fed soy formulas. It is clear that progressive mucosal damage also occurs during the feedings of both hydrolyzed protein formulas and/or electrolyte solutions.

Similarities in mucosal pathology exist between gluten-sensitive enteropathy and AMI. This suggests the possibility that the infantile disorder is mediated by gluten intolerance. The age at which infants are exposed to gluten varies in different geographic areas; the typical onset of gluten-sensitive enteropathy is during the second semester of infancy. The infants in Houston who present with AMI seldom have been exposed to any wheat products before the onset of illness. Similarly, in Mexico, gluten was not a factor (1).

European investigators have advanced the allergy theory (Chapter 11). The intolerance of these infants to cow's milk has led to the hypothesis that the mucosal atrophy is mediated by protein hypersensitivity. This is an attractive and time-honored hypothesis among pediatricians. Kuitunen et al. reported three infants who grew better on breast milk than on cow's milk and who demonstrated a modest atrophy of the mucosal histology during a month's challenge to cow's milk (18). They argued that mucosal atrophy is a sign of protein intolerance in infants fed whole cow's milk. Others reported similar responses to whole cow's milk feeding (19). In these observations, the use of whole cow's milk has made it difficult to separate carbohydrate intolerance from milk protein hypersensitivity. The allergy hypothesis is opposed by the observation that many infants have received "hypoallergenic" formulas such as Pregestimil early in their hospitalization when mucosal atrophy was progressive (Table 3). The hydrolyzed casein formulas often are used because of the substitution of sucrose or glucose for lactose. In addition, the transient nature of the mucosal lesion and its failure to recur with challenge when the infants have recovered nutritionally is difficult to explain from the classic

continuing dietary insult (Table 4).

Since malnutrition is a universal concomitant of this disease (Chapter 2), the jejunal atrophy could be the result of nutritional deficits. The more frequent form of malnutrition is the marasmic type and edematous forms usually are a consequence of nutritional mismanagement. These patients commonly are fasted during attempts to restore water balance after successive failures of empirical management with untolerated formulas. Recovery of

hypersensitive point of view. Finally, it also is difficult to explain why progressive mucosal lesions can occur with the prolonged feeding of oral hydrating solutions which have no protein content.

In the context of the allergy theory, it is important to comment on the osmolar load associated with hydrolyzed formulas and "elemental" diets. The osmolar load associated with these formulas makes it difficult to provide adequate caloric intakes during the oral or nasogastric feedings of infants with mucosal atrophy. Although success has been reported with this form of feeding (20), the volumes of fluid intake necessary to reach caloric balance with diluted forms of these diets often are impossible to achieve without partial intravenous nutritional support. The fluid intakes of these infants usually exceed 200 ml/kg per day.

The infectious agent theory entertains the possibility that a continuing infection could account for the persistence of mucosal atrophy. To date there has been no consistency in the identification of etiological agents in our AMI subjects. Certainly, there is no evidence of continuing infection with any of the known etiological agents associated with epidemic diarrhea. However, the children with AMI frequently are susceptible to nosocomial infections and we have observed that *Salmonella* and rotaviral infections occur in these infants during nutritional rehabilitation. The response to these intercurrent infections does not reveal any unusual persistence of the organisms, although they were associated with transient deterioration of mucosal function. Similarly, there may be small bowel mucosal damage in AMI associated with proliferation of fecal and colonic bacteria into the upper segments of the small intestine (21). Bacterial overgrowth usually occurs in the small bowel under the conditions of reduced motility. There is an increased deconjugation of bile acids as a consequence of the bacterial overgrowth. It has been postulated that free bile acids in the upper small bowel may have a toxic effect on the mucosal morphology, although this theory has been questioned because similar levels of free bile acids have been observed in the upper small bowel of infants who have benign courses and acute viral diarrheas (22–24). However, deconjugated bile salts in small concentrations (0.5 mM/liter) may be injurious to the small bowel of a malnourished host and not to that of a well-nourished control (25), so other factors may exist which account for the susceptibility to injury of the small bowel under the stress of malnutrition and diarrhea (26). The suspicion of bacterial overgrowth has led to the use of cholestyramine to bind the free bile acids (27). In our experience, this approach has not simplified the nutrition management.

It has long been taught that diarrhea can be a response to respiratory infections. This has led to the "parenteral diarrhea" concept in which circulating "toxins" from respiratory tract infections are believed to be a cause of chronic diarrhea. Today it is understood that respiratory symptoms are prevalent in viral diarrheas of infants. At one time, mastoidectomies were done in children with chronic diarrhea to prevent the circulation of "parenteral toxins." This practice is still followed in some pediatric departments in Europe (28). It is possible that "silent infections" do play a role in the resistance of some infants to nutritional rehabilitation. The effect of parenteral toxins on mucosal function, however, remains enigmatic.

There is little doubt that host defense is reduced in patients with AMI which may account for the severe infections of intestinal and extraintestinal origin. This immune defect is consistent with the type of altered defense seen in other children with malnutrition but without symptomatic mucosal atrophy. It is probable that the defect host defense mechanism is a symptom of the associated malnutrition because of its prompt recovery with nutritional rehabilitation.

## Final Considerations

In reviewing these etiological hypotheses, some conclusions can be determined. If a unified hypothesis is required, however, it is probable that there is some truth in each of the hypotheses that has been advanced and that the development of precise quantitative assays of mucosal function and structure will open a second generation of feeding trials in which the dietary management of this disease can be improved and a more specific hypothesis will result.

In the formulation of a unified hypothesis, it is striking to note that AMI has been extremely rare in breast-fed infants, even those living under severe privations (29). There may be factors in breast milk of a trophic nature and protective value that provide a cascade of complimentary levels of protection to the infant. These functional factors may play a role in mucosal development and maturation and undoubtedly may influence the ability of colonic flora to scavenge the nutrients reaching the distal intestine. It also is striking that AMI is a disease that develops after initial refeeding. As shown in Table 3, glucose intolerance was not more prevalent during the initial dietary management of children who subsequently developed AMI. Further progress in this field will require a quantitative evaluation of the response of the immature infant to these factors in human development. Present knowledge is at a qualitative level and is not applicable to pediatric practice.

## Acknowledgments

This work is a publication of the USDA/ARS Children's Nutrition Research Center in the Department of Pediatrics at Baylor College of Medicine and Texas Children's Hospital. The author wishes to thank former Fellows in the Section of Nutrition and Gastroenterology for their contributions to the study: W. J. Klish, J. T. Rodriguez, R. Calvin, G. Daoud, and F. Jalili. The author also wishes to thank Drs. A. A. Mintz and G. S. Gopalakrishna for permission to study their patients at the Ben Taub General Hospital.

## References

1. Lifshitz, F., Coello-Ramirez, P., Gutierrez-Topete, G., and Contreras-Gutierrez, M. L. (1970). Monosaccharide intolerance and hypoglycemia in infants with diarrhea. I. Clinical course of 23 infants. *J. Pediatr.* 77:595–603.
2. Jalili, F., Smith, E. O., Nichols, V. N., and Nichols, B. L. (1982). A comparison of acquired monosaccharide intolerance and acute diarrheal syndrome. *J. Pediatr. Gastroenterol. Nutr.,* in press.
3. Klish, W. J., Udall, J. N., Rodriguez, J. T., Singer, D. B., and Nichols, B. L. (1978). Intestinal surface area in infants with acquired monosaccharide intolerance. *J. Pediatr. 52*:566–571.
4. Daoud, G., Hawkins, E., Klish, W., Calvin, R., Ferry, G., and Nichols, B. L. (1978). Histologic criteria for differentiation of acquired monosaccharide intolerance (AMI) and gluten sensitive enteropathy (GSE). *Pediatr. Res. 12*:433 (Abstr.).
5. Calvin, R., Klish, W., Garza, C., Daoud, G., and Nichols, B. L. (1978). Jejunal morphology and disaccharidase activities in children with chronic diarrhea. *Pediatr. Res. 120*:431 (Abstr.).
6. Klish, W. J., Potts, E., Ferry, G. D., and Nichols, B. L. (1976). Modular formula: An approach to management of infants with complex food intolerances. *J. Pediatr. 88*:948–952.
7. Klish, W. J., Udall, J. N., Calvin, R. T., and Nichols, B. L. (1980). The effect of intestinal solute load on water secretion in infants with acquired monosaccharide intolerance. *Pediatr. Res. 14*:1343–1346.
8. Fisher, S. E., Leone, G., and Kelley, R. H. (1978). Chronic protracted diarrhea: Intolerance to dietary polymers. *Pediatrics 67*:271–273.
9. Launiala, K. (1968). The mechanism of diarrhea in congenital disaccharide malabsorption. *Acta Paediatr. Scand. 57*:425–432.
10. Toccalino, H., Licastro, R., Garcia Cardo, A., and Williams, M. (1972).

Histological alterations of the small intestine in normal infants with acute diarrhea. *Acta Gastroenterol. Latinoam.* *4*:129–134.

11. Torres-Pinedo, R., Rivera, C., and Garcia-Castineiras, S. (1974). Intestinal exfoliated cells in infants: A system for the study of microvillus particles. *Gastroenterology* *66*:1154–1160.

12. James, W. P. T. (1970). Sugar absorption and intestinal motility in children when malnourished and after treatment. *Clin. Sci.* *39*:305–318.

13. Brunser, O., Reid, A., Monckeberg, F., Maccioni, A., and Contreras, I. (1968). Jejunal mucosa in infant malnutrition. *Am. J. Clin. Nutr.* *21*:976–983.

14. Bowie, M. D., Brinkman, G. L., and Hansen, J. D. L. (1965). Acquired disaccharide intolerance in malnutrition. *J. Pediatr.* *66*:1083–1091.

15. Green, H. L., McCabe, D. R., and Merenstein, G. B. (1975). Protracted diarrhea and malnutrition in infancy: Changes in intestinal morphology and disaccharidase activity during treatment with total intravenous nutrition on oral elemental diets. *J. Pediatr.* *87*:695.

16. Lifshitz, F., Coello-Ramirez, P., Gutierrez-Topete, G., and Coronado-Cornet, M. C. (1971). Carbohydrate intolerance in infants with diarrhea. *J. Pediatr.* *79*:760–767.

17. Alvarez, J. R., and Torres-Pinedo, R. (1981). Soybean lectin and soyasaponins cooperatively stimulate the penetration of glycinin in rabbit jejunal epithelium. *Pediatr. Res.* *15*:524 (Abstr.).

18. Kuitunen, P., Rapola, J., Savilahti, E., and Visakorpi, J. K. (1973). Response of the jejunal mucosa to cow's milk in the malabsorption syndrome with cow's milk intolerance. *Acta Paediatr. Scand.* *62*:585–595.

19. Shiner, M., Ballard, J., Brook, C. G. D., and Herman, S. (1975). Intestinal biopsy in the diagnosis of cow's milk protein intolerance with acute symptoms. *Lancet* *3*:1060–1063.

20. Sherman, J. O., Hamly, C. A., and Khachadurian, A. K. (1975). Use of an oral elemental diet in infants with severe intractable diarrhea. *J. Pediatr.* *86*:518–523.

21. Coello-Ramirez, P., and Lifshitz, F. (1972). Enteric microflora and carbohydrate intolerance in infants with diarrhea. *Pediatrics* *49*:233–242.

22. Rodriguez, J. T., Mastromarino, A., Darby, W., Flores, N., Ordonez, J. V., Huang, T. L., Alvarado, J., Wilson, R., Soriano, H., and Nichols, B. L. (1974). Alteration of intestinal flora and function in acute nonspecific diarrhea of infancy. *Am. J. Clin. Nutr.* *27*:435 (Abstr.).

23. Rodriguez, J. T., Huang, T. L., Alvarado, J., Klish, W. J., Darby, W. E., Flores, H., and Nichols, B. L. (1974). Role of free bile acids in acquired monosaccharide intolerance. *Pediatr. Res.* *8*:111 (Abstr.).

24.  Rodriguez, J. T., Mastromarino, A. J., Ordonez, J. V., Alvarado, J., Flores, N., Wilson, R., and Nichols, B. L. (1979). Role of altered anaerobic microflora in acquired monosaccharide intolerance (AMI). *Pediatr. Res. 13*:111 (Abstr.).

25.  Teichberg, S., Fagundes-Neto, U., Bayne, M. A., and Lifshitz, F. (1981). Jejunal macromolecular absorption and bile salt deconjugation in protein-energy malnourished rats. *Am. J. Clin. Nutr. 34*:1281–1291.

26.  Lifshitz, F., Teichberg, S., and Wapnir, R. (1981). Malnutrition and the intestine in nutrition and child health. In *Perspectives for the 80s*, R. C. Tsang and B. L. Nichols (Eds.), Alan Liss, New York, pp. 1–24.

27.  Tamer, M. A., Santora, T. R., and Sandberg, D. H. (1974). Cholestyramine therapy for intractable diarrhea. *Pediatrics 53*:217–220.

28.  Sousa, J. S., Silva, A., and Ribeiro, V. C. (1980). Intractable diarrhea of infancy and latent otomastoiditis. *Arch. Dis. Child. 55*:937–940.

29.  Okuni, M., Okinaga, K., and Baba, K. (1972). Studies on reducing sugars in stools of acute infantile diarrhea, with special reference to the difference between breast-fed and artificially fed babies. *Tohoku J. Exp. Med. 101*:395–402.

# 9

# INTESTINAL OSMOTIC AND KINETIC EFFECTS OF CARBOHYDRATE MALABSORPTION

RAUL A. WAPNIR
*Cornell University Medical College, New York
and North Shore University Hospital, Manhasset, New York*

Digestible carbohydrates constitute the main source of energy for humans. Alterations in the effectiveness of their small intestinal absorption, particularly early in life, may result in diarrheal disease and long-term deleterious consequences for the health of the individual.

The absorptive process requires a solubilization or emulsification step for solid foodstuffs. Prior to absorption, hypertonic gastric contents are diluted and osmotically equilibrated by an intestinal efflux of water. At the termination of the digestive sequences, the elimination of solid excreta and retention of body water balances demand an inverse process of water resorption. The exchanges of water and solutes across the apical membrane of the enterocyte are subject to the same physicochemical and thermodynamical laws that regulate the movement of substances across all biological semipermeable membranes. Chemical, electric, and osmotic gradients act in concert or in opposition to energy-consuming processes. An understanding of their interplay may lead to intelligent measures for the therapy of conditions causing malabsorption of carbohydrates and diarrheal illness (1,2).

In this chapter we present some concepts describing mechanisms of intestinal absorption, how water and sodium transport are altered by carbohydrate malabsorption, and a description of some experimental models of this condition. Finally, we consider how other substances can alter absorption kinetics of glucose and water fluxes across the small intestine, and their clinical relevance.

## Malabsorption of Carbohydrates

### Effects on Intestinal Transport of Water and Sodium

If malabsorption of carbohydrate occurs, normal water and sodium fluxes in the intestine are disrupted because of the hyperosmotic load. Carbohydrate, sodium, and water transport processes are intimately linked. The answer to the clinical problems of malabsorption resides in the resolution of the hyperosmosis, either by removal of the poorly absorbed solute, or by achieving normalization of electrolyte and fluid uptake by the mucosa.

On a molar basis, water and sodium fluxes across the small intestinal mucosa have the greatest quantitative significance among all exchanges in the gut (3). Under normal absorptive conditions, the transport of sodium will entail water absorption. But even in the absence of dietary sodium, ingested water will be rapidly absorbed by the gastrointestinal tract, by both trans- and by paracellular routes, that is, across "pores" in the apical membrane and through the tight junctions. The small intestine can absorb water, even against an osmotic pressure difference. Parsons and Wingate (4) demonstrated with in vitro experiments that the mucosal solution had to be made about 110 mosmol/kg hypertonic with respect to the serosal side in order to stop water influx. With an artificial membrane, approximately 480 mM of sucrose was needed to abolish "uphill" water transfer (5).

Several factors determine the osmotic load exerted by a dietary disaccharide (Table 1). Three elements will control the velocity of its luminal disappearance: the concentration of the disaccharide, the enzymatic capability of the disaccharidase ($V_{max}$), and the resistance presented by the unstirred layer and the mucus. Disaccharides are not absorbed directly, unless they have been previously split to their constituent monosaccharides.

**Table 1**   Factors Influencing the Osmotic Load Exerted by a Disaccharide in the Gut

| | | | |
|---|---|---|---|
| Osmotic load | $\sim$ | $\dfrac{1}{\text{gastric emptying rate}}$ | |
| of a | $\sim$ | Electrolyte (Na) fluxes | |
| disaccharide in | $\sim$ | Disaccharide concentration | Rate |
| the small | $\sim$ | $\dfrac{1}{V_{max} \text{ disaccharidase}}$ | of |
| intestine | $\sim$ | $\dfrac{1}{\text{unstirred layer} + \text{mucus thickness}}$ | luminal disappearance |

Their molecular weight is too high to allow for a substantial penetration into the enterocyte by diffusion. A steric linkage in the sites of disaccharidase activity and the translocation carrier for glucose and/or galactose has been postulated (6). This means that hydrolysis and active transport follow each other and take place in contiguous sites of the membrane.

It should be pointed out that the concentration of a solute at its absorption site on the small intestinal mucosa differs from that in the bulk phase of the intestinal lumen (Table 2a,b). A layer of mucus (7) and glycoproteins with their products of partial hydrolysis (8), secreted or extruded by both goblet and absorptive cells, constitute a functional cushion to the surface of the small intestinal epithelium.

In the zone contiguous to the microvilli, with a depth of tens to hundreds of microns, there is a fluid film "unstirred layer" (9) through which the passage of solutes occurs by diffusion. Once the barrier of the unstirred layer is traversed, small molecules such as electrolytes, monosaccharides, amino acids, and dipeptides may be translocated into the enterocyte by active transport carriers (10-12) (Fig. 1).

In the absence of the appropriate disaccharidase or when the hydrolysis of the sugar becomes the limiting factor, the disaccharide acts as a nonabsorbable substance creating an osmotic load that can only be relieved by dilution and/or eventual absorption. The hyperosmosis then produces an acceleration of the transit time of the small intestinal contents. This, for

**Table 2** Kinetic Expressions Relating Intestinal Absorption, Diffusional Transport, and Active Transport

(a)    Rate of diffusional transport: $J_D = \dfrac{D}{d}(C - C^*)$

(b)    Concentration of solute at the mucosal surface:

$$C^* = C - J_D\left(\dfrac{d}{D}\right)$$

(c)    Rate of active transport: $J' = \dfrac{J_{max} \cdot C^*}{K_t + C^*}$

(d)    Linear transformation of active transport kinetics:

$$C^*/J' = \dfrac{K_t}{J_{max}} + \dfrac{1}{J_{max}} \cdot C^*$$

(e)    "Resistance" r of the unstirred layer: $\dfrac{d}{D}$

(f)    "Resistance" r' of carrier-mediated (active) transport:

$$\dfrac{K_t}{J_{max}}$$

(g)    Absorption rate of an actively transported solute:

$$J = \dfrac{K_t}{(d/D) + (K_t/J_{max})}$$

d = Thickness of unstirred layer; D = diffusion constant of solute; C = concentration of solute in bulk phase; $J_{max}$ = maximum transport rate of the carrier; $K_t$ = affinity constant of the carrier for the solute.
*Source*: Refs. 31 and 32.

example, is the effect of sucrose in patients affected by congenital sucrose-isomaltose malabsorption (13,14). In normal individuals or experimental animals, an analogous effect can be obtained by instillation of mannitol, a poorly absorbed polyol.

Hyperosmosis due to carbohydrate malabsorption can be further complicated by a variety of factors. Unabsorbed carbohydrate is attacked by intestinal bacteria, which break down complex sugars and produce oligosaccharides, organic acids, and other fermentation products with even higher osmotic activity. In general, conditions which generate an excess of protons will disrupt the barrier function of the intestinal epithelium (15). Intestinal

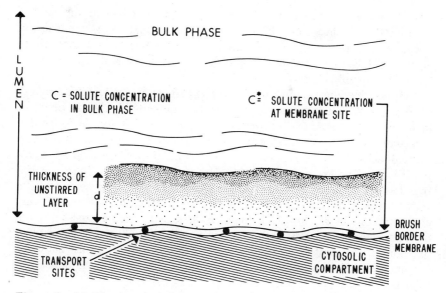

**Figure 1**   Idealized representation of the small intestinal lumen. A solute at concentration C in the bulk phase will be at concentration C* after traversing an unstirred layer of thickness d.

injuries due to bacterial or viral infection, and products of bacterial action, that is, deconjugated bile salts, organic acids, and hydroxylated fatty acids, among other agents, perpetuate the absorptive impairment of the individual.

### Alterations of Intestinal Absorption Kinetics by a Reduction of Active Transport Resistance

Excess disaccharide in the gut may have a considerable disruptive effect not only on the transport of electrolytes and water, but also on mechanisms of active transport in the small intestine. Such an effect could be inferred from experiments in which rats were fed diets containing 16.7% of either lactose or maltose for 21 days, with a commercial ration as the complement of their diet. Although these animals did not develop diarrhea and grew at a normal rate, when their intestinal absorption capacity was investigated by in vivo procedures, the kinetic data showed a loss of carrier-mediated glucose transport ability. The experimental data were compatible with an apparent entire dependency on a diffusional process rather than on diffusion plus a saturable active transport mechanism (16). Another consequence of the long-term disaccharide feedings was an approximate doubling of the rate of macromolecular penetration in rats fed lactose or maltose over animals fed a commercial ration containing complex carbohydrates. The question of macromolecular absorption in pathological conditions is discussed extensively in Chapters 11–13.

The possible clinical relevance of the experimental disaccharide feedings of young adult animals mimicks the situation presented by lactase-deficient individuals given amounts of the disaccharides they are unable to handle, even without signs of intolerance. The excess oligosaccharide in the diet or the products of hydrolysis overwhelm or inhibit the hydrolysis-active transport sequence necessary for normal carbohydrate absorption. The result is a functional malabsorption of carbohydrate and loss of brush-border enzymatic activity which can only be uncovered by exposing the mucosa to increasing concentrations of glucose. In humans, as in experimental animals, the loss of glucose-active transport ability by hyperosmolar feedings can deprive the organism of the most effective means of solute absorption and also allow for the uptake of macromolecules even when there may be no symptoms of intolerance.

### Experimental Models of Carbohydrate Malabsorption

Malabsorption could be causing physiological and cellular damages which are not easy to identify in the sick individual. Some answers with general validity have been obtained from animal models of this condition. When rats are force-fed a hyperosmotic solution of mannitol (1300 mosmol/kg), the dilution of the solute in the lumen occurs rapidly and is reflected in the reduction of the concentration of the high molecular weight nonabsorbable marker, polyethylene glycol, with a comparable influx of sodium into the lumen (Fig. 2). The osmotic shock can induce loss of cellular material into the lumen. This, in turn, will decrease the disaccharidase activity of the intestinal mucosa, therefore disrupting the hydrolysis-absorption sequence and perpetuating the malabsorption of carbohydrate (17).

However, not only poorly absorbed organic substances in hypertonic loads can induce malabsorption. A slowly hydrolyzed disaccharide such as lactose, at physiological concentrations and under isotonic conditions, can produce a reduction of water and sodium absorption typical of solute malabsorption. Such a decrease in water fluxes could be a component in the onset of diarrhea and be a salient feature in lactose intolerance. This was demonstrated in vivo, in the rat jejunum, using perfusion procedures similar to those described earlier (18,19). As shown in Figure 3A, these exchanges were unaltered by the

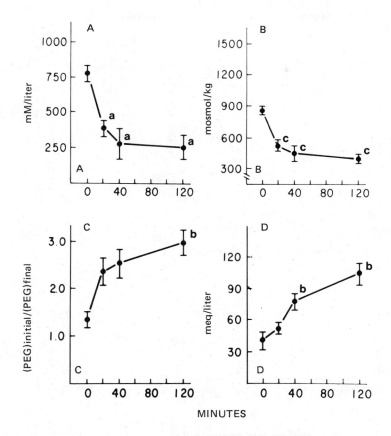

**Figure 2**    Jejunal luminal fluid changes after force-feeding rats hyperosmotic mannitol solutions. (A) Mannitol concentration. (B) Osmolality. (C) Water flux. (D) Na flux. Means ± SEM at each point. a = $P < 0.05$; b = $P < 0.01$. All values compared against zero time levels. (Data from Ref. 17.)

presence of 60 mM maltose in the solution. However, when perfusing 60 mM lactose, a severe reduction of water absorption was noted. For comparative purposes, solutions of mannitol were tested under identical conditions. This substance produced the sharpest drop in water absorption, as expected. In contrast, the absorption of water from the lumen was stimulated by the inclusion of 60 mM sucrose in the fluid.

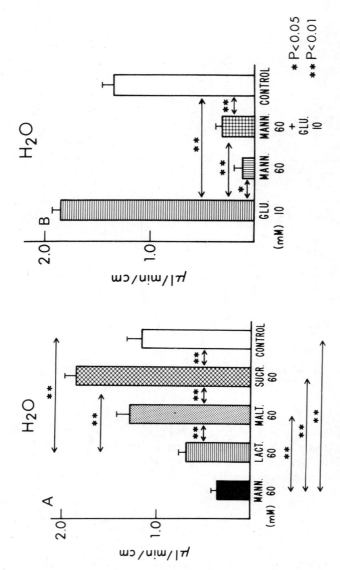

**Figure 3** (A) Water absorption of isotonic solutions containing 60 mM each of either mannitol, lactose, maltose, or sucrose. The control contained a buffered Krebs-phosphate solution. All perfusates were adjusted to pH 6.9. (B) Absorption of water of balanced salt solutions containing either 10 mM glucose, 60 mM mannitol, or 60 mM mannitol plus 10 mM glucose. The control was as indicated in A.

Since chemically pure sucrose is generally contaminated with substantial amounts of glucose, we investigated whether glucose per se, when added to a nonabsorbable polyol solution, would normalize   the rates of water and sodium transport, shown to be reduced by poorly absorbed substances under isotonic conditions. In the presence of 60 mM mannitol, in isotonic solution, the severe impairment of water absorption was only marginally improved by the addition of 10 mM glucose into the perfusate (Fig. 3B). Malabsorption of a poorly absorbed sugar, therefore, can be partially relieved by the active "solute-coupled" transport of glucose which enhances the lumen-to-blood movement of water. This approach has been extensively used in oral rehydration therapy for childhood diarrhea. The most frequently used commercial preparations for oral rehydration marketed in the United States contain glucose or corn syrup solids. Glucose is also a component of the formula for oral rehydration recommended by the World Health Organization (20). The inclusion of a sugar originally added for palatability has, in fact, a physiological role that was empirically verified and which has been substantiated by experimental studies.

This information suggests that the inclusion of an actively transported solute, that is, glucose, may also have a role in the therapy of carbohydrate malabsorption. Later we discuss the stimulation of water fluxes by other actively transported solutes, such as amino acids and small peptides.

## Alterations of Intestinal Absorption Kinetics by Nonabsorbable Substances

In agreement with the concepts presented under Malabsorption of Carbohydrates, the current understanding of the physiology of the small intestinal mucosa, recent studies have shown that it is possible to change the absorption rate of glucose by altering the characteristics of the intestinal milieu. We will review below (see Increased Absorption) a situation in which the absorption of the monosaccharide is enhanced by a reduction of the resistance offered by the unstirred layer. This approach could be relevant for the improvement of malabsorption syndromes. We also consider an opposite condition (see Delayed Absorption), when the absorption rate of glucose is decreased as a result of changes in the viscosity of the intestinal fluid.

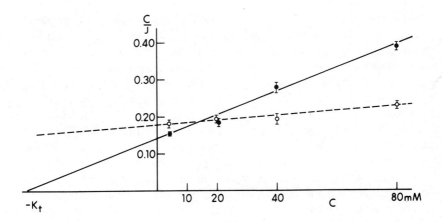

**Figure 4**   Representation of the glucose absorption kinetics as the ratio of solute concentration (C) and absorption rates (J) versus solute concentration (see Table 2d) for rats fed either a commercial feed (closed circles) or the same diet but containing 5% magnesium trisilicate (open circles). The regression lines were drawn by the least-squares method. (Data from Ref. 23.)

## Increased Absorption by Reduction of the Unstirred Layer Resistance

Most pharmacopoeias include various intestinal adsorbents of mineral or vegetable origin as antidiarrheal agents for adults (21). Their mode of action has not been well elucidated. Another use for inert substances was empirically found by ranchers and breeders who managed to improve weight gain in cattle by feeding them pulverized mineral solids, such as cement kiln slag, mixed with their rations (22). In experiments conducted with rats, long-term ingestion of substances such as activated charcoal, bismuth subcarbonate, kaolin plus pectin, or magnesium trisilicate, not only changed the rate of weight gain, but also the intestinal absorption of glucose (23). For example, with 5% magnesium trisilicate in the diet, the kinetics of glucose absorption becomes markedly different from that of control animals (Fig. 4). The maximum absorption rate $J_{max}$ is increased fivefold but the glucose affinity constant $K_t$ also rises from 43 to 277 mM, indicating a loss in the affinity between active transport sites and substrate. These changes in the properties of the rat jejunal mucosa were concomitant with greater water and sodium fluxes and were tentatively explained by a thinning of the glycocalyx and/or the unstirred fluid layer. This change would reduce the overall "resistance" (Table 2e) and allow for a greater absorption rate of the solute.

The potential application of these findings to the problem of malabsorption has not been tested yet. It is conceivable that nonabsorbable substances, including dietary fiber, may have a role in the treatment of carbohydrate malabsorption by a regularization of intestinal motility, control of water fluxes, and reduction of turbulent propulsion of the chyme.

### Delayed Absorption by the Enhancement of the Unstirred Layer Resistance

Certain soluble polysaccharides, also classified as dietary fiber, reduce postprandial glycemia in normal and diabetic individuals (24). A galactomannan, guar gum, has proven to be particularly interesting. One of its postulated modes of action is the delay of gastric emptying (25). However, the main direct effect of guar gum, as well as of carboxymethylcellulose, is an increased viscosity of the liquid film surrounding the villi, with a consequent expansion of the unstirred layer. The addition of 0.25% of guar gum was shown to be very effective in reducing the transport of glucose in vitro (26). Similar results were obtained when the jejunum of rats was pretreated with a solution containing 6 g/liter of guar gum prior to the determination of glucose transport in vivo (27).

In these instances, the reduction of solute absorption is explainable by an elevation of the "resistance" of the unstirred layer (Table 2e). This can be due either to an increase of its thickness (Table 2d) (26) or to an apparent decrease of the diffusion constant D. These two explanations are not mutually exclusive and could both result in a lower absorption rate (Table 2g).

A reduction of intestinal absorption rates may be clinically useful in cases when the intestinal mucosa's exposure to a carbohydrate needs to be "cushioned." This could be desirable during recovery from transient carbohydrate intolerance, when the introduction of a specific sugar may still produce adverse symptoms and diarrhea. Delaying absorption could prevent the overwhelming of disaccharidase enzymatic capacity with subsequent malabsorption of carbohydrate.

## Modification of Water Fluxes Across the Small Intestinal Mucosa by Protein Breakdown Products

Water movement across the intestinal epithelium will follow the passage of sodium in and out of the enterocyte. This has been abundantly shown since

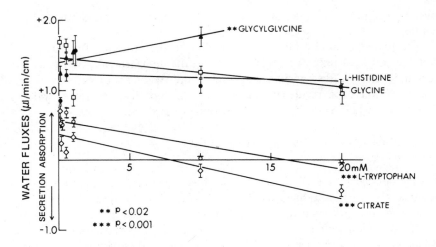

**Figure 5**    Water fluxes during in vivo intestinal perfusion as a function of solute concentration. Buffered, isotonic solutions of sodium chloride with variable concentrations of the substances indicated were perfused through a rat ileal segment (see text). The points represent the means ± SEM for 30–40 determinations each.

the early 1960s (9,10,28). The most quantitatively significant way to modify the fluxes of sodium is by solute-coupling. Knowledge of the linkage between sodium and amino acids and sodium and monosaccharides dates back to the work of Csáky (29) and Schultz and Zalusky (30). Therefore, the possibility exists that water absorption, which is reduced in carbohydrate malabsorption, could be stimulated by other solutes, such as amino acids or small peptides. This, in turn, could alleviate the osmotically induced water loss which can develop into diarrhea.

Recently we have explored the relationship between the concentration of some amino acids and dipeptides and water movement across the ileum of the rat. Using in vivo procedures described earlier (18,19), we found that increasing concentrations of glycylglycine, from 0.08 to 10 mM, did produce a significant increase in water fluxes proportional to the concentration of the dipeptide (Fig. 5). Certain amino acids, such as L-histidine or glycine, up to 20 mM, did not alter the rate of water absorption, which did not differ from the values obtained with isotonic, balanced salt solutions. Another amino acid, tryptophan, depressed water uptake, with levels of 20 mM causing a cessation of water transfer from the lumen to the circulation. This cathartic effect was not as marked as in the case of citrate, a typical nonabsorbable anion, included in this series of experiments for comparative purposes. As expected, an increasing concentration of citrate inversely correlated with water absorption and, when perfused at concentration greater than 8 mM, produced significant secretion of water into the lumen.

These preliminary results in regard to water fluxes may reflect the rate of amino acid or peptide absorption. It can be predicted that the faster the intestinal absorption process for each different solute, the more rapid the water disappearance from the lumen will be. How this relates to the chemical nature of the protein breakdown product and the identity of specific carriers remains to be elucidated. This effect, if properly applied, may allow for the improvement of water and solute absorption by dietary means in diarrheal disease and carbohydrate intolerance.

## Conclusions

Malabsorption of carbohydrates produces a reduction or reversal of normal lumen-to-blood water fluxes. The presence of lactose in the gut, even under isotonic conditions, decreases water and sodium transport. In an experimental animal model, chronic disaccharide feedings can disrupt saturable absorptive mechanisms. Experimental studies suggest that the stasis produced by a poorly absorbed disaccharide, such as lactose, could be reversed, in part, by the presence of solutes stimulating water and sodium absorption, using principles similar to those applied for oral rehydration therapy.

The natural resistance barriers to the transport of glucose and, possibly, amino acids and small peptides, may be manipulated to achieve an increase or a decrease of intestinal absorptive rates. Substances modifying the absorptive capacity of the gut may have a therapeutic potential in carbohydrate malabsorption and diarrhea. This clinical approach has been explored only to a very limited extent.

## Acknowledgments

I thank the technical assistance of Mrs. Mary Ann Bayne and Miss Debra Khani.

This work was supported in part by NIH Grant S08 RR 09128-03.

References

1. Lifshitz, F. (1980). Secondary carbohydrate intolerance in infancy. In *Clinical Disorders in Pediatric Gastroenterology and Nutrition*. F. Lifshitz (Ed.), Marcel Dekker, New York, pp. 327–340.
2. Hirschhorn, N. (1980). The treatment of acute diarrhea in children. An historical and physiological perspective. *Am. J. Clin. Nutr. 33*:637–663.
3. Phillips, S. F. (1973). Fluid and electrolyte fluxes in the gut. *Hosp. Pract. 8*(3):137–146.
4. Parsons, D. S., and Wingate, D. L. (1961). The effect of osmotic gradients on fluid transfer across rat intestine in vitro. *Biochim. Biophys. Acta 46*:170–183.
5. Curran, P. F., and MacIntosh, J. R. (1962). A model system for biological water transport. *Nature (London) 193*:347–348.
6. Crane, R. K. (1975). Fifteen years of struggle with the brush border. In *Intestinal Absorption and Malabsorption*, T. Z. Csáky (Ed.), Raven Press, New York, pp. 127–142.
7. Smithson, K. W., Millar, D. B., Jacobs, L. R., and Gray, G. M. (1981). Intestinal diffusion barrier: unstirred layer or membrane surface mucous coat? *Science 214*:1241–1244.
8. Walker, W. A. (1980). Intestinal defenses in health and disease. In *Clinical disorders in Pediatric Gastroenterology and Nutrition*, F. Lifshitz (Ed.), Marcel Dekker, New York, pp. 99–119.
9. Winne, D. (1973). Unstirred layer, source of biased Michaelis constant in membrane transport. *Biochim. Biophys. Acta 298*:27–31.
10. Curran, P. F. (1960). Na, Cl and water transport by rat ileum in vitro. *J. Gen. Physiol. 43*:1137–1148.
11. Fordtran, J. S., and Dietschy, J. M. (1966). Water and electrolyte movement in the intestine. *Gastroenterology 50*:263–285.
12. Erlij, D. (1976). Solute transport across isolated epithelia. *Kidney Intl. 9*:76–87.
13. Launiala, K. (1968). The effect of unabsorbed sucrose and mannitol on the small intestinal flow rate and mean transit time. *Scand. J. Gastroenterol. 3*:665–671.
14. Launiala, K. (1969). The effect of unabsorbed sucrose or mannitol-induced accelerated transit on absorption in the human small intestine. *Scand. J. Gastroenterol. 4*:25–32.
15. Powell, D. W. (1981). Barrier function of epithelia. *Am. J. Physiol. 241*:G275–G288.
16. Teichberg, S., Lifshitz, F., Fagundes-Neto, U., and Bayne, M. A. (1979). Increased jejunal macromolecular absorption induced by 'low dose' lactose feedings in rats. *Gastroenterology 76*:1260.

17. Teichberg, S., Lifshitz, F., Pergolizzi, R., and Wapnir, R. A. (1978). Response of rat intestine to a hyperosmotic feeding. *Pediatr. Res. 12*: 720–725.

18. Wapnir, R. A., and Lifshitz, F. (1974). Absorption of amino acids in malnourished rats. *J. Nutr. 104*:843–849.

19. Wapnir, R. A., Exeni, R. A., McVicar, M., and Lifshitz, F. (1977). Experimental lead poisoning and intestinal transport of glucose, amino acids and sodium. *Pediatr. Res. 11*:153–157.

20. Parker, R. L., Rinehart, W., Piotrow, P. T., and Doucette, L. (1980). Oral rehydration therapy (ORT) for childhood diarrhea. *Pop. Rep. 8* (6):L41–L75.

21. Swinyard, E. A. (1975). Surface acting drugs. In *The Pharmacological Basis of Therapeutics,* 5th ed., L. S. Goodman and A. Gilman (Eds.), Macmillan, New York, pp. 948–949.

22. Maugh, T. H. (1978). The fatted calf. II. The concrete truth about beef. *Science 199*:413.

23. Wapnir, R. A., and Lifshitz, F. (1981). Weight gain and intestinal absorption of nutrients in rats: effect of antidiarrheal agents (astringents). *Nutr. Rep. Intl. 23*:557–564.

24. Alberti, K. G. M. M., Swolever, T. M., Gassul, M. A., and Hockaday, T. D. R. (1976). Unabsorbable carbohydrates and diabetes: decreased post-prandial hyperglycemia. *Lancet 2*:172–174.

25. Holt, S., Heading, R., Carter, D., Prescott, L., and Tothill, P. (1979). Effect of gel fibre on gastric emptying and absorption of glucose and paracetamol. *Lancet 1*:636–639.

26. Johnson, I. T., and Gee, J. M. (1981). Effect of gel-forming gums on the intestinal unstirred layer and sugar transport in vitro. *Gut 22*:398–403.

27. Blackburn, N. A., and Johnson, I. T. (1981). The effect of guar gum on the viscosity of the gastrointestinal contents and on glucose uptake from the perfused jejunum in the rat. *Br. J. Nutr. 46*:239–246.

28. Diamond, J. M., and Bossert, W. H. (1967). Standing gradient osmotic flow. A mechanism for coupling water and solute transport in epithelia. *J. Gen. Physiol. 50*:2061–2083.

29. Csáky, T. Z. (1963). A possible link between active transport of electrolytes and nonelectrolytes. *Fed. Proc. 22*:3–7.

30. Schultz, S. G., and Zalusky, R. (1964). Ion transport in isolated rabbit ileum. II. The interaction between sodium and active sugar transport. *J. Gen. Physiol. 47*:1043–1059.

# 10

# CARBOHYDRATE INTOLERANCE AND THE ENTERIC MICROFLORA

JAY A. PERMAN
*University of California, San Francisco
and University of California Hospital, San Francisco, California*

*From man's point of view the most interesting function of a given microbe may be to cause a disease, or to form a desired chemical compound. From its own point of view, however, the basic function of a microbe is simply to grow, in one or another environment (1).*

The enteric microflora comprise a complex ecosystem largely confined to the colon but in certain states proliferating in the upper small bowel as well. Within these environments, bacteria derive energy for growth from available fuels, principally carbohydrates. The sugar-containing compounds degraded by intestinal microbes originate exogenously from the host's diet or are synthesized endogenously by host cells. Bacterial requirements for growth thereby dictate a relationship between intestinal organisms and their host which, although usually symbiotic, may become adversarial.

The role of the enteric microflora in the host's ability to tolerate and absorb dietary sugars is a significant example of both harmful and beneficial effects of the intestinal ecosystem. Evidence is presented to show that the establishment of a fecal-type flora in the upper small bowel results in carbohydrate malabsorption by the action of microbes on brush-border carbohydrate-containing proteins and on intestinal transport mechanisms. In contrast, the metabolic activities of the colonic ecosystem toward carbohydrates escaping small bowel absorption may reduce host *intolerance* to malabsorbed sugars. Thus, the nature of the host-microbe interaction in carbohydrate absorption and tolerance depends to a large extent on the location of bacterial proliferation within the gastrointestinal tract, and the metabolic activities of the organisms present in a specific location.

### The Small Bowel Flora

The duodenal aspirates of infants from 2 weeks to 10 months of age without intestinal disorders may be sterile or contain a sparse microflora, generally gram-positive aerobic organisms characteristic of mouth flora whose number rarely exceeds $10^4$/ml duodenal fluid (2). Colonization of the gastrointestinal tract occurs following birth in a rostral-caudal direction (3), but retrograde colonization from the colon to the small bowel may occur in disease states (4). Mechanisms thought to prevent more extensive colonization of the upper small bowel include gastric acidity, normal small intestine motility, and enteric secretions.

It is difficult to assign a number indicative of abnormal growth in the upper small bowel, since colony counts of $10^6$ or greater/ml, generally considered abnormal, have been described in apparently healthy infants and adults (2,5). The qualitative characteristics of the flora appear more important than numbers, and investigators generally agree that translocation of a fecal-type flora (e.g., *Escherischia coli*, *Klebsiella*, *Enterococci*) to the proximal small intestine is consistent with bacterial overgrowth (6-8).

### Small Bowel Flora and Carbohydrate Malabsorption

Clinical Observations

Multiple studies have supported an association between malabsorption of mono- and disaccharides and an abnormal small bowel flora (9-11). The association has been documented in infants following surgical repair of congenital abnormalities of the small intestine including atresias, gastroschisis, malrotations, and meconium ileus (7,9). Disordered motility induced either by the primary abnormality or by its surgical repair appears to be a likely mechanism for stasis-induced overgrowth. Sugar malabsorption in association

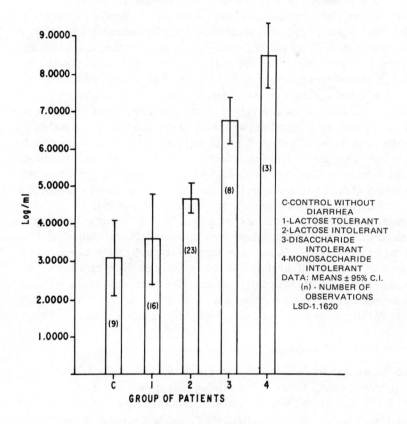

**Figure 1**  Duodenal flora in infants with diarrhea. The cultures of the duodenal fluid obtained at the time of the diagnosis of the capacity to tolerate
carbohydrates are shown. The differences in bacterial counts between diarrheal groups were significant ($P < 0.01$). LSD = Least significant difference
at 0.05% level. (From Ref. 11, © 1972)

with bacterial overgrowth has also been reported in nonsurgical infants with
acute and chronic diarrhea ranging in duration from days to months (10,11).
In 50 infants with diarrhea who had bacterial proliferation in the small intestine, Coello-Ramirez et al. (11) demonstrated carbohydrate malabsorption

in 68%. Lactose malabsorption alone was present in 46%, sucrose and lactose malabsorption in 16%, and malabsorption of all test carbohydrates, including glucose, fructose, and glucose-galactose combinations, in 6%. As shown in Figure 1, the degree of bacterial proliferation paralleled the severity of sugar malabsorption in this and other studies (10). However, the association between presence and severity of bacterial overgrowth and carbohydrate malabsorption has not been uniformly demonstrated in infants with sugar tolerance (7,12), and variation in results may be due to ethnic differences of the populations studied, administration of total parenteral nutrition prior to duodenal aspiration for bacterial culture (7), or nutritional status. Although Coello-Ramirez et al. (11) found no correlation between bacterial counts and nutritional deficits in Mexican infants with carbohydrate malabsorption, bacterial counts in duodenal fluid decrease with repair of protein-calorie malnutrition (13). Thus, nutritional status cannot be excluded as a variable in the association between overgrowth and sugar malabsorption.

Clinical data therefore indicate that a fecal-type flora exists in the proximal small intestine of *some* infants with carbohydrate malabsorption. Proliferation of bacteria in this site may occur secondarily to processes which increase the quantity of unabsorbed sugars available to organisms in the lumen, but direct evidence for this is lacking. However, considerable evidence exists demonstrating that the organisms themselves can, by their metabolic activity, directly cause or exacerbate carbohydrate malabsorption.

### Depression of Brush-Border Disaccharidase Activity

Disaccharidase activity in the small intestine of rats with bacterial overgrowth resulting from surgically created blind loops is depressed approximately twofold (14-16). Lactase activity in mucosal homogenates is most severely affected, comparable to the clinical situation, and the severity of the abnormality parallels the degree of bacterial proliferation (14). Patchy ultrastructural abnormalities of the villi have been associated with bacterial overgrowth (16). However, Jonas et al. (16) have demonstrated that the lactase, sucrase, and maltase activity per unit *brush-border membrane* is significantly reduced, while alkaline phosphatase activity is preserved, thus establishing that enzyme deficiency is attributable to degradation of exposed brush-border disaccharidases and not solely due to damaged surface microvilli.

Disaccharidases are sugar-containing proteins, and Prizont (17) has demonstrated that degradation of brush-border glycoproteins by bacteria results from glycoprotein-degrading glycosidases present in high concentrations in the jejunum of blind loop rats. Release of volatile fatty acids from carbohydrates present in rat intestinal brush border provides evidence of energy-yielding fermentative reactions by the bacteria, leading to the speculation that glycosidase action may provide a mechanism by which blind loop bacteria obtain sugar from intestinal glycoproteins, thus permitting survival independent of exogenous sources (17). A similar process may occur in humans with bacterial overgrowth. Experiments in our laboratory indicate that when bacteria present in the human intestinal tract ferment endogenous glycoproteins, gaseous $H_2$ is released (18). We have observed that individuals with bacterial overgrowth syndromes have markedly elevated fasting $H_2$ concentrations in breath compared to normal controls (103.7 ± 74.9 ppm versus 17.5 ± 13.7 ppm; mean ± SD), suggesting degradation of endogenous carbohydrate-containing substrates such as disaccharidases.

## Effect on Monosaccharide Transport

Transport of glucose and fructose is impaired in the presence of bacterial overgrowth when stasis is induced either surgically (14,19) or pharmacologically by a $\beta$-adrenergic blocking agent which impairs intestinal motility (20). The transport defect is correlated with the degree of overgrowth (14,19). Unconjugated bile acids, resulting from deconjugated enzymes present in a variety of bacterial species (21–23), are commonly found in the contaminated jejunum (21–23), and considerable evidence implicates these compounds in the impairment of monosaccharide transport associated with bacterial overgrowth. In a series of in vitro and in vivo experiments using rat intestine, Gracey et al. (19,24–26) have demonstrated reversible inhibition of monosaccharide uptake by the small intestine upon addition of physiologically realistic concentrations of deoxycholate. Administration of the conjugated bile acid taurocholate had no such effect, nor was the inhibitory effect of deoxycholate modified by the simultaneous addition of conjugated bile salts to the perfusate. The specific mechanism by which deconjugated bile acids inhibit monosaccharide transport remains unknown.

Bacterial overgrowth occurs in infants with protein-calorie malnutrition. Schneider and Viteri (22,27) have documented high unconjugated/conjugated bile acid ratios in their duodenal fluids. Carbohydrate tolerance studies were not reported, but these subjects had frequent diarrheal episodes. Carbohydrate malabsorption occurs in protein-calorie malnutrition (28), and it is tempting to speculate that unconjugated bile acids in the duodenal fluid of these infants may be causative. However, a direct association between bacterial overgrowth and sugar malabsorption in this setting has not been demonstrated.

Antibiotic or Cholestyramine Administration Effects

Administration of oral antibiotics in the experimental animal with bacterial overgrowth, associated with reduction in numbers of organisms, has been correlated with a rise in brush-border disaccharidase activity, although lactase recovered more slowly than sucrase and maltase. Interestingly, monosaccharide transport remained depressed (14). Antibiotic therapy in infants with monosaccharide malabsorption has resulted in symptomatic improvement in some, but not all, patients (7,29).

Administration of nonabsorbable resins, like cholestyramine, may also prevent the effects of enteric proliferation of microflora. These resins are able to sequester injurious products of bacterial metabolism which would alter the normal gastrointestinal function (30). Under experimental conditions, Berant et al. showed that feedings of 4% cholestyramine to rats under conditions of bacterial overgrowth in the jejunem, induced by a $\beta$-adrenergic blocking agent, resulted in lowering luminal concentrations of free fatty acids and deconjugated bile salts. These experiments suggest that intestinal derangements induced by fecal and colonic proliferation of bacteria in the upper segments of small intestine were ameliorated by decreasing levels of the injurious products (31). However, the use of such resins for treatment of patients with blind loop syndrome, diarrheal disease, or carbohydrate intolerance must be restricted and applied judiciously in very selected instances.

## Role of Colonic Flora in Carbohydrate Intolerance

Conversion of Malabsorbed Carbohydrate to
Absorbable Organic Acids

Malabsorption of sugars results in an appreciable osmotic load reaching the colon. It is estimated that if only 5% of the average American adult's daily intake of carbohydrate (350 g) were deposited in the colon as monosaccharide, an osmotic load of approximately 95 mosmol would result, holding 300 ml of water in nonabsorbable form and causing diarrhea (32). In a series of investigations, Bond and co-workers (33–35) demonstrated, however, that 65–85% of mono- and disaccharides reaching the colon were converted by enteric flora fermentation reactions to short-chain organic acids which are rapidly absorbed. Approximately two-thirds of the remaining carbohydrate was converted to larger molecules limited in osmotic activity, so that little

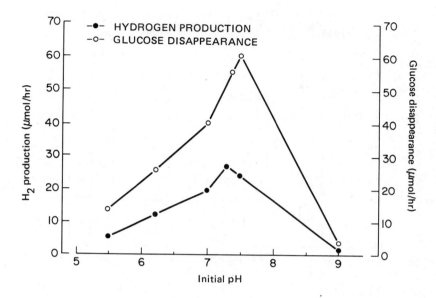

**Figure 2** Relationship between pH and $H_2$ production from glucose by colonic flora. A fecal specimen was divided, homogenized in a series of phosphate-saline solutions at pH 3.0–11.0, and incubated for 1 hr in 1 ml 1.25% glucose (69 $\mu$mol). The pH values represent the actual pH at the start of incubation. (From Ref. 37.)

of the carbohydrate reaching the colon appeared in an osmotically active form in the feces (35). Thus, fecal water resulting from malabsorbed carbohydrate is reduced by bacterial metabolism of dietary sugars to osmotically active but absorbable particles in the form of organic acids, and conversion of much of the remaining substrate to osmotically less active forms.

Chronic diarrheal states in domestic animals have been attributed to alteration in colonic microbial fermentative activity (36). Levitt and Bond have speculated that quantitative and qualitative differences in fermentation of sugars by individual colonic ecosystems could account for variation in susceptibility to symptoms resulting from carbohydrate malabsorption, especially diarrhea (32,33).

Intraluminal colonic pH may account for some of these differences. In vitro experiments in our laboratory (37) have indicated that glucose degrada-

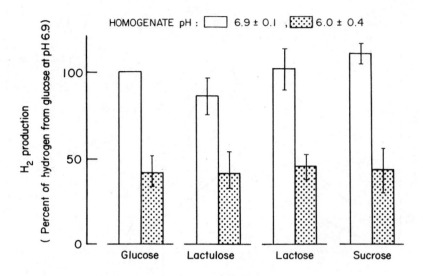

**Figure 3**  Fecal specimens from neonates were homogenized in either saline or phosphate-buffered saline (pH 7.0) and incubated for 1 hr with each of four substrates. The mean pH (±SEM) of the incubates were 6.0 ± 0.4 and 6.9 ± 0.1 when specimens were homogenized in saline or phosphate-buffered saline (7.0), respectively. The differences were statistically significant ($P <$ 0.005) for each sugar. (From Ref. 37.)

tion by fecal homogenates from normal adults is pH-dependent in the range 5.5-7.6 (Fig. 2). Optimal degradation of glucose, paralleled by release of the fermentation product $H_2$, occurred at pH 7.0-7.45. Inhibition of both bacterial glucose metabolism and $H_2$ production occurred at acid pH. $H_2$ per hour from glucose at pH 6.2 and 5.5 averaged 60 and 24%, respectively, of $H_2$ per hour produced at neutral pH. The effect of pH on $H_2$ production from glucose was reproduced with lactulose, lactose, and sucrose using fecal incubates from infants (Fig. 3). In vivo acidification of colonic contents by repeated administration of the nonabsorbable disaccharide, lactulose, significantly reduced excess breath $H_2$ excretion, an index of intraluminal $H_2$ production, from 55.4 ± 11.1 (SE) to 12.2 ± 3.1 ml/4 hr ($P < 0.05$) following administration of a test dose of lactulose. Since $H_2$ production is correlated with carbohydrate degradation (Fig. 4) by $H_2$-producing fermentative

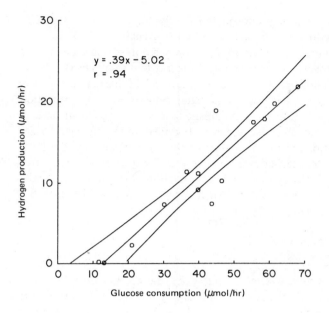

**Figure 4** Relationship between glucose consumption and $H_2$ production. Fecal specimens from five adult subjects were homogenized in a series of phosphate-saline solutions resulting in initial pHs ranging from 5.5 to 7.6, and incubated for 1 hr in 1 ml 1.25% glucose (69 $\mu$mol). The 95% confidence limits are indicated.

reactions, the in vivo data likewise indicate an inhibition of these processes at acid pH.

These data suggest that the intraluminal colonic pH operant at the time malabsorbed sugar reaches the colon influences the fate of the carbohydrate and, on the basis of the observations of Bond and Levitt, its osmotic activity. If the colonic pH is above a limiting level, $H_2$-producing fermentative reactions occur leading to extensive conversion of sugars to absorbable organic acids. Conversely, an acidic colonic pH inhibits extensive metabolism of sugar and may result in an osmotic diarrhea. The factors regulating colonic pH are incompletely understood, but long-term maintenance of an acidic pH by dietary means could eventually result in conversion of the enteric flora to an acidophilic type able to efficiently degrade carbohydrate by alternate fermentative pathways. This may explain the widely accepted observations of increasing tolerance to malabsorbed carbohydrate, such as lactulose, over time. However, deliberate attempts to alter composition of the enteric flora by administration of lactulose have met with inconsistent results (38).

Fermentative reactions reducing the osmotic load of malabsorbed carbohydrate may also benefit the host by salvaging calories escaping absorption in the small intestine (33,39). This ruminant function is dependent on bacterial metabolism of nonabsorbed sugar as described above followed by absorption and oxidation of resulting short-chain organic acids by the host. The adult human colon can absorb up to 540 kcal/day as short-chain fatty acids (40), but the efficiency of colonic conservation of calories reaching the colon as malabsorbed sugar has not been evaluated in infants with carbohydrate malabsorption.

Adverse Effects of Metabolism of
Intraluminal Carbohydrates

In contrast to the beneficial effects exerted by the colonic flora, it is also possible that intraluminal metabolism of dietary carbohydrates by the enteric flora may exert a negative influence on the physiology of the host. Acidosis has been described in the prematurely born neonate following lactose loading (41). Although neomycin administration did not modify this response, it remains unknown whether the acidosis of premature infants following carbohydrate loading and the late metabolic acidosis of prematures occurring at 3–4 weeks of age are secondary to generation of anions within tissues or due to intraluminal bacterial fermentation. However, the production of organic acids by intestinal bacteria has been demonstrated to have a role in the development of acidosis in cattle (42). Similarly, D-lactic acidosis thought to be secondary to intraluminal bacterial metabolism of sugars has been described in an adult (43) and a child (44) with short bowel syndrome. Proliferation of fecal and colonic flora in jejunum may also enhance the secretion of NA+ and water in the small intestine through stimulation of cAMP. This may be due to the generation of free fatty acids and deconjugated bile salts resulting from bacterial action on host secretions and foodstuffs (31). Increased water delivered to the colon from the upper segments of the small intestine, which surpasses the reabsorptive ability of the colon, results in diarrhea. Thus, intraluminal bacterial metabolism of sugars may exert a negative effect on host metabolism.

**Table 1**  Clinical Conditions in Infancy Associated with
Bacterial Overgrowth

| Column | Reference |
|---|---|
| Chronic diarrhea | |
|    Mono- and disaccharide malabsorption | 9–11 |
|    Protein-calorie malnutrition | 13 |
|    Intestinal pseudo-obstruction | 51 |
| Postoperative diarrhea | |
|    Tracheoesophageal fistula | 7 |
|    Esophageal atresia | 9 |
|    Gastroschisis | 7 |
|    Small bowel atresia, stenosis, stricture | 7, 9, 12 |
|    Meconium ileus | 9 |
|    Malrotation | 7 |
|    Hirschprung's disease | 12 |
| Alternative feeding routes | |
|    Gastrostomy | 9 |
|    Nasojejunal tube | 52 |

## Final Considerations

Carbohydrate malabsorption may occur when a fecal-type flora is present
in the upper small bowel. Inability of enterocytes to hydrolyze disaccharides
and transport monosaccharides appears to be mediated by the metabolic
activities of microbes, specifically degradation of brush-border glycoproteins
and deconjugation of bile acids. While colonic microbial conversion of malabsorbed carbohydrates to absorbable short-chain fatty acids may in some
situations induce systemic acidosis, the resulting reduction in osmotic load
appears likely to increase tolerance to sugars escaping the small intestine.

A variety of clinical conditions in infancy predispose to bacterial overgrowth (Table 1). Since carbohydrate malabsorption can result from an abnormal small bowel flora, the presence of carbohydrate malabsorption in

these conditions warrants aspiration of duodenal fluid for culture. Falsely negative cultures may occur in instances when overgrowth is confined to areas distal to the site sampled. Indirect screening methods for the presence of an abnormal small bowel flora include the $[^{13}C]$ glycocholate breath test (45, 46), and measurement of serum folate and $B_{12}$ levels (47). Elevation of fasting $H_2$ levels may indicate overgrowth in the older infant and child. Antibiotic therapy is indicated when an abnormal flora is documented, and surgical correction is indicated when feasible if stasis is due to an anatomical abnormality (48).

Wide individual differences in tolerance, that is, symptoms, occur following ingestion of lactose by children with lactose malabsorption (49,50). In addition, the younger child with lactose malabsorption often presents with chronic diarrhea and the older child may present with recurrent abdominal pain (50). These differences may in part be due to individual variations in the amount of sugar escaping small bowel absorption. However, in view of the studies of Levitt and Bond (32), it appears entirely reasonable to speculate that symptomatic differences among infants and children with carbohydrate malabsorption may also be mediated by the metabolic activities of the colonic ecosystem.

### Acknowledgment

The studies performed in the author's laboratory were supported by a research grant (HD12449) and Research Career Development Award HD00297 from the National Institute of Child Health and Human Development.

### References

1. Davis, B. D., Dulbecco, R., Eisen, H. N., Ginsberg, H. S., and Wood, W. B. (1967). *Microbiology.* Harper and Row, New York, p. 56.
2. Challacombe, D. N., Richardson, J. M., and Anderson, C. M. (1974). Bacterial microflora of the upper gastrointestinal tract in infants without diarrhea. *Arch. Dis. Child. 49*:264–269.
3. Donaldson, R. M., Jr. (1964). Normal bacterial populations of the intestine and their relation to intestinal function. *New Engl. J. Med. 270*: 938–45, 994–1000, 1050–1056.
4. Althausen, T. L., Gunnison, J. B., Marshall, M. S., and Shipman, S. J. (1935). Carbohydrate intolerance and intestinal flora. *Arch. Int. Med. 56*:1263–1286.

5. Bjorneklett, A., and Midtvedt, T. (1981). Influence of three antimicrobial agents—penicillin, metronidazole, and doxycyclin—on the intestinal microflora of healthy microflora of healthy humans. *Scand. J. Gastroenterol. 16*;473–480.

6. Challacombe, D. N., Richardson, J. M., Rowe, B., and Anderson, C. M. (1974). Bacterial microflora of the upper gastrointestinal tract in infants with protracted diarrhea. *Arch. Dis. Child. 49*:270–277.

7. Lloyd-Still, J. D., and Shwachman, H. (1975). Duodenal microflora: a prospective study in pediatric gastrointestinal disorders. *Am. J. Dig. Dis. 20*:708–715.

8. Burke, V., and Anderson, C. M. (1975). Bacterial flora of the upper gastrointestinal tract. In *Pediatric Gastroenterology,* C. M. Anderson and V. Burke (Eds.), Blackwell Scientific, Oxford, pp. 397–410.

9. Burke, V., and Anderson, C. M. (1966). Sugar intolerance as a cause of protracted diarrhea following surgery of the gastrointestinal tract in neonates. *Aust. Paediatr. J. 2*:219–227.

10. Gracey, M., Burke, V., and Anderson, C. M. (1969). Association of monosaccharide malabsorption with abnormal small intestinal flora. *Lancet ii*:384–385.

11. Coello-Ramirez, P., Lifshitz, F., and Zuniga, V. (1972). Enteric microflora and carbohydrate intolerance in infants with diarrhea. *Pediatrics 49*:233–242.

12. Challacombe, D. N., Richardson, T. M., and Edkins, S. (1974). Anaerobic bacteria and deconjugated bile salts in the upper small intestine of infants with gastrointestinal disorders. *Acta Pediatr. Scand. 63*:581–587.

13. Mata, L. J., Jiminez, F., Cordon, M., Rosales, E. P., Schneider, R. E., and Viteri, F. (1972). Gastrointestinal flora of children with protein-calorie malnutrition. *Am. J. Clin. Nutr. 25*:1118–1126.

14. Gianella, R. A., Rout, W. R., and Toskes, P. P. (1974). Jejunal brush border injury and impaired sugar and amino acid uptake in the blind loop syndrome. *Gastroenterology 67*:965–974.

15. Gracey, M., Thomas, J., and Houghton, M. (1975). Effect of stasis on intestinal enzyme activities. *Aust. N.Z. J. Med. 5*:141–144.

16. Jonas, A., Flanagan, P. R., and Forstner, G. G. (1977). Pathogenesis of mucosal injury in the blind loop syndrome. *J. Clin. Invest. 601*: 1321–1330.

17. Prizont, R. (1981). Glycoprotein degradation in the blind loop syndrome. *J. Clin. Invest. 67*:336–344.

18. Perman, J. A., and Modler, S. (1981). Hydrogen ($H_2$) and methane ($CH_4$) are products of glycoprotein catabolism by colonic flora. *Gastroenterology 80*:1251.

19. Gracey, M., Burke, V., Oshin, S., Barker, J., and Glasgow, E. F. (1971). Bacteria, bile salts and intestinal monosaccharide malabsorption. *Gut 12*:683–692.

20. Lifshitz, F., Wapnir, R. A., Wehman, H. J., Diaz-Bensussen, S., and Pergolizzi, R. (1978). The effects of small intestinal colonization by fecal and colonic bacteria on intestinal function in rats. *J. Nutr.* 108:1913–1923.

21. Hill, M. J., and Drasar, B. S. (1968). Degradation of bile salts by human intestinal bacteria. *Gut* 9:22–27.

22. Schneider, R. E., and Viteri, F. C. (1974). Luminal events of lipid absorption in protein calorie malnourished children; relationship with nutritional recovery and diarrhea. II. Alterations in bile acid content of duodenal aspirates. *Am. J. Clin. Nutr.* 27:788–796.

23. Watkins, J. B., and Perman, J. A. (1977). Bile acid metabolism in infants and children. *Clin. Gastroenterol.* 6:201–218.

24. Gracey, M., Burke, V., and Anderson, C. M. (1969). Association of monosaccharide malabsorption with abnormal small-intestinal flora. *Lancet ii*:384–385.

25. Gracey, M., Burke, V., and Oshin, A. (1971). Influence of bile salts on intestinal sugar transport in vivo. *Scand. J. Gastroenterol.* 6:273–276.

26. Gracey, M., Burke, V., and Oshin, A. (1971). Reversible inhibition of intestinal active sugar transport by deconjugated bile salt in vitro. *Biochim. Biophys. Acta* 225:308–314.

27. Schneider, R. E., and Viteri, F. E. (1974). Luminal events of lipid absorption in protein calorie malnourished children; relationship with nutritional recovery and diarrhea. I. Capacity of the duodenal content to achieve micellar solubilization of lipids. *Am. J. Clin. Nutr.* 27:777–787.

28. Wharton, B. S. (1975). Gastroenterological problems in children of developing countries. In *Pediatric Gastroenterology,* C. M. Anderson and V. Burke (Eds.), Blackwell Scientific, Oxford, pp. 569–610.

29. Lifshitz, F., Coello-Ramirez, P., and Guiterrez-Topete, G. (1970). Monosaccharide intolerance and hypoglycemia in infants with diarrhea. I. Clinical course of 23 infants. *J. Pediatr.* 77:595–603.

30. Berant, M. (1980). Non-absorbable resins in the management of gastrointestinal disease. In *Clinical Disorders in Pediatric Gastroenterology and Malnutrition,* F. Lifshitz (Ed.), Marcel Dekker, New York, pp. 169–181.

31. Berant, M., Lifshitz, F., Bayne, M. A., and Wapnir, R. A. (1981). Jejunal CAMP activated sodium secretion via deconjugated bile salts and fatty acids. *Biochem. Med.* 25:327–336.

32. Levitt, M. D., and Bond, J. H. (1979). Role of fetal bacteria in diarrhea associated with carbohydrate malabsorption. In *Frontiers of Knowledge in the Diarrheal Diseases.* H. D. Janowitz and D. B. Sachar (Eds.), Projects in Health, Inc., Upper Montclair, N.J., pp. 327–331.

33. Bond, J. H., Jr., and Levitt, M. D. (1976). Fate of soluble carbohydrate in the colon of rats and man. *J. Clin. Invest.* 57:1158–1164.

34. Bond, J. H., and Levitt, M. D. (1976). Quantitative measurement of lactose absorption. *Gastroenterology 70*:1058–1062.

35. Bond, J. H., Currier, B. E., Buchwald, H., and Levitt, M. D. (1980). Colonic conservation of malabsorbed carbohydrate. *Gastroenterology 78*:444–447.

36. Minder, H. P., Merritt, A. M., and Chalupa, W. (1980). In vitro fermentation of feces from normal and chronically diarrheal horses. *Am. J. Vet. Res. 41*:564–567.

37. Perman, J. A., Modler, S., and Olson, A. C. (1981). Role of pH in production of hydrogen from carbohydrates by colonic flora: studies in vivo and in vitro. *J. Clin. Invest. 67*:643–650.

38. Conn, H. O., and Lieberthal, M. M. (1979). Formulation and pharmacology of lactulose. In *The Hepatic Coma Syndromes and Lactulose*, Williams and Wilkins, Baltimore, pp, 248–277.

39. Chiles, C., Watkins, J. B., Barr, R., Tsai, P. Y., and Goldman, D. A. (1979). Lactose utilization in the newborn: role of colonic flora. *Pediatr. Res. 13*:365.

40. Ruppin, H., Bar-Meir, S., Soergel, K. H., Wood, C. M., and Schmitt, M. G., Jr. (1980). Absorption of short chain fatty acids by the colon. *Gastroenterology 78*:1500–1507.

41. Lifshitz, F., Diaz-Bensussen, S., Martinez-Garza, V., Abdo-Bassols, F., and Diaz del Castillo, E. (1971). Influence of disaccharides on the development of systemic acidosis in the premature infant. *Pediatr. Res. 5*:213–225.

42. Dunlop, R. H., and Hammond, P. B. (1965). D-Lactic acidosis of ruminants. *Ann. N.Y. Acad. Sci. 119*:1109–1132.

43. Oh, M. S., Phelps, K. R., Traube, M., Barbosa-Saldivar, J. L., Boxhill, C., and Carroll, H. J. (1979). D-Lactic acidosis in a man with the short-bowel syndrome. *New Engl. J. Med. 301*:249–252.

44. Schoorel, E. P., Giesberts, M. A. H., Blom, W., and Van Gelderen, H. H. (1980). D-Lactic acidosis in a boy with short-bowel syndrome. *Arch. Dis. Child. 55*:810–812.

45. Barr, R. G., Perman, J. A., Schoeller, D. A., and Watkins, J. B. (1978). Breath tests in pediatric gastrointestinal disorders: new diagnostic opportunities. *Pediatrics 62*:393–401.

46. Watkins, J. B., Park, R., Perman, J. A., Schoeller, D. A., and Klein, D. D. (1980). Ileal dysfunction vs. bacterial overgrowth: detection by [13]C glycocholate breath test and fecal combustion. *Pediatr. Res. 14*:578.

47. Perman, J. A. (1978). Contaminated small bowel syndrome. In *Principles of Pediatrics: Health Care of the Young*, R. Hoekelman (Ed.), McGraw-Hill, New York, pp. 808–809.

48. Watkins, J. B., and Perman, J. A. (1980). Malabsorptive syndromes. In *Current Pediatric Therapy*, S. S. Gellis and B. M. Kagan (Eds.), W. B. Saunders, Philadelphia, pp. 230–240.

49. Barr, R. G., Levine, M. D., and Watkins, J. B. (1979). Recurrent abdominal pain (RAP) in children due to lactose intolerance: A prospective study. *N. Engl. J. Med. 300*:1449.

50. Barr, R. G., Watkins, J. B., and Perman, J. A. (1981). Mucosal function and breath hydrogen excretion: comparative studies in the clinical evaluation of children with nonspecific abdominal complaints. *Pediatrics 68*:526–533.

51. Byrne, W. J., Cipel, L., Euler, A. R., Halpin, T. C., and Ament, M. E. (1977). Chronic idiopathic intestinal pseudo-obstruction syndrome in children—clinical characteristics and prognosis. *J. Pediatr. 90*:585–589.

52. Challacombe, D. (1974). Bacterial microflora in infants receiving nasojejunal tube feeding. *J. Pediatr. 85*:113.

# CARBOHYDRATE INTOLERANCE AND PROTEIN HYPERSENSITIVITY

# 11

# INTERRELATIONSHIP BETWEEN COW'S MILK PROTEIN INTOLERANCE AND LACTOSE INTOLERANCE

JOHN A. WALKER-SMITH
Queen Elizabeth Hospital for Children, London, England

It is widely accepted that clinical lactose intolerance is a common and important cause of postenteritis diarrhea in infancy (1–3). Studies over several years at Queen Elizabeth Hospital for Children indicate that lactose intolerance in these circumstances is often associated with cow's milk protein intolerance. Our experience indicates that persistent lactose intolerance may often be a secondary result of cow's milk protein intolerance (CMPI). The following clinical evidence supports this hypothesis. Following gastroenteritis in infancy, feedings of breast milk that contains 7% lactose do not induce diarrhea, whereas feedings of cow's milk with the same lactose load do (Table 1). Diarrhea induced by cow's milk was accompanied by abnormal amounts of stool-reducing substances despite a normal rise in the blood sugar level. Harrison (4) originally reported four infants with lactose intolerance complicating

**Table 1**   Milk Tolerance Test in Infants (Lactose Content 7 g/100 ml)

|  | Expressed human breast milk | Cow's half cream national dried milk |
|---|---|---|
| Plasma glucose rise (mg %) | 31 | 32 |
| Stool-reducing substances | Negative | Abnormal |
| Weight (g) ↓ | 10 | 350 |
| No. of stools after test | 2 | 6 |
| No. of vomitings | – | 4 |

*Source*: Walker-Smith, J. A. (1975). Gastroenteritis. In *Diseases of the Small Intestine in Childhood,* 1st ed., Pitman Medical, London. p. 98.

acute nonbacterial gastroenteritis successfully treated with Nutramigen, a lactose-free casein-hydrolysate formula. After recovery all these infants had normal lactose tolerance tests but redeveloped diarrhea, with excess stool-reducing substances in three, when recommenced on cow's milk. Similar studies from Queen Elizabeth Hospital extended these observations for an additional 13 patients following gastroenteritis. These patients were all lactose tolerant, yet 10 showed a relapse of diarrhea with increased stool-reducing substances and low stool pH on challenge with cow's milk. Liu et al. (5) demonstrated that this response is specifically the result of the protein fraction in cow's milk (bovine serum albumin or beta lactoglobulins). This evidence suggests that the protein in cow's milk may be responsible for the development of clinical lactose intolerance following an episode of acute gastroenteritis.

**Figure 1**   Serial small intestinal biopsies in a child, aged 4 months at initial diagnosis. (a) Untreated on cow's milk, abnormal mucosa; (b) well on a milk-free diet 4 months later, normal mucosa; (c) after relapse following a clinical challenge with cow's milk, 4 days after (b).

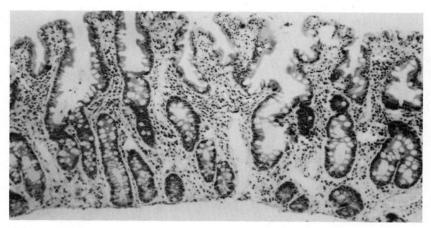

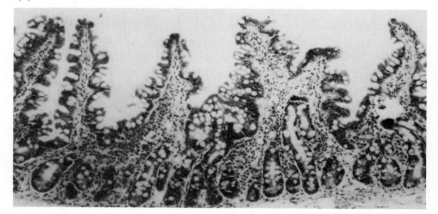

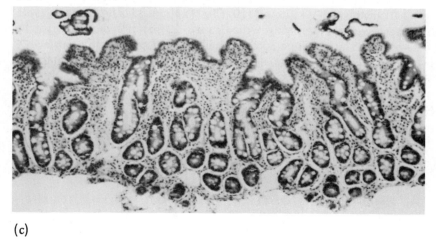

## Cow's Milk-Sensitive Enteropathy (CMSE)

CMSE refers specifically to the intestinal pathology and diarrhea induced by what is presumably cow's milk protein, whereas CMPI refers to other reactions as well. The notion that CMSE following gastroenteritis in infancy is the result of small intestinal mucosal damage due to cow's milk protein was demonstrated by serial biopsies of the small bowel (6,7). An example of the effects of cow's milk feedings following gastroenteritis in one infant with CMPI is shown in Figure 1. The small bowel shows an abnormal morphology at the time of diagnosis of CMSE (Fig. 1a), with improvement following elimination of cow's milk (Fig. 1b). Following a cow's milk challenge, the small intestinal epithelial morphology deteriorated (Fig. 1c), confirming the diagnosis of CMSE. The altered mucosa was generally thin (8), suggesting a decreased capacity of crypt cells to regenerate the enterocyte. Concomitantly, the intestinal disaccharidase levels were low at the time of diagnosis, rose during recovery, and fell on relapse induced by cow's milk challenge (Fig. 2). The changes in lactase concentrations of the small bowel paralleled the changes in epithelial surface area and the histologic integrity of the mucosa. Phillips et al. have shown that these enzyme changes paralleled alterations in the microvillous surface area as assessed with electron microscopy (9). These serial small intestinal biopsies thus provide hard evidence not only that cow's milk-sensitive enteropathy does exist, but that this disorder is associated with acquired lactase deficiency, paralleling small intestinal mucosal damage. Therefore, it could be concluded that there may be clinical lactose intolerance after a clinical relapse of the disease produced by cow's milk feedings.

The lesion of the intestinal mucosa induced by cow's milk protein in sensitive patients is usually "patchy" (10) (Fig. 3). From 33 children studied with untreated cow's milk-sensitive enteropathy, 22 biopsies showed a patchy enteropathy. Thus, interpretation of small bowel biopsies is most satisfactory when the largest area possible is sampled (in our hands using the double port capsule), and the largest area examined of the biopsy itself (using the dissecting microscope and taking serial sections when possible). Failure by some workers to show consistent changes related to cow's milk challenge in such children may relate to these patchy changes. Such errors are especially likely

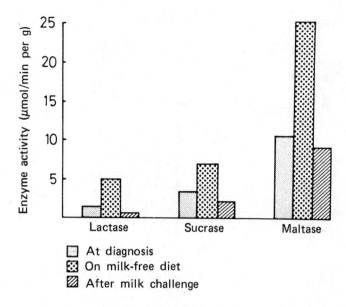

**Figure 2**  Mean disaccharidase activity related to cow's milk intake in five infants with cow's milk-sensitive enteropathy.

to occur when only single biopsies are used. These patchy changes are also important in relation to interpretation of intestinal disaccharidase results. Campbell et al. (11) have shown that significant variation in lactase levels occurred between paired biopsy samples obtained with a double port capsule when a patchy lesion was present with significant differences between the two samples.

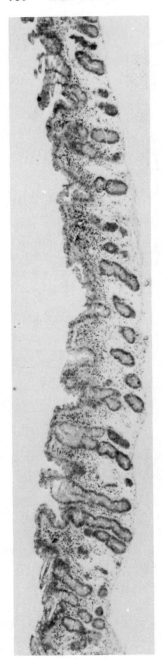

**Figure 3**  Patchy enteropathy. Two histological sections of biopsies taken simultaneously with a double port capsule. Above, moderate uniform enteropathy; below, on left, normal mucosa; on right, severe enteropathy.

## Postenteritis CMSE and Lactose Intolerance

The correlation between the intestinal morphological and enzymatic alterations in CMSE with the clinical syndrome of lactose intolerance and/or milk
intolerance is compounded. There are many factors which must be considered when addressing this issue, as reviewed in Chapters 1, 12, and 13. In
postenteritis CMSE there is usually a positive correlation among the intestinal
morphological alterations, small intestinal lactase levels, and clinical milk or
lactose intolerance when considering groups of patients. However, there is a
great variability in individual patients with lack of correlation among these
variables (12). This is usually the case in patients who exhibit marked patchy
enteropathy as described above. There may be clinical lactose intolerance
with normal lactase levels in the small intestinal biopsy, and there may be low
lactose levels with or without morphological alterations of the epithelial
cells. However, on electron microscopy there may be a reduction in microvillus surface area to account for the lactase deficiency in samples with normal histological appearance (9).

From these studies it is clear that levels of lactase on a single biopsy speci-
ment may not consistently correlate with clinical lactose intolerance in
CMSE.

This failure of a consistent correlation between lactase levels on biopsy
and clinical lactose intolerance in postenteritis CMSE may also be related to
the unrepresentative nature of proximal biospy as a guide to morphology
along the small gut as a whole, and so, of lactase activity further along the
intestine. Clearly a single proximal biopsy often does not represent the morphology of the entire small intestine. The mucosal damage along the total
intestine was shown to be variable in 10 children dying from gastroenteritis,
at postmortem (13). In contrast, patients with limited proximal jejunal lesions
as in celiac disease there may be lactase deficiency on a limited portion of the
jejunum, but the patient may be lactose tolerant, as the remainder of the
intestine may be normal with normal levels of intestinal disaccharidases.
Therefore, the total extent of mucosal damage and so the total depression of
lactase activity in the small intestine as a whole, is what determines whether
clinical lactose intolerance develops.

## Hypothesis Interrelating CMSE and Lactose
## Intolerance Following Gastroenteritis

We have proposed two hypotheses to explain how CMSE may develop after
an attack of acute gastroenteritis in infancy (Fig. 4): (a) the result of transient

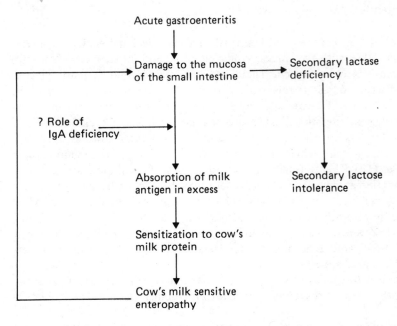

**Figure 4** Hypothesis, interrelating acute gastroenteritis, cow's milk protein intolerance, and lactose intolerance.

lactose or monosaccharide intolerance due to mucosal damage related to the immediate infection and (b) a persistent enteropathy due to primary CMSE or sensitivity to some other food proteins. In the latter hypothesis there may or may not be lactose intolerance.

How can these syndromes be distinguished? The time of onset of lactose intolerance may be helpful. If lactose intolerance after gastroenteritis merely reflects the extent and severity of the small intestinal damage at the time of the acute attack, it should manifest as soon as the amount of lactose in the diet after the acute attack is increased and should be relatively brief in duration. In contrast if lactose intolerance postenteritis reflects persistent intestinal damage by CMSE, it should manifest later after sensitization occurs. In fact, Gribbin et al. (14) (Fig. 5) reported both possibilities in infants with gastroenteritis. In some patients the time of onset of lactose intolerance following diarrhea was immediate, which agreed with the concept of acute

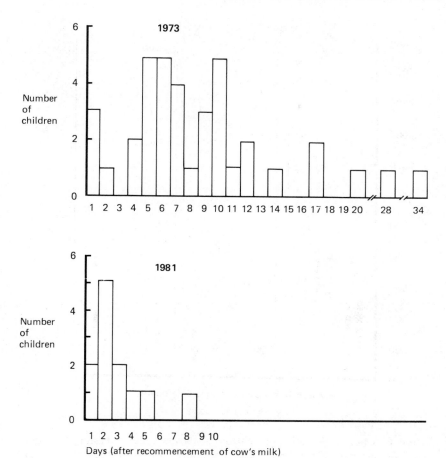

**Figure 5** Interval after return to cow's milk feedings when lactose intolerance appeared (return of diarrhea with excess reducing substances).

gastroenteritis-induced lactase deficiency, secondary to acute mucosal damage. In other patients with diarrhea there was quite a considerable time interval before lactose intolerance developed, agreeing with the concept of secondary cow's milk protein-induced damage. This interval could represent the time required to sensitize the mucosa to cow's milk protein. However, this interval is clearly variable, as a few infants who develop signs of clinical

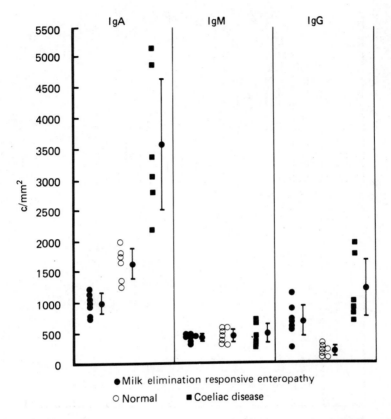

**Figure 6** Quantitation of lamina propria plasma cells containing IgA, IgM, and IgG, using a direct horseradish peroxidase antibody technique, in six histologically normal biopsies, in seven biopsies from milk elimination-responsive postenteritis enteropathy, and in six biopsies from untreated celiac disease. (Permission, A. Haidas.)

lactose intolerance immediately after acute gastroenteritis also proved to have cow's milk-sensitive enteropathy. It was already known from the observations of Gruskay and Cook (15) that excess antigen absorption may occur rapidly; in their study, egg albumin crossed into the circulation in infants with acute gastroenteritis, presumably related to small intestinal mucosal damage at the time of acute infection. In Chapter 12, evidence is put forward linking unabsorbed lactose with intestinal damage of the barrier which protects the host

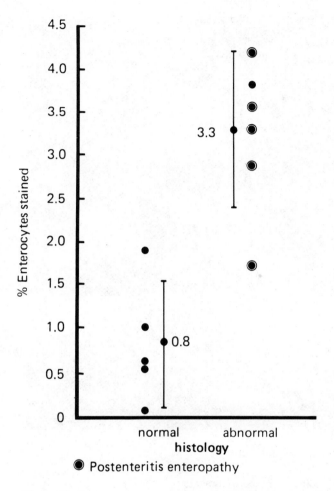

**Figure 7**  Percentage of enterocytes taking up horseradish peroxidase in fixed biopsies, histologically normal and abnormal.

from the passage of intact proteins across the intestine. Also, evidence is presented for the possible interactions between the dietary proteins and mucosal damage, particularly as it relates to oligodisaccharidases in milk and soy protein feedings (Chapter 13), which may contribute to the problem of protein-sensitive enteropathy following gastroenteritis in children.

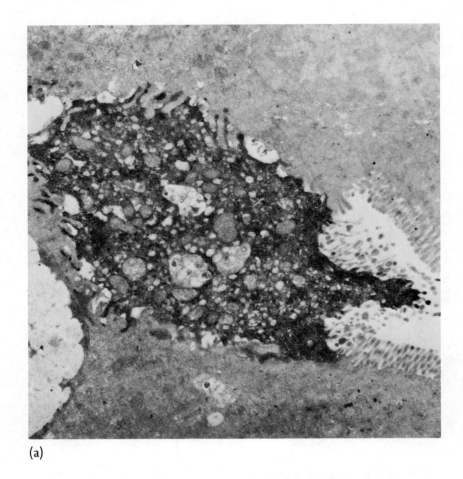

(a)

**Figure 8a**  Extruding cell penetrated by horseradish peroxidase. Unstained section X 11,250.

Local small intestinal IgA deficiency could also be a factor in excess anti-gen absorption. By using a direct horseradish peroxidase antibody technique on paraffin sections of small intestinal biopsies, IgA-, IgM-, and IgG-contain-ing plasma cells were quantitated in the small intestinal lamina propria (Fig. 6). Patients with CMSE all tended to have fewer numbers of secretory IgA-producing plasma cells in the lamina propria  than was found in coeliac

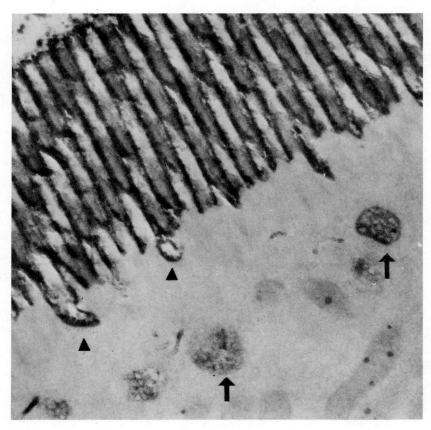

(b)

**Figure 8b**   Horseradish peroxidase uptake in biopsy organ culture of abnormal mucosa. Peroxidase is seen in pinocytotic vesicles (arrowheads) and in mulivesibular bodies (arrows). Unstained section X 41,000.

disease, whereas the number of IgA- and IgM-producing cells were normal (16). Serum IgA levels were low in only two of the six CMSE children studied.

Evidence was then sought that antigen could enter damaged mucosa by a morphological study with light and electron microscopy. The passive and active permeability of the small intestinal mucosa to antigens was studied using horseradish peroxidase as a tracer molecule using fixed tissue (17). Significantly more cells were passively permeable in children with postenteritis CMSE. The intestinal mucosa of these patients took up horseradish peroxidase more than histologically normal mucosa of other patients (Fig. 7). There was increased penetration both into enterocytes and from them into the lamina propria (Fig. 8a). Thus these studies show that anatomical pathways exist for increased antigen entry via passive diffusion through damaged enterocytes. Studies of active uptake of horseradish peroxidase in biopsy organ culture in these children also showed increased diffuse penetration of damaged enterocytes, but there was a more varied pattern of horseradish peroxidase uptake in pinocytotic vesicles. That is, less evidence of pinocytosis occurred in the more disrupted enterocytes although normal or increased uptake of horseradish was evident in more normal enterocytes (18) (Fig. 8b). The significant increase in the number of enterocytes diffusely penetrated with horseradish peroxidase in biopsies of CMSE patients suggests that passive diffusion of macromolecules into the mucosa may be important in these children. These findings may be of significance for the pathogenesis of some patients with CMSE as a sequel to gastroenteritis.

### Sensitizing Capacity of Milk Feedings

However, another factor of importance in the development of a postenteritis cow's milk-sensitive enteropathy may be the sensitizing capacity of the type of feed the infant is given. In recent years there has been in our gastroenteritis unit an overall decline in the incidence of delayed recovery after acute gastroenteritis and of lactose intolerance specifically. In infants under 6 months of age admitted with acute gastroenteritis, in 1973 18.9% developed lactose intolerance, whereas in 1981 this level had fallen to 13.5% (a reduction of approximately one-quarter) (Fig. 5). Furthermore, the time of onset after acute gastroenteritis has changed with a gross reduction in the number of children developing lactose intolerance a week or more after the acute attack.

This decrease in the delay of recovery may be due to alterations in the sensitizing capacity of current low solute milks. The anaphylactic sensitizing capacity of various milk feeds has been studied in Cambridge (19) in guinea pigs. The newer low-solute milks such as gold cap SMA are significantly less sensitizing than the older high-solute formulas such as full cream Cow & Gate used in our unit in 1973 (20), when the incidence of delayed recovery was much higher than at present. A study of delayed recovery after gastroenteritis and the relationship to the milk feeding at Queen Elizabeth Hospital showed that the type of milk fed significantly influenced the development of delayed recovery (20). A modern formula such as SMA is clearly less sensitizing. It is possible that further treatment of such milks could make them even less sensitizing.

## Relevance of CMSE to the Developing World

Chronic diarrhea with or without excess reducing substances in infants with malnutrition (marasmus in particular) is a very common problem in the developing world in cow's milk-fed children. It often appears to occur as a sequel to acute gastroenteritis (20). Indeed, the potential importance of this problem in the developing world has already been suggested by Iyngkaran et al. (21). who has prospectively studied the role of cow's milk protein intolerance as a complication of acute gastroenteritis in Malaysia. This observation has been confirmed and extended by Manuel et al. (22), who found cow's milk-sensitive enteropathy to be present in a significant number of infants with chronic diarrhea in Indonesian children in Surabaja. Serial measurements of morphological parameters clearly established cow's milk-sensitive enteropathy as an important cause of chronic diarrhea in Surabaja.

## Conclusions

Food-sensitive enteropathy and CMSE in particular, with or without lactose intolerance, as a sequel to gastrointestinal infection may be one of the most important causes of chronic infantile diarrhea in much of the world. The hypothesis put forward, therefore, is that persistent diarrhea due to lactose intolerance as well as chronic diarrhea without excretion of carbohydrates in stools following gastroenteritis is often due to CMSE. Currently, its prevalence at Queen Elizabeth Hospital for Children has fallen due to the introduction of less-sensitizing cow's milk feedings such as modern SMA and other low-solute milks.

Does this distinction between lactose intolerance and CMSE matter if they can coexist? Yes. If this hypothesis is correct, it should be possible to very significantly reduce the morbidity of complications of gastroenteritis by feeding babies with milk formulas of low-sensitizing capacity, rather than by promoting soy formulas which could also be sensitizing. If the above hypothesis is correct, consideration should be given to providing infants who develop gastroenteritis a milk feeding which is less sensitizing than those currently available to reduce the prevalence of postenteritis milk intolerance. Of course, when CMSE does develop, the temporary use of a casein hydrolysate formula such as Pregestimil may be preferable to the use of other proteins such as soy.

However, every effort should be made to promote human breast-feeding and so reduce the incidence of gastroenteritis and its morbidity, and also every effort be made to improve hygiene.

# References

1.  Sunshine, P., and Kretchmer, N. (1964). Studies of small intestine during development. *Pediatrics 34*:38–50.
2.  Burke, V., Kerry, K. R., and Anderson, C. M. (1965). The relationship of dietary lactose to refractory diarrhoea in infancy. *Aust. Paediatr. J. 1*:147–160.
3.  Lifshitz, F., Coello-Ramirez, P., Cutierrez Topete, G., and Cornado Cornet, M. C. (1971). Carbohydrate intolerance in infants with diarrhea. *J. Pediatr. 79*:760–767.
4.  Harrison, M. (1974). Sugar malabsorption in cow's milk protein intolerance. *Lancet i*:360–361.
5.  Liu, H-Y., Tsao, M. U., Moore, B., and Giday, Z. (1968). Bovine milk protein induced malabsorption of lactose and fat in infants. *Gastroenterology 54*:27–34.
6.  Harrison, B. M., Kilby, A., Walker-Smith, J. A., France, N. E., and Wood, C. B. S. (1976). Cow's milk protein intolerance: a possible association with gastroenteritis, lactose intolerance, and IgA deficiency. *Br. Med. J. 1*:1501–1504.
7.  Walker-Smith, J. A., Harrison, M., Kilby, A., Phillips, A., and France, N. E. (1978). Cow's milk sensitive enteropathy. *Arch. Dis. Child. 53*: 375–380.
8.  Maluenda, C., Phillips, A. D., Briddon, A., and Walker-Smith, J. A. (1980). Quantitative analysis of small intestinal mucosa in cow's milk protein intolerance (Cow's milk allergy). The American College of Allergists Third International Food Allergy Symposium.
9.  Phillips, A. D., Avigad, S., Rice, S. J., France, N. E., and Walker-Smith, J. A. (1980). Microvillous surface area in secondary disaccharidase deficiency. *Gut 21*:44–48.
10.  Manuel, P. D., Walker-Smith, J. A., and France, N. E. (1979). Patchy enteropathy. *Gut 20*:211–215.
11.  Campbell, C. A., Clay, P., and Walker-Smith, J. A. (1980). Disaccharidase activity in patchy enteropathy in children. *British Paediatric Association Meeting, York.*

12. Harrison, M., and Walker-Smith, J. A. (1977). Reinvestigation lactose intolerant children: lack of correlation between lactose intolerance and small intestinal morphology, disaccharidase activity and lactose tolerance tests. *Gut 18*:48–52.
13. Walker-Smith, J. A. (1979). Gastroenteritis. In *Diseases of the Small Intestine in Childhood,* 2nd ed. Pitman Medical, London, p. 182.
14. Gribbin, M., Walker-Smith, J. A., and Wood, C. B. S. (1976). Delayed recovery following acute gastroenteritis. *Acta Paediatr. Belg. 26*:167–176.
15. Gruskay, F. L., and Cook, R. E. (1955). The gastrointestinal absorption of unaltered protein in normal infants and in infants recovering from diarrhoea. *Pediatrics 16*:763–768.
16. Haidas, A. (1982). In preparation.
17. Jackson, D., Walker-Smith, J. A., and Phillips, A. D. (1982). *Histopathology,* in press.
18. Phillips, A. D. (1981). Small intestinal mucosa in childhood in health and disease. *Scand. J. Gastroenterol. 16*:70 (Suppl.) 65–85.
19. McLaughlan, P., Anderson, K. J., Widdowson, E. M., and Coombs, R. R. A. (1981). Effect of heat on anaphylactic-sensitising capacity of cow's milk, goat's milk and various infant formulae fed to guinea-pigs. *Arch. Dis. Child. 56*:165–171.
20. Manuel, P. D., and Walker-Smith, J. A. (1981). A comparison of three infant feeding formulae for the prevention of delayed recovery after infantile gastroenteritis. *Acta Paediatr. Belg. 34*:13–20.
21. Iyngkaran, N., Robinson, N. J., Sumithran, E., Lam, S. K., Putchucheary, S. D., and Yadv, M. (1978). Cow's milk protein-sensitive enteropathy an important factor in prolonging diarrhoea in acute infective enteritis in early infancy. *Arch. Dis. Child. 53*:150–153.
22. Manuel, P. D., Walker-Smith, J. A., and Soeparto, P. (1980). Cow's milk sensitive enteropathy in Indonesian infants. *Lancet ii*:1365.

# 12

# JEJUNAL MACROMOLECULAR ABSORPTION IN DIARRHEAL DISEASE

SAUL TEICHBERG
*Cornell University Medical College, New York
and North Shore University Hospital, Manhasset, New York*

Clinical studies strongly suggest that the integrity of the intestinal barrier to potentially antigenic molecules may be altered during gastroenteritis. Walzer (1), Wilson and Walzer (2), and Gruskay and Cooke (3) all reported increased circulating serum precipitins to dietary milk and egg protein during gastroenteritis. And, many studies have documented an association between cow's milk or soy protein hypersensitivity and gastroenteritis (4-6) (Chapters 11 and 13). The possible interrelationships between gastroenteritis and the development of cow's milk, soy, or other food protein hypersensitivities are outlined in Figure 1.

In clinical studies of gastroenteritis it is not always possible to delineate the sequence of events leading to a sensitivity to food protein. Damaging luminal physiological agents generated during diarrhea, dying enterocytes,

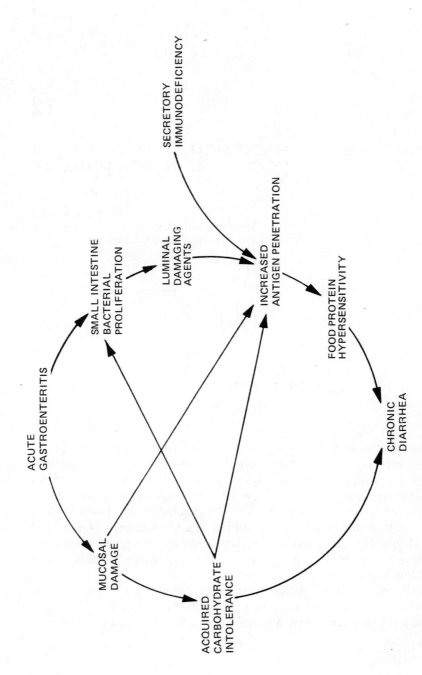

**Figure 1** Diagrammatic representation of some of the possible routes by which acute gastroenteritis may lead to food protein hypersensitivity and chronic diarrhea.

and deficiencies in secretory immune factors may all, at times, play a role in altering intestinal absorption of potential antigens. Some workers have stressed the importance of secretory IgA deficiency (4,5) in the development of cow's milk protein hypersensitivity and further complications including acquired lactose intolerance. The role of food protein hypersensitivity leading to postenteritis chronic diarrhea is discussed in Chapter 11. Evidence described below suggests that specific luminal pathophysiological agents seen in gastroenteritis and its sequelae may damage the normal epithelial barrier of the small intestine and permit increased antigen penetration; this could lead to sensitization of a susceptible host (7). These luminal agents include (a) malabsorbed carbohydrates that generate hyperosmolar luminal gradients and secretion of water during acquired carbohydrate intolerance (8-10) and (b) the products of bacterial metabolism, such as deconjugated bile salts, found in the upper small intestine during chronic diarrhea induced by overgrowth of fecal and colonic flora (11-14).

This chapter focuses on the organization of the normal small intestinal barrier to intact macromolecules and how the epithelial cell barrier may be damaged during diarrheal disease by specific luminal pathophysiological agents.

### Gastrointestinal Barrier to Macromolecules

General

One of the major functions of the lining of the gastrointestinal tract is to form a barrier selectively excluding a variety of foreign antigenic or toxigenic substances as well as infectious agents from entry into the internal environment of the body (15,16). This barrier role is essential because the lumen of the gastrointestinal tract is in physical continuity with the external world, containing an enormous surface area interface between the external and internal environment. The gastrointestinal barrier is composed of the following physiological and anatomical components. (a) Few foreign organisms or antigens can survive the acidic conditions and enzymatic digestive processes of the stomach (17). (b) Peristaltic bowel movements propel materials through the intestinal tract fairly rapidly and restrict their time of contact with the cell surface, decreasing the opportunity for absorption. (c) Intestinal digestive enzymes hydrolyze potentially antigenic substances into amino acids, dipeptides, and monosaccharides in the normal absorptive process. (d) Mucus secretion of goblet cells may "wash" potential antigens off the epithelial surface (18). (e) Secretory immuno-

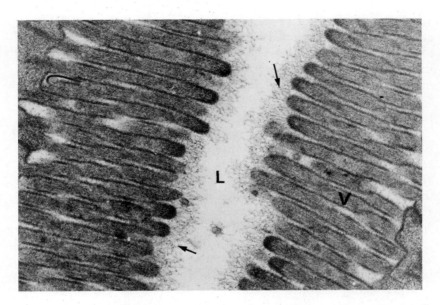

**Figure 2** Electron micrograph of the microvillar brush border from the rat jejunal epithelium. The jejunal lumen is at L, microvilli at V. The arrows point to the fuzzy coat surface of the microvilli. The projections of the fuzzy coat are mucopolysaccharide polymers. The oligodisaccharidases are located proximal to the microvillar plasma membrane. Intact proteins, glycoproteins, or partially digested polypeptide fragments clearly must first bind to and transverse the fuzzy coat layer before they have an opportunity to gain access to the absorptive epithelial cell surface at the base of the microvilli. X 30,000.

globins produced by gut-associated lymphoid tissue (19,20) inhibit absorption of foreign antigens; experimental studies have demonstrated that prefeeding of an antigen will inhibit its subsequent absorption (21), and Porter has shown that calves may even be orally immunized against viral enteric infection by stimulation of their gut secretory immune system (22). In neonates, secretory immunological factors in mother's milk play a similar role in preventing antigen absorption (15,19). The gut immunological barrier to potentially antigenic substances has been extensively reviewed elsewhere (19).

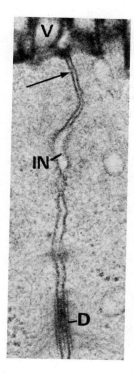

**Figure 3**  Electron micrograph of the zone of apposition between two jejunal absorptive epithelial cells which have been exposed at their luminal surface to a 40,000 mol wt glycoprotein, horseradish peroxidase (HRP). The black reaction product for HRP is seen on the external surface of the microvilli (V). Note that there is no HRP seen in the intercellular space between the two epithelial cells (IN). The arrow points to the tight junctional zone where the plasma membranes of the adjacent cells come into close contact forming a barrier to the diffusion of large molecules, from either the lumen to blood, or, blood to lumen. A desmosome is at D. × 55,000.

## Barrier Characteristics of the Small Intestinal Epithelium

In addition to the immunological and physiological aspects of the small intestinal barrier to macromolecular absorption, the epithelial cell surface membranes, the intercellular tight junctions formed between the gastrointestinal epithelial cells and the hydrolytic activity of the intracellular lysosomes in the epithelial cells also contribute to normally restricting the penetration of potentially antigenic or toxigenic substances from the lumen of the gut into the blood. This epithelial cell barrier is described in detail below.

*Fuzzy Coat*  Before infectious agents or potentially antigenic substances are absorbed, they must adsorb to and reach the plasma membrane of the epithelial cells lining the intestine. The sulfated mucopolysaccharide "fuzzy" coat (Fig. 2) of carbohydrate (23,24) projecting into the lumen of the gut from the microvillar plasma membrane surface may play an important role in regulating the absorption of macromolecules by controlling their access to the intraluminal space between the microvilli. It is clear that endocytotic vesicles and tubules containing exogenous materials form deep in the "pits" of the microvilli (Fig. 3) (15,16,25,26). The sulfated, sialic acid-containing residues on the carbohydrate polymers of the glycoproteins composing the fuzzy coat appear to contain considerable numbers of negatively charged sites (27). As in a variety of other cell types, this could result in a more ready adsorption and subsequent absorption of net positively charged proteins (28). It is also possible that the physical constraints of the fuzzy coat meshwork, at least partially, restrict diffusion of large molecules towards the deeper pit zone of the microvilli. Therefore, modifications of fuzzy coat size and charge distribution might alter the access of exogenous protein to the microvillar membrane surface. This notion remains to be experimentally tested in the small intestine. Alterations in luminal conditions that affect the integrity of the "unstirred" layer may allow easier diffusional access of foreign antigenic substances into the fuzzy coat layer. Experimental observation of this process are described below and in Chapter 9.

*Plasma Membrane*  In the absence of damage to the selective permeability properties of the plasma membrane, macromolecules are not freely permeable across the plasma membrane (25,29). In the normal small intestine it is clear that some of the dying epithelial cells at the villus tip extrusion zone come to be diffusely labeled with luminally applied macromolecular tracer molecules (26). In general, however, equal numbers of such cells are found on all normal villi under normal physiological conditions (13,26). This type of permeation should not be pathologically significant, unless the numbers of such diffusely permeated cells are shown to increase. This may be the case in severe acute infectious diarrhea involving increased numbers of dying enterocytes, (Chapter 11) and under some severe experimental conditions described below (13,30).

*Tight Junctions*  The tight junction forms an apical belt surrounding the intestinal epithelial cells and functions as a barrier to the transport of large molecules between the cells (23). In thin-section electron micrographs (Fig. 3), the plasma membranes of adjacent epithelial cells appear as if focally fused in this zone. Freeze-fracture studies show that the junctions are formed by an array of intramembranous particles that form a continuous network (31). Several physiological and anatomical features of the jejunal epithelial tight junctions are of note with respect to the potential paracellular transport of intact proteins. The jejunal epithelium is generally considered to be of the "leaky" type, with a relatively low resistance to the flux of ions and

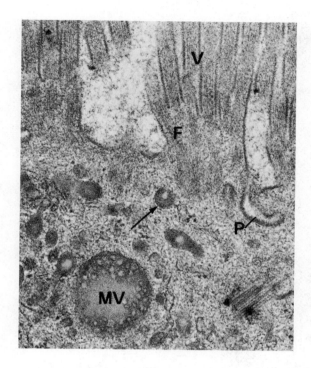

**Figure 4** Electron micrograph of the apical surface of a human jejunal epithelial cell. Microvilli are at V, microvillar filaments at F. At P, the image suggests an invagination of the epithelial cell surface, as if in the process of forming a pinocytotic or endocytotic vesicle. This is a "pinocytotic pit." A multivesicular body with small internal vesicles is seen at MV, and newly forming multivesicular bodies are seen at arrow (see also Refs. 36 and 40). X 35,000.

water in comparison with more distal regions of the intestine such as the colon. This relatively leaky physiological property of the jejunal epithelium may in part be related to the anatomical features of its tight junctions (31,32). As demonstrated by Madara et al. (32), the jejunal junctions are substantially shorter than ileal junctions. They also show a heterogeneity found in all regions of the gut; crypt-crypt cell junctions are shorter than junctions between mature absorptive epithelial cells, and goblet cell-absorptive epithelial cell junctions are the most disorganized. The relative leakiness to

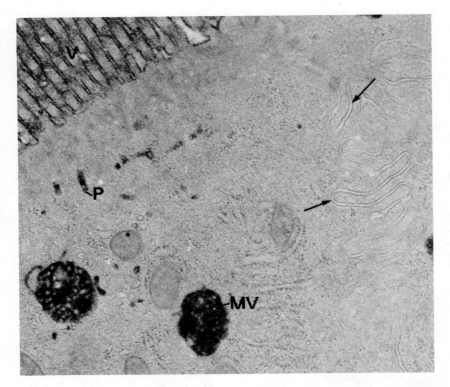

**Figure 5** Jejunal epithelial cell from a control preparation exposed at its lumen to HRP. The protein tracer is seen on the microvillar brush border (V), in pinocytotic vesicles and tubules (P), and in multivesicular bodies (MV). Note that the small internal vesicles of the MVs are clear while the HRP is seen in the luminal space of the MV. This occurs because the internal vesicles of the MV form by invaginations from its surface, while the MVs acquire HRP by fusion with pinocytotic vesicles (36,40). Also, note that there is no HRP found in the intercellular space (arrows) between adjacent epithelial cells. X 24,000.

ions and anatomical shortness of jejunal tight junctions suggests that they theoretically might be more easily modified than the junctions of tighter epithelia like the colon. Some evidence for penetration across the tight junctions of jejunal epithelia under experimental conditions including those related to diarrheal disease (13, 14, 25, 26, 33-35) has been reported and are described below.

*Lysosomes and Endocytosis*  In the jejunal epithelium large molecules enter endocytotic vesicles or tubules forming at the base of microvilli in "pinocytotic pits" (Fig. 4). Most often these endocytotic vesicles or tubules that bud into the epithelial cells fuse with preexisting multivesicular bodies (MVB) (Figs. 4 and 5), depositing their contents into the interior of lumen of the MVB, where they are degraded. Multivesicular bodies are membrane-delimited vacuolar structures filled with numerous internal small vesicles. The contents of foreign material deposited in MVBs is generally hydrolyzed because MVBs are eventually converted to acid hydrolase containing active lysosomes (25, 36,37). This also occurs by a process of fusion with other membrane-delimited vesicles that are primary lysosomes produced in the Golgi apparatus (36,38). The contents of the MVB are thereby subjected to degradation with the appearance of small molecules such as amino acids and dipeptides that cross the lysosomal membrane and contribute to the cell's metabolic pool (37).

Although endocytotic vesicles are externally coated with the protein clathrin (39), the "coats" may be lost and are not always seen morphologically (36,40,41). Morphological coats are also found on Golgi apparatus-derived vesicles en route to the cell surface (36). Therefore, the presence or absence of a coat is not necessarily evidence of an endocytotic process. Endocytosis is best demonstrated by the use of exogenous macromolecular tracers (25,26,36) including those with peroxidatic enzyme activities such as horseradish peroxidase, catalase and cytochrome, and other electron-dense proteins such as ferritin. The molecular size differences and potential for net charge modification of these proteins (42) add substantially to their usefulness.

Factors affecting the rates of endocytotic vesicle formation, fusion properties of the endocytotic vesicles with MVBs, and the available numbers of MVBs may play some role in regulating the extent of antigen penetration across the jejunal epithelium. Studies on the role of endocytosis in the excess absorption of potential antigens is under current investigation and are described below.

## Normal Macromolecular Absorption

Despite the elaborate barrier described above, there is normally some penetration of intact macromolecules across the small intestine. The principal normal route for this absorption is thought to be by bulk flow in endocytotic vesicles (15,16,25,26,43). These vesicles are transported around the tight junction, and fuse with the plasma membrane of the lateral cell margin releasing their contents by exocytosis (25,43); beyond the tight junctional

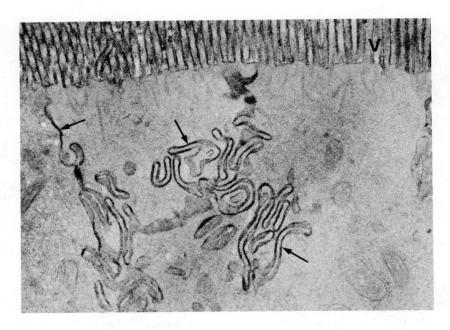

**Figure 6** From a jejunal preparation perfused with 0.5 mM deoxycholate, a deconjugated bile salt, and HRP. Microvilli, at V, contain HRP on their surface, and HRP has penetrated into the intercellular space (arrows) between the epithelial cells. The tracer is then free to diffuse into the lamina propria. X12,000.

zone, large molecules are freely permeable into the lamina propria zone and into the circulation (Fig. 6). This process is beautifully illustrated in some neonatal mammals, where specific immunoglobins are endocytosed by the intestinal epithelium in vesicles and tubules by a receptor-mediated process. These vesicles and tubules are able to avoid fusion with multivesicular bodies and lysosomal degradation by a mechanism that is not well understood (43). This absorption plays an important role in the acquisition, by the neonate, of immunoglobins from breast milk (15,44). In human neonates this process may be less important because IgG is able to cross the placenta during intra-uterine development (45).

In postweaning and adult mammals, including humans, there also normally appears to be a quantitatively small absorption of intact protein. Evidence for this process comes from studies on the intestinal absorption of oral insulin (46), food proteins (1-6) and tracer proteins in experimental studies (16,25, 43). Some antigens that reach the ileum may also cross the thin specialized "M" cell epithelium that lies over Peyers patches and may thereby interact with the intestinal lymphoid system. This topic is reviewed elsewhere by Owen (47).

## Abnormal Absorption of Macromolecules

When the integrity of the intestinal barrier to macromolecular absorption is compromised, allowing increased penetration of antigens, toxins or infectious agents there may be significant pathological consequences. Increased absorption of potentially antigenic macromolecules across the intestinal epithelium has been speculated to underlie a number of pathological entities: these include food protein sensitivity, celiac disease, inflammatory bowel disease, and enterotoxin absorption (16,25). In addition, failure of the secretory immunological system and the small intestinal epithelial barrier to prevent penetration of infectious agents, bacterial or viral, or their toxigenic products may result in severe infectious diarrheal disease.

A number of pathophysiological conditions may lead to an increased penetration of intact antigenic or toxigenic substances across the intestine. For example, gastric achlorohydria may permit increased concentrations of intact antigens or infectious organisms to reach the lumen of the small intestine (48) where they may be absorbed. Alterations in the efficiency of digestion, as seen, for example, in pancreatic insufficienty (49), may also lead to an elevation of luminal antigen concentrations. Congenital or acquired immunodeficiencies, like those seen in protein-energy malnutrition, may also compromise the capacity of the intestinal secretory immune system to protect against absorption of antigenic or toxigenic substances (50-52). Severe malnutrition may also affect the epithelial cell junctional and intracellular barrier of the intestine (14,34). In addition, as noted above, evidence from clinical studies indicates that there is an increased intestinal absorption of potential antigens during gastroenteritis (1-6). Experiments concerning the role of luminal pathophysiological conditions in damaging the integrity of the intestinal epithelial barrier to macromolecules during diarrhea, and the cellular pathways mediating this increased absorption of potential antigens are reviewed below.

**Table 1**   Some Conditions Altering the Integrity
of the Barrier to Macromolecules in Small
Intestinal Epithelium

Surgical trauma

Secretory antibody deficiency

Malnutrition

Diarrhea

Dihydroxy, deconjugated bile salts

Luminal hyperosmolality

Alcohol feedings

Disaccharide feedings

## Alterations in the Jejunal Epithelial Barrier to Macromolecules: Experimental Studies

### General

Numerous experimental conditions have been shown to damage the integrity
of the small intestinal barrier to macromolecules (Table 1). Investigations
from our group have been directed to the following question: Do specific
luminal pathophysiological agents seen in diarrhea alter the integrity of the
mammalian intestinal epithelial barrier to macromolecules, and what aspects
of the cellular barrier are affected? The experimental designs have involved
(a) direct in vivo perfusion of the rat jejunal lumen with solutions containing
specific potentially damaging agents and (b) the effects of feeding these
agents to the animals followed by perfusion under normal physiological conditions. Our interest has principally focused on the potential role of malabsorbed carbohydrate and deconjugated bile salts as barrier-altering agents.

### Altered Epthelial Barriers

*Plasma Membrane and Fuzzy Coat Alterations*   Clearly, invasive infectious
diarrheas that cause epithelial cell disruption and necrosis and lead to flat
mucosae would allow a relatively easy passage of intact protein from the gut
lumen to circulation (Chapter 11). This type of protein leak will occur across
necrotic epithelia that have lost their selective permeability properties towards large molecules.

In our experimental studies diffuse permeability of intact protein across damaged absorptive epithelial cells is only seen under relatively severe experimental conditions. These include feeding of 60% lactose to lactase-deficient rats. Under this stress the animals develop a very severe watery osmotic diarrhea, and lose weight (30). Cytological examination of villi from perfused jejunal loops of these animals shows a loss of epithelial cells and marked ultrastructural damage to enterocytes that could account for the increased absorption of a 40,000 mol wt protein tracer, horseradish peroxidase, that occurs under these conditions. The effects of lower-dose disaccharide feedings that do not produce cytological damage on the integrity of the endocytotic-lysosomal cellular barrier are detailed below. Diffuse staining of enterocytes with horseradish peroxidase, indicative of a destroyed plasma membrane permeability barrier, is also seen when the jejunum of well-nourished rats is directly perfused with the 7-α-dihydroxy deconjugated bile salt, deoxycholate (dch), at a 5 mM level (13). At this concentration dch is strikingly cytotoxic, inducing vesiculation of the endoplasmic reticulum, loss of epithelial cell cytoplasmic matrix, and producing severe intestinal sodium and water secretion.

When the jejunum of well-nourished rats is perfused with 0.5 mM dch, there is no histological or ultrastructural evidence of cytotoxicity, although these preparations do show an increased absorption of intact protein. In contrast, when the jejunum of protein-energy malnourished (PEM) rats is perfused with 0.5 mM dch, there is ultrastructural evidence of damage to the membranes of the epithelial cells (14); this includes an increased number of lysosomes filled with membranous swirls. PEM rats perfused with 0.5 mM dch also showed serum horseradish peroxidase levels greater than in well-nourished animals. These observations may be relevant to the clinical problem of chronic diarrhea due to fecal and colonic bacterial overgrowth of the small bowel in malnourished children living under conditions of poor sanitation and hygiene (51,52). These patients have duodenal aspirate levels of deconjugated bile salts that reach 0.5 mM (11) and they may be at an increased risk for the absorption of intact antigens.

No direct studies on experimental alterations in the glycoprotein fuzzy coat that affect the absorption of intact protein are available at this time. Indirect studies, however, indicate that chronic feedings of poorly absorbed disaccharides, such as lactose, decrease the resistance of the unstirred layer, suggesting that macromolecules may gain easier access into the fuzzy coat layer under these conditions (30). This view is based on the experimental observation that an increase in diffusional noncarrier-mediated monosaccharide transport induced by chronic disaccharide feedings is paralleled by an increased absorption of an intact protein tracer (Chapter 9).

*Tight Junctional Alterations*  Alterations in the tight junctional barrier of the small intestinal epithelium have been reported in a variety of experimental conditions, including surgical trauma (33) and chronic-severe malnutrition (34). Since malabsorbed carbohydrates, and other nutrients, induce hyperosmotic luminal gradients (8), we evaluated the effect of perfusing a hypertonic solution of a nonabsorbable solute, mannitol, on the jejunal barrier to macromolecules. In these studies we demonstrated penetration of horseradish peroxidase across the apical tight junctional zone and into deeper regions of the intercellular space (26). Hyperosmolar solutions have been reported to alter the tight junctional integrity of other cellular barriers, including hepatocytes (53) and cerebral endothelium (54).

We have also noted penetration of a protein tracer across the tight junctional zone of rat jejunum perfused with 0.5 or 5 mM α-dihydroxy deconjugated bile salts (13,14). This penetration appears to occur very occasionally with perfusion of 0.5 mM levels of deoxycholate or chenodeoxycholate, that produce no evidence of diffuse tracer leakage across enterocytes and no evidence of ultrastructural damage to the jejunal epithelium (13). The 0.5 mM levels are similar to the levels of deconjugated bile salts found in the duodenal aspirates of children with chronic diarrhea (11), in patients with small bowel stasis syndromes (12), and in experimental animals with drug-induced bacterial proliferation in the upper small intestine (55).

As we have repeatedly noted, in these studies the protein tracer is only infrequently seen in the tight junctional zone, but is usually present only on the microvillar brush border and in deeper regions of the intercellular space (13,25). These observations have been interpreted as indicating that small focal breaks in the functional integrity of the tight junctional belt may allow more substantial leakage of protein into the intercellular space (33). More direct confirmation of this process requires freeze-fracture studies of junctions that are not yet available.

*Endocytosis-Lysosomal Alterations*  Endocytosis normally appears to be the physiological route that mediates the quantitatively small intact protein absorption (16,25,43) in the intestine. Endocytosis may also play a role in the increased levels of intact lumen-to-blood protein absorption that we have observed under experimental conditions that include feedings of poorly absorbed disaccharides and hyperosmolar perfusions. For example, long-term feedings of maltose or lactose to rats at concentrations that do not produce symptoms of intolerance lead to increased intact protein penetration in the absence of cytological damage or evidence of tight junctional alterations. In these studies, tracer protein can be demonstrated in endocytotic vesicles and in deeper regions of the intercellular space between enterocytes (30).

Other studies on either hyperosmolar perfusions (26) or with feedings of high concentrations of disaccharides (30), such as maltose, suggest increased levels of endocytotic vesicles accumulating in the enterocytes. In other epithelia such as the toad bladder (56,57), exocytosis coupled to increased endocytosis is thought to play a role in peptide hormone-mediated regulation of water fluxes; this process is believed to represent exchanges of surface membrane with differing water permeability properties. A similar process, operating in the intestine, would provide a cellular mechanism for regulating water transport and might be of importance in the pathophysiology of diarrhea. If this view were correct, then endocytotic absorption of intact protein from lumen to blood might be a reflection of responses of the intestinal surface to altered water transport conditions. Clearly, this notion remains to be experimentally tested.

## Conclusions

The experimental studies focus our attention on the multiplicity of potential pathways that may all result in increased antigen penetration across the small intestinal epithelium during diarrheal disease (Fig. 1). The factors responsible for increased antigen absorption during gastroenteritis may include not only secretory immunodeficiency and frank loss of mucosal integrity; secondary effects of the initial insults of acute gastroenteritis, including carbohydrate intolerance and small bowel bacterial overgrowth syndromes, may generate pathophysiological agents or conditions that alter the normal barrier of the jejunal epithelium to intact macromolecules. Evidence from our experimental studies on enhanced macromolecular absorption produced by deconjugated bile salts and feedings of poorly absorbed disaccharides all support this view.

The precise role or importance of each one of these barrier-altering factors in a clinical setting still needs to be defined. Regardless of which factors affect the integrity of the macromolecular barrier of the small intestine, it is clear that the evolution of an immunologically mediated disease such as food protein hypersensitivity is complex and depends upon a susceptible host (58).

## Acknowledgment

Some of the work described here was supported by NIH Grant S08-09128-03.

## References

1. Walzer, M. (1927). Studies in absorption of undigested proteins in human beings. I. A simple direct method of studying the absorption of undigested protein. *J. Immunol. 14*:143–149.
2. Wilson, S. J., and Walzer, M. (1935). Absorption of undigested proteins in human beings. *Am. J. Dis. Child. 50*:49–57.
3. Gruskay, F. L., and Cooke, R. E. (1955). The gastrointestinal absorption of unaltered protein in normal infants and in infants recovering from diarrhea. *Pediatrics 16*:763–768.
4. Harrison, H., Kilby, A., Walker-Smith, J. A., Frace, N. E., and Wood, C. B. S. (1976). Cow's milk protein intolerance: a possible association with gastroenteritis, lactose intolerance, and IgA deficiency. *Br. Med. J. 1*:1501–1504.
5. Iyngkaran, J., Abdin, Z., Davis, K., Boey, C. G., Prathap, M. B., Yadav, M., Lam, S. K., and Puthucheary, S. D. (1979). Acquired carbohydrate intolerance and cow's milk protein-sensitive enteropathy in young infants. *J. Pediatr. 95*:373–377.
6. Goel, K., Lifshitz, F., Kahn, E., and Teichberg, S. (1978). Monosaccharide intolerance and soy-protein hypersensitivity in an infant with diarrhea. *J. Pediatr. 93*:617–619.
7. Walker, W. A. (1980). Intestinal defenses in health and disease. In *Clinical Disorders in Pediatric Gastroenterology and Nutrition*, F. Lifshitz (Ed.), Marcell Dekker, New York, pp. 99–119.
8. Launalia, K. (1968). The effect of unabsorbed sucrose and mannitol in the small intestinal flow rate and mean transit time. *Scand. J. Gastroenterol. 39*:655–671.
9. Lifshitz, F., Coello-Ramirez, P., Gutierrez-Topete, G., and Coronado-Coronet, M. C. (1971). Carbohydrate intolerance in infants with diarrhea. *J. Pediatr. 79*:760–767.
10. Teichberg, S., Lifshitz, F., Pergolizzi, R., and Wapnir, R. A. (1978). Response of rat intestine to an acute hyperosmotic feeding. *Pediatr. Res. 12*:720–725.
11. Schneider, R. E., Contreras, C., and Viteri, F. E. (1974). Studies on the luminal events of lipid absorption in protein calorie malnourished (PCM) in children; its relation with nutritional recovery and diarrhea. I. Capacity of the duodenum content to achieve micellar solubilization of lipids. *Am. J. Clin. Nutr. 27*:777–787.
12. Challacombe, D. N., Richardson, J. M., and Edkins, S. (1974). Anaerobic bacteria and deconjugated bile salts in the upper small intestine of infants with gastrointestinal disorders. *Acta Pediatr. Scand. 63*:581–587.
13. Fagundes-Neto, U., Teichberg, S., Bayne, M. A., Morton, B., and Lifshitz, F. (1981). Bile salt-enhanced rat jejunal absorption of a macromolecular tracer. *Lab. Invest. 44*:18–26.

14. Teichberg, S., Fagundes,-Neto, U., Bayne, M. A., and Lifshitz, F. (1981). Jejunal macromolecular absorption and bile salt deconjugation in protein-energy malnourished rats. *Am. J. Clin. Nutr. 34*:1281-1291.

15. Walker, W. A. (1976). Host defense mechanisms in the gastrointestinal tract. *Pediatrics 57*:901-916.

16. Walker, W. A., and Isselbacher, K. J. (1974). Uptake and transport of macromolecules by the intestine: possible role in clinical disorders. *Gastroenterology 67*:531-550.

17. Dupont, H. L., Formal, S. B., and Hornick, R. S. (1971). Pathogenesis of *Escherichia coli* diarrhea. *New Engl. J. Med. 285*:1-9.

18. Walker, W. A., Wu, M., and Bloch, K.-J. (1977). Stimulation by immune complexes of mucus release from goblet cells of the rat small intestine. *Science 197*:370-372.

19. Walker, W. A., and Isselbacher, K. J. (1977). Intestinal antibodies. *New Engl. J. Med. 297*:767-773.

20. Walker, W. A., Wu, M., Isselbacher, K. J., and Bloch, K. J. (1975). Intestinal uptake of macromolecules. III. Studies on the mechanism by which antibodies interfere with antigen uptake. *J. Immunol. 115*:854-861.

21. Walker, W. A., Isselbacher, K. J., and Bloch, K. J. (1972). Intestinal uptake of macromolecules: effect of oral immunization. *Science 177*: 608-610.

22. Allen, W. D., and Porter, P. (1977). The relative frequencies and distribution of immunoglobin bearing cells in the intestinal mucosa of neonatal and weaned pigs and their significance in the development of secretory immunity. *Immunology 32*:819-826.

23. Trier, J. (1968). Morphology of the epithelium of the small intestine. In *Handbook of Physiology, Sect. 6, The Alimentary Canal, Vol. 3*, The American Physiological Society, Washington, D.C., pp. 1125-1175.

24. Ito, S. (1965). The enteric surface coat on the cat intestinal microvilli. *J. Cell Biol. 27*:475-491.

25. Teichberg, S. (1980). Penetration of epithelial barriers by macromolecules: The intestinal mucosa. In *Clinical Disorders in Pediatric Gastroenterology and Nutrition*, F. Lifshitz (Ed.), Marcel Dekker, New York, pp. 185-202.

26. Cooper, M., Teichberg, S., and Lifshitz, F. (1978). Alterations in rat jejunal permeability to a macromolecular tracer during a hyperosmotic load. *Lab. Invest. 38*:447-454.

27. Le Blond, C. P., and Bennet, G. (1977). Role of the Golgi apparatus in terminal glycosylation. In *International Cell Biology*, Rockefeller Univ. Press, New York, pp. 326-336.

28. Farquhar, M. G. (1978). Recovery of surface membrane in anterior pituitary cells. *J. Cell Biol. 77*:R35-R42.

29. Novikoff, A. B., and Holtzman, E. (1976). *Cells and Organelles,* Holt Rinehart, Winston, New York.

30. Teichberg, S., Lifshitz, F., Bayne, M. A., Fagundes-Neto, U., Wapnir, R. A., and McGarvey, E. (1982). Disaccharide feedings enhance rat jejunal macromolecular absorption, in preparation.

31. Staehlin, L. A., and Hall, B. E. (1978). Junctions between living cells. *Sci. Am. 238*(5):141–152.

32. Madara, J. L., Trier, J. S., and Neutra, M. R. (1980). Structural changes in the plasma membrane accompanying differentiation of epithelial cells in human and monkey small intestine. *Gastroenterology 78*:963–975.

33. Rhodes, R. S., and Karnovsky, M. J. (1971). Loss of macromolecular barrier function associated with surgical trauma to the intestine. *Lab. Invest. 25*:220–229.

34. Worthington, B. S., Boatman, E. S., and Kenny, G. E. (1974). Intestinal absorption of intact proteins in normal and protein-deficient rats. *Am. J. Clin. Nutr. 27*:276–286.

35. Worthington, B. S., Meserole, L., and Syrotuck, J. A. (1978). Effect of daily ethanol ingestion on intestinal permeability to macromolecules. *Digest. Dis. 23*:23–32.

36. Holtzman, E. (1976). *Lysosomes: A Survey,* Springer-Verlag, Vienna.

37. deDuve, C. (1969). The lysosome in retrospect. In *Lysosomes in Biology and Pathology,* Vol. 1, J. T. Dingle and H. B. Fell (Eds.), Elsevier-North-Holland, Amsterdam, pp. 3–40.

38. Holtzman, E., Novikoff, A. B., and Villaverde, H. (1967). Lysosomes and GERL in normal and chromatolytic neurons of the rat ganglion nodosum. *J. Cell. Biol. 33*:419–436.

39. Pearse, B. M. F. (1976). Clathrin: a unique protein associated with intracellular transfer of membrane by coated vesicles. *Proc. Natl. Acad. Sci. U.S.A. 73*:1255–1259.

40. Holtzman, E., Teichberg, S., Abrahams, S., Citkowitz, E., Crain, S. M., Kawai, N., and Peterson, E. R. (1973). Notes on synaptic vesicles and related structures, endoplasmic reticulum, lysosomes and peroxisomes in nervous tissue and the adrenal medulla. *J. Histol. Cytol. 21*:349–385.

41. Teichberg, S., Holtzman, E., Crain, S. M., and Peterson, E. R. (1975). Circulation and turnover of synaptic vesicle membrane in cultured fetal mammalian spinal cord neurons. *J. Cell Biol. 67*:215–230.

42. Rennke, H., Patel, Y., and Venkatachalam, M. A. (1978). Glomerular filtration of proteins: clearance of anionic, neutral, and cationic horseradish peroxidase in the rat. *Kidney Int. 13*:324–328.

43. Rodewald, R. (1978). Intestinal transport of antibodies in the newborn rat. *J. Cell Biol. 58*:189–211.

44. Hanson, L. A. (1979). Immune response in the mammary gland. In *Immunology of Breast Milk,* Raven Press, New York, pp. 145–157.

45. Johnson, P. M. (1979). Membrane receptors for IgG in the human placental. In *Protein Transmission through Living Membranes,* Elsevier-North Holland, Amsterdam, pp. 45–54.

46. Danforth, E., and Moore, R. D. (1959). Intestinal absorption of insulin in the rat. *Endocrinology 65*:118–126.

47. Owen, R. L. (1977). Sequential uptake of horseradish peroxidase by lymphoid follicle epithelium of Peyer's patches in the normal unobstructed mouse intestine. *Gastroenterology 72*:440–451.

48. Kraft, S. C., Rothberg, R. M., Kramer, C. M., Svoboda, A. C., Monroe, L. S., and Farr, R. S. (1967). Gastric output and circulating antibovine serum albumin in adults. *Clin. Exp. Immunol. 2*:321–330.

49. Walker, W. A., Wu, M., Isselbacher, K. J., and Bloch, K. J. (1975). Intestinal uptake of macromolecules. IV. The effect of pancreatic duct ligation on the breakdown of antigen and antigen-antibody complexes on the intestinal surface. *Gastroenterology 69*:1223–1229.

50. Chandra, R. K. (1980). *Immunology of Nutritional Disorders,* Edward Arnold, London.

51. Campos, J. V., Fagundes-Neto, U., Patricio, F. R. S., Wehba, J., Carvalho, A. A., and Shriner, M. (1979). Jejunal mucosa in marasmic children. Clinical, pathological and fine structural evaluation of the effect of protein-energy malnutrition and environmental contamination. *Am. J. Clin. Nutr. 32*:1575–1591.

52. Mata, L. J., Urritia, J. J., and Lechtig, A. (1971). Infection and nutrition of children of a low socio-economic rural community. *Am. J. Clin. Nutr. 24*:249–259.

53. Goodenough, D. A., and Gilula, N. B. (1974). The splitting of hepatocyte gap junctions and zonulae occludentes with hypertonic disaccharides. *J. Cell Biol. 61*:575–590.

54. Brightman, M. W., Hori, M., Rappaport, S. I., Reese, T. S., and Westergaard, E. (1974). Osmotic opening of tight junctions in cerebral endothelium. *J. Comp. Neurol. 152*:317–325.

55. Berant, M., Lifshitz, F., Bayne, M. A., and Wapnir, R. A. (1981). Jejunal cAMP-activated sodium secretion via deconjugated bile salts and fatty acids. *Biochem. Med. 25*:327–336.

56. Masur, S. K., Holtzman, E., Schwartz, I. L., and Walter, R. (1971). Correlation between pinocytosis and hydroosmosis induced by neurohypophyseal hormones and mediated by adenosine 3'-5'-cyclic monophosphate. *J. Cell Biol. 49*:582–594.

57. Gronowicz, G., Masur, S. K., and Holtzman, E. (1980). Quantitative analysis of exocytosis and endocytosis in the hydroosmotic response of toad bladder. *J. Membr. Biol. 52*:221–235.

58. Eastham, E. J., and Walker, W. A. (1977). Effect of cow's milk on the gastrointestinal tract: a persistent dilemma for the pediatrician. *Pediatrics 60*:477–481.

# 13

# SOY AND BOVINE MILK PROTEIN-SUGAR ASSOCIATIONS AND THEIR CLINICAL RELEVANCE

EDUARDO CICHOWICZ-EMMANUELLI and RAMON TORRES-PINEDO
*University of Oklahoma Health Sciences Center
and Children's Memorial Hospital, Oklahoma City, Oklahoma*

The precise structure and natural conformation of carbohydrate immuno-determinants in glycoproteins can now be determined through a combination of analytical and immunological techniques and by theoretical computer calculations. This approach is already being applied to investigations of breast milk oligosaccharides and comparative studies of milk oligosaccharide immunodeterminants in mammalian species (1–4). Knowledge of the precise structure of reactive terminal sugar chains in glycoproteins and the use of lectins and monoclonal antibodies have permitted detailed characterizations of cell-macromolecule interactions and mechanisms of macromolecular penetration into cells. This field of work is now beginning to be applied to the study of antigen penetration into intestinal epithelium (5,6).

Cow's milk and soy extracts are the most common base materials for the preparation of infant formulas. Thus, it seems appropriate to present a brief review of their oligosaccharide components. With this in the background, we briefly discuss some partly well-documented, partly speculative pathways for penetration of milk proteins into intestinal epithelium in which oligo-saccharide structures may play a direct or indirect role. Finally, we review some clinical aspects of soy protein intolerance, emphasizing the significant allergenic potential of this protein and the need to reexamine the rationale behind its widespread use.

## Oligosaccharides in Human and Bovine Glycoprotein Fractions

Most milk glycoproteins are components of the milk fat globule (MFG). This structure originates in the mammary gland at the time of milk secretion and consists of an envelopment of secreted lipids in apical plasma membrane from the lactating cells (7). The origin and nature of the MFG glycoproteins explain why these substances exhibit considerable species specificity in their oligosaccharide chains. Newman and Uhlenbruck (1) have conducted detailed comparative studies of oligosaccharide structures in human and bovine MFG glycoproteins. Alkali-labile oligosaccharides were investigated by a combina-tion of direct analysis and hemagglutination tests. A summary of the results of these studies is shown in Table 1. In brief, terminal D-Gal$\beta\rightarrow$3GalNAc existed in sialyl-substituted and -unsubstituted forms in both human and bovine MFG glycoprotein, but it was more abundant in bovine glycoproteins.

**Table 1**   Alkali-Labile Oligosaccharide Sequences in Human and Bovine Milk Fat Globule (MFG) Glycoproteins

| Oligosaccharide | | |
| --- | --- | --- |
| Sial | Sial | |
| Gal ($\beta$1–3) – GalNAc | | Human, bovine |
| Sial | | |
| Gal ($\beta$1–3) – GalNAc | | Human, bovine |
| Gal ($\beta$1–3) – GalNAc | | Human, bovine |
| | GalNAc | Bovine |

*Source*: Ref. 1.

**Table 2**  Comparison Between Human and Bovine MFG Glycoproteins: Inhibition of Agglutinins Acting on Alkali-Stable Oligosaccharide Chains

| | Inhibition by Glycoproteins From: | | | |
| | Human MFG | | Bovine MFG | |
| Agglutinin | Native | Desyalated | Native | Desyalated |
| --- | --- | --- | --- | --- |
| Triticum vulgaris | 0 | – | $2^9$ | – |
| Myxovirus | $2^1$ | 0 | $2^6$ | 0 |
| *Ulex Europeus* | $2^3$ | – | 0 | – |
| Anti-type 14 pneumococcus | 0 | 0 | $2^3$ | $2^4$ |

The initial concentration of inhibitors was 5 mg/ml, and the hemagglutination inhibition titers were measured, from serial dilutions, as the minimal amount of substance able to inhibit four agglutination doses of lectin or serum.
*Source*: Ref. 1.


**Table 3**  Representative Oligosacchairdes of Human Milk[a]

| | |
| --- | --- |
| Lacto-N-tetraose | Gal$\beta$1→3GlcNAc$\beta$1→3-(lactose) |
| Lacto-N-neotetraose | Gal$\beta$1→4GlcNAc$\beta$1→3-(lactose) |

Lacto-N-hexaose

$$\begin{array}{c} \text{Gal}\beta1\rightarrow4\text{GlcNAc}\beta1 \\ \downarrow \\ 6 \\ \text{Gal}\beta1\rightarrow3\text{GlcNAc}\beta1\rightarrow3\text{-(lactose)} \end{array}$$

Lacto-N-neohexaose

$$\begin{array}{c} \text{Gal}\beta1\rightarrow4\text{GlcNAc}\beta1 \\ \downarrow \\ 6 \\ \text{Gal}\beta1\rightarrow4\text{GlcNAc}\beta1\rightarrow3\text{-(lactose)} \end{array}$$

Difucosyl-para-lacto-N-hexaose

$$\begin{array}{cc} \text{Fuc}\alpha1 & \text{Fuc}\alpha1 \\ \downarrow & \downarrow \\ 3 & 3 \\ \end{array}$$
$$\text{Gal}\beta1\rightarrow3\text{GlcNAc.\ldots.GlcNAc}\beta1\rightarrow3\text{-(lactose)}$$

Difucosyl-para-lacto-N-neohexaose

$$\begin{array}{cc} \text{Fuc}\alpha1 & \text{Fuc}\alpha1 \\ \downarrow & \downarrow \\ 3 & 3 \\ \end{array}$$
$$\text{Gal}\beta1\rightarrow4\text{GlcNAc.\ldots.GlcNAc}\beta1\rightarrow3\text{-(lactose)}$$

[a]All monosaccharides have a D configuration, except for fucose.
*Source*: Ref. 3.

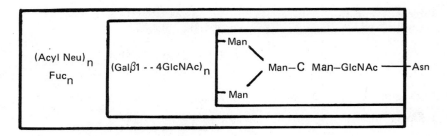

**Figure 1** General structure for asparagine-linked oligosaccharides suggested by Montrenil (9).

Terminal unsubstituted D-GalNAc was also present in MFG glycoproteins from both species but it seemed to differ significantly in the nature of its linkage to the rest of the molecule. In bovine MFG glycoproteins the sugar residue was probably linked directly to the protein backbone, whereas in human glycoproteins it seemed to be part of group A substance, which was absent in bovine glycoproteins. Newman and Uhlenbruck also investigated some of the alkali-stable oligosaccharides (Table 2). Two observations were of special interest: (a) oligosaccharides in bovine MFG glycoproteins were predominantly sialyl-substituted, whereas in human MFG glycoproteins they were predominantly fucosyl-substituted, and (b) the terminal sequence D-Gal$\beta$1→4GlcNAc (lactosamine) was found in bovine but not in human MFG glycoproteins. This last observation was based on the lack of inhibition by human glycoproteins of hemagglutination by anti-type 14 pneumococcus serum. However, several workers (3,4,8) have subsequently demonstrated the existence of several human milk oligosaccharides with high specificity for type 14 pneumococcal antipolysaccharide. The structures of these oligosaccharides are shown in Table 3.

From the above studies, one may conclude that many human and bovine MFG glycoproteins probably conform in their oligosaccharide structure with the general model for asparagine-linked oligosaccharide proposed by Montrenil (9) (Fig. 1), but differ significantly in the structure of their predominant terminal chains, specially in relation to substituting sialic acid and L-fucose.

Studies on the potential antigenicity of bovine milk to infant small bowel has focused on the skim-phase proteins (caseins, $\beta$-lactoglobulin, $\alpha$-lactalbumin, serum albumin) (10–12), and little or no attention has been paid to the MFG glycoproteins. Although milk glycoproteins are likely to undergo pro-

**Table 4**   Major Carbohydrate-Containing
Constituents of Soybeans

| Substance | Carbohydrate |
|-----------|--------------|
| Glycinin (11S) | Xylose, mannose, glucose, galactose, arabinose, rhamnose |
| Soyasaponins | Glucuronic acid, arabinose, rhamnose, galactose |
| Soybean lectin | Glucosamine, mannose |

*Source*: Data from Refs. 17, 19, and 29.

found changes during processing, including a high degree of polymerization (13), their oligosaccharide components should resist heat treatment as well as other denaturing procedures. It is likely that during the early stages of mucosal digestion the oligosaccharide chains are protected from oligosaccharidase attack by their protein matrices. If so, the conditions would exist for specific interactions with combining sites at the intestinal surface, as a possible first step toward internalization of the macromolecule. (This of course would require an incomplete antibody barrier for certain glycoproteins.) Such considerations, although purely speculative, underscore the potential importance of MFG glycoproteins as intestinal antigens.

## Carbohydrate-Containing Constituents in Soybean Extracts

A detailed description of oligosaccharides in soybean protein fractions is beyond the scope of this chapter. We limit our discussion to three components of defatted soy extract, in which we have developed an interest, namely glycinin, soyasaponins, and soybean lectin (Table 4). Soybean lectin is a glycoprotein tetramer of two kinds of subunits (mol wt 120,000) (14) containing two binding sites for terminal D-GalNAc and D-Gal. Glycinin, the major storage protein of the soybean (mol wt 320,000) (15), consists of two protomers, each a hexamer of alternating acidic and basic subunits. Glycinin has at least one hydrophobic site which accepts amphiphiles such as soyasaponins. When isolated by the usual method (16), glycinin contains the saccharides shown in Table 4, but such saccharides are noncovalently bound (17) and represent sugar residues from glycoside contaminants. Soyasaponins are quantitatively the most important among these contaminants

**Table 5**  Glycoside Contaminants in Glycinin (11S Globulin)
Preparations (Alcohol Extractables)

| Glycoside | Carbohydrate Moiety |
|---|---|
| Soyasaponins | Galactose, rhamnose, arabinose, glucuronic acid |
| Sitosterol | Glucose |
| Genistein | Glucose |

*Source*: Data from Refs. 18 and 29.

(18,19) (Table 5). Soyasaponins are a heterogenous mixture of triterpenoid glycosides having sapogenol B as the aglycone, and glucuronic acid, arabinose, and terminal rhamnose or galactose as carbohydrates (20). Figure 2 illustrates how these three molecules can interact with each other in solution.

Soybean lectin binds to terminal D-GalNAc or D-Gal in cell surface components, and in the case of red blood cells, it causes hemagglutination. Soyasaponins are strong hemolytic agents (21), and their hemolytic action in soy extracts increases with heat-processing or auto-claving. The hemolytic effect has been shown to involve binding of the aglycone moiety to an unknown membrane component (different from cholesterol) (22), followed by cleavage of the sugar moiety by a membrane glycosidase (23). The type of membrane lesion caused by soyasaponins has not been investigated, but is probably similar to that produced by other saponins, i.e., membrane holes (24–26). We have isolated soyasaponins from defatted infant soy formula in the expected amounts (27).

Although soyasaponins have been shown not to be absorbable (28), and apparently to be devoid of harmful effects to the bowel in experimental animals (28), we have shown these substances to be capable of altering rabbit jejunal epithelium in vitro (29). In these studies, we tested the effects of soyasaponins and soybean lectin on the uptake of $[^{125}I]$ glycinin by jejunal mucosa. Our results can be summarized as follows: (a) the uptake of $[^{125}I]$ glycinin by control tissue was negligible, (b) soyasaponins produced a significant increase in uptake, (c) soybean lectin markedly stimulated the soyasaponin-induced uptake, and (d) this stimulation by the lectin was blocked by N-acetylgalactosamine. The postulated mechanism for the cooperative effect of soybean lectin and soyasaponins is represented in Figure 3. We have assumed that soybean lectin binds to sugar sites at the

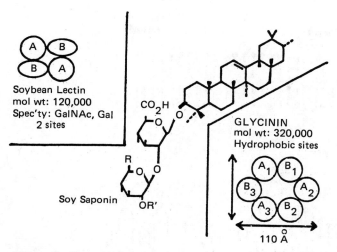

**Figure 2**  General characteristics of soybean lectin soyasaponins, and glycinin (11S globulin).

epithelial surface and causes membrane alterations that result in an increased exposure of saponin-sensitive sites in the bilayer.

Pathways for Protein Internalization
into Intestinal Epithelium

Table 6 shows three possible pathways for intestinal uptake of milk proteins in which oligosaccharide residues may participate directly or indirectly. In pathway 1, the oligosaccharide is a component of glycoproteins at the apical membrane surface. Binding of macromolecular ligands to these components may be followed by receptor-mediated endocytosis (30). Certain breast milk macromolecules, such as IgG and IgG-antigen complexes, are internalized in the jejunum of newborn rats by this mechanism. As shown by Rodewald and coworkers (6), these macromolecules cross the cytoplasmic matrix inside coated vesicles, avoiding lysosomal digestion, and are exocytosed into the lamina propria. From work on other cell populations (30), it is also quite possible that other breast milk macromolecules, such as lipoproteins and hormones, are also transported through the epithelial membrane by receptor-mediated endocytosis. Finally, lectins may be among foreign (nonmilk) substances which may have adapted themselves to the existence of these

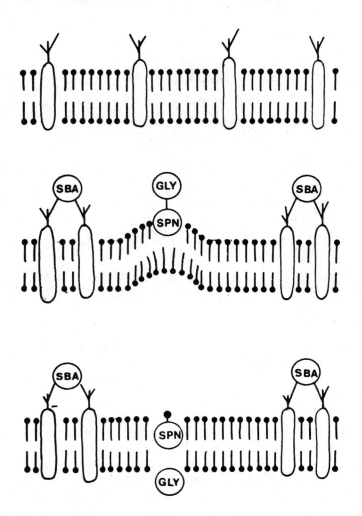

**Figure 3** Hypothetical mechanisms of glycinin penetration into jejunal epithelium.

oligosaccharide sites on the cell surface and have developed the ability to enter into the cells. In pathway 2, the oligosaccharide is a component of milk glycoproteins that carries specificity for lectin-like affinity sites in the membrane. These proteins are likely to be internalized by fluid-phase endo-cytosis. Proteins entering the cell in fluid phagosomes are rapidly attacked

**Table 6** Pathways of Protein Internalization into Intestinal Epithelium

| I | II | III |
|---|---|---|
| IgG, antigen-IgG, hormones, lectins | Glycoproteins | Proteins with no specific affinities |
| ↓ | ↓ | ↓ |
| Binding to membrane glycoproteins | Binding to "lectin-like" sites in membrane | Membrane lesions caused by inter- acting agent |
| ↓ | ↓ | ↓ |
| Receptor-mediated endocytosis | "Fluid-phase" endocytosis | Leak into cell |
| ↓ | ↓ | |
| Transepithelial transport | Lysosomal degradation | |
| or | | |
| Lysosomal degradation | | |

by the lysosomes (30) and should not normally cross the intestinal epithelium. For example, as shown by Steinman and coworkers (31), in the jejunum of newborn rats IgG-bound horseradish peroxidase crossed the epithelial cell inside coated vesicles, while free horseradish peroxidase remained in large residual bodies at the apical cytoplasm and never entered into the tissue's extracellular fluid. Nevertheless, the uptake of horseradish peroxidase through intact epithelium has been demonstrated by Walker and coworkers in nonimmunized newborn rats (32). Thus, it appears that under certain situations such as inadequate immunological barrier or excessive antigenic load, glycoproteins may traverse intact intestinal epithelium by fluid-phase endocytosis. In pathway 3, the protein is inert, in the sense that it does not carry specificity or affinity for membrane sites. The protein enters into the cell at lytic points produced by damaging agents. Studies with other cell populations have shown that bacterial and plant lysins (33,34), as well as viruses (35), may act on the cell membrane, altering its permeability and causing leakiness to external macromolecules. Although no conclusive proof for similar effects on intestinal epithelium has been presented, such a mechanism might arise in some clinical situations involving damaging agents in infant bowel.

Table 7    Soy Protein-Based Formulas

| | |
|---|---|
| CHO-free | Nursoy |
| C.I.B. | Nutri 1000 LF |
| Ensure | Osmolite |
| Isocal | Prosobee |
| Isomil | Sustacal |
| Neo-Mullsoy | Vital |

## Clinical Aspects of Soy Protein Intolerance

Adverse reactions following exposure to soy protein products (Table 7), either through the respiratory or digestive tracts, have been well documented. Reports of intolerance, allergy, or hypersensitivity to soy protein-based formulas (SPF) are now appearing regularly in the pediatric literature. Physicians who care for infants need to be aware of the diverse symptomatology, sometimes life-threatening, which has been associated with soy protein intolerance (SPI), since serious injury to the gastrointestinal tract may well be averted by simple dietary manipulation.

### Clinical Presentation

SPI, frequently accompanying cow's milk intolerance (CMI) (36,37), most commonly presents within the first 6 months of life, usually shortly after breast feeding has been abandoned. Symptoms may be limited to the gastrointestinal tract, but are often accompanied by rhinitis, dermatitis, asthma, or other atopic manifestations. Gastrointestinal symptoms vary from benign cyclic bouts of loose stools to a fulminant enterocolitis. SPF has also been reported to produce anaphylaxis (38). Regardless of the severity of the reaction, however, most infants develop tolerance to soy and other offending dietary proteins by the second or third year of life. A very common situation involves an infant who has intolerance to cow's milk protein (CMP) or a viral gastroenteritis while on cow's milk formula (CMF) and is switched to a SPF. This is tolerated briefly or not at all and the patient promptly "stools out." Depending on how severe the mucosal lesion is at that time, a number of conditions causing recurrent diarrhea may be considered: acidic stools may

**Table 8**  Spectrum of Gastrointestinal
Response to Soy Intolerance

Postinfectious diarrhea

Chronic nonspecific diarrhea

Carbohydrate malabsorption

Intractable diarrhea

Colitis

Necrotizing enterocolitis

Anaphylaxis

suggest carbohydrate malabsorption; mucousy stools with polymorphonu-
clear leukocytes and positive for occult blood may suggest an infectious enteritis; a flat jejunal mucosal biopsy (39) may suggest celiac disease. Faced
with these possibilities, the physician should recognize that SPI may be the
mechanism behind the damage, and that SPF should be discontinued in favor
of a protein hydrolysate. It is more common, though, for the mucosal lesion
to be mild and patchy, and for the accompanying diarrhea not to produce
malabsorption or weight loss. In these cases, SPF may be safely continued
until the infant "outgrows" the diarrhea.

Several reports in recent years have described different symptom complexes arising from the use of SPF (Table 8). Ament and Rubin (39) reported a 6-week-old infant who, within 24 hr of being exposed to SPF, developed fever, leukocytosis, cyanosis, vomiting, massive blood-tinged mucoid
diarrhea, dehydration, metabolic acidosis, and a flat jejunal mucosal biopsy.
Whitington and Gibson (36) presented four patients with intractable diarrhea
of infancy who responded to a SPF challenge with diarrhea, vomiting, hypo-
tension, lethargy, and fever. Halpin et al. (40) describe a group of infants who
presented with vomiting, diarrhea, hematochezia, and weight loss after a trial
of SPF. Rectal biopsy performed within 24 hr of the challenge showed an
acute colitis with crypt abscesses, findings which precluded distinguishing
these cases histologically from infectious colitis or mild ulcerative colitis.
Finally, Powell (41) reported two low-birth-weight infants who developed
vomiting, abdominal distension, a septic appearance, and bloody diarrhea
after ingestion of CMF and subsequently SPF. Their clinical picture was
obviously very similar to that of neonatal necrotizing enterocolitis. It is most

important that physicians, when encountered with similar clinical presentations, consider SPF as the possible culprit. Failure to do so may lead to catastrophic results when SPF is reintroduced at a later date.

## Allergenic Potential of Soy

The immunological events leading to sensitization against a major food protein, and how reexposure leads to tissue damage, are subjects of active investigation. It is known that, during the first few months of life, there exists a facilitated internalization of foreign macromolecules through the intestinal mucosa (42,43). So much so, that during the first 3 years of life 95% of bottle-fed infants will have circulating antibodies to CMP (44). An equally striking increase in antibody titer to soy protein is seen in infants fed SPF (45). Why only about 0.5% of the infant population manifest milk intolerance clinically is not well understood.

Acute damage to the intestinal mucosa, such as occurs with viral gastroenteritis, has been shown to open the way for increased macromolecular absorption (46). In this regard, Powell (37) has noted a marked tendency for infants to develop SPI when SPF was offered immediately after CMP-induced intestinal damage. She cautions against this common practice.

Another situation where SPF has been seen as the formula of choice is in feeding infants born into strongly atopic families. To evaluate if SPF was truly hypoallergenic, Halpern et al. (47) studied 1753 infants fed breast, soy, or cow's milk from birth to 6 months of age. In infants with an immediate family history of atopy, and who were followed for varying periods of up to 7 years, the incidence of allergy in the CMF and SPF groups was identical (16%). Kjellman and Johanson (48) studied the same problem and concluded that soy, given instead of CMF from weaning until 9 months of age, did not lower the incidence of atopic symptoms or postpone the development of such symptoms.

The conclusions to be drawn regarding the allergenicity of SPF may be found to be surprising. First, there is no evidence that soy protein is any less capable than cow's milk of producing gastrointestinal sensitization, and upon continued use, mucosal damage. Second, the practice of using SPF to refeed infants with viral gastroenteritis or CMI may be counterproductive, as a setup for hypersensitization is present in these circumstances. Last, the concept of SPF as hypoallergenic should be abandoned and, therefore, using SPF to feed newborns with a strong family history of atopy is unwarranted.

SPI and Chronic Diarrhea

Butler et al. (49) have recently studied 11 infants with active CMI and/or SPI and found their neutrophils to exhibit depressed chemotaxis and enhanced random migration. Interestingly, these same defects had been described some years before by Hill et al. (50) in 14 infants with chronic diarrhea who were intolerant to numerous formulas. This last group of patients also suffered from recurrent otitis media, as did Powell's (37) cases with SPI-induced enterocolitis. In our series of 102 infants with chronic recurrent diarrhea (unpublished data), 26% had sufficient middle ear disease as to require tympanostomy tube replacement compared to 2% among controls.

What the above means in terms of the role of the phagocyte in allergic reactions to dietary proteins is that there seems to be an intimate relation between CMI and SPI and those prolonged diarrhea states referred to as postinfectious diarrhea or chronic nonspecific diarrhea. Our impression is that the latter two conditions make their appearance clinically when a damaged mucosa is repeatedly challenged with new foreign proteins, which are then internalized and sensitize the infant to a subsequent exposure. After a few weeks of changing formulas, without allowing time for the gut to heal completely, predisposed infants exhibit multiple protein intolerance and will react accordingly to any milk product offered. Should the hypersensitivity reactions be too severe, intravenous nutrition may be required to allow for "gut rest."

We hope this short review on milk and soy protein-sugar associations, their possible role in determining protein uptake into intestinal mucosa, and the clinical relevance of these and related alterations will sensitize both the infant formula manufacturers as well as general practitioners to the importance of these molecular entities and to the selective use of soy products.

# References

1. Newman, R. A., and Uhlenbruck, G. G. (1977). Investigation of the occurrence and structure of lectin receptors on human and bovine erythrocyte, milk-fat globule and lymphocyte-plasma-membrane glycoproteins. *Eur. J. Biochem. 76*:149–155.
2. Brown, R. C., Fish, W. W., Hudson, B. G., and Ebner, K. E. (1977). Isolation and characterization of rat α-lactalbumin: a glycoprotein. *Biochim. Byophys. Acta 491*:82–92.
3. Yamashita, K., Tachibana, Y., and Kobata, A. (1977). Oligosaccharides of human milk. Structural studies of two new octasaccharides,

difucosyl derivatives of para-lacto-N-hexaose and para-lacto-N-neohexaose. *J. Biol. Chem. 252*:5408–5411.

4.  Biswas, M., and Rao, V. S. R. (1980). Conformational analysis of the milk oligosaccharides. *Byopolymers 19*:1555–1566.

5.  Walker, W. A., Isselbacher, K. J., and Bloch, K. J. (1972). Intestinal uptake of macromolecules: effect of oral immunizations. *Science 177*: 608–610.

6.  Abrahamson, D. R., Powers, A., and Rodewald, R. (1979). Intestinal absorption of immune complexes by neonatal rats: a route of antigen transfer from mother to young. *Science 206*:567–569.

7.  Patton, S., and Keenan, T. W. (1975). The milk fat globule. *Biochim. Biophys. Acta 415*:273–309.

8.  Kabat, E. A. (1976). *Structural Concepts in Immunology and Immunochemistry*, 2nd ed., Holt, Rinehart and Winston, New York, Chap. 6.

9.  Montrenil, J. (1975). Recent data on the structure of the carbohydrate moiety of glycoproteins: metabolic and biochemical implications. *Pure App Chem. 42*:431–477.

10.  Goldman, A. S., Anderson, D. W., Jr., Sellers, W. A., Saperstein, S., Kniker, W. T., Halpern, S. R., et al. (1963). Milk allergy. I. Oral challenge with milk and isolated milk proteins in allergic children. *Pediatrics 32*:425–442.

11.  Fallstrom, S., Ahlstedt, S., and Hanson, L. A. (1978). *Int. Arch. Allergy Appl. Immunol. 56*:97–105.

12.  Bahna, S. L., and Heiner, D. C. (1978). Cow's milk allergy: pathogenesis, manifestations, diagnosis and management. Year Book Medical Publishers, Chicago, pp. 1–37.

13.  Mulder, H., and Walstra, P. (1974). The Milk Fat Globule. Emulsion Science As Applied to Milk Products and Comparable Foods. Commonwealth Agricultural Bureaux, Farnham Royal, Bucks, England, pp. 1–296.

14.  Lotan, R., Siegelman, H. W., Lis, H., and Sharon, N. (1974). Subunit structure of soybean agglutinin. *J. Biol. Chem. 249*:1219–1224.

15.  Badley, R. A., Atkinson, D., Hauser, J., Oldani, D., Green, J. P., and Stubbs, J. M. (1975). The structure, physical and chemical properties of the soybean protein glycinin. *Biochim. Biophys. Acta 412*:214–228.

16.  Thanh, V. H., and Shibasaki, K. (1976). Major proteins of soybean seeds. A straight forward fractionation and their characterization. *J. Agr. Food Chem. 24*:1117–1121.

17.  Koshiyama, I., and Fukushima, D. (1976). A note on carbohydrates in the 11 S globulin of soybean seeds. *Cereal Chem. 53*(5):768–769.

18.  Nash, A. M., Eldridge, A. C., and Wolf, W. J. (1967). Fractionation and characterization of alcohol extractables associated with soybean proteins. *J. Agr. Food Chem. 15*:102–108.

19. Eldridge, A. C., and Wolf, W. J. (1969). Crystalline saponins from soybean protein. *Cereal Chem. 46*:344–349.
20. Kitawaga, I., Yoshikawa, M., and Yosioka, I. (1976). Saponin and sapogenol. XIII. Structures of three soybean saponins: soyasaponin I, soyasaponin II, and soyasaponin III. *Chem Pharmacol. Bull 24*(1):121–129.
21. Birk, Y., Bondi, A., Gestetner, B., and Ishaaya, I. (1963). A thermostable haemolytic factor in soybeans. *Nature 197*:1089–1090.
22. Gestetner, B., Assa, Y., Henis, Y., Tencer, Y., Rotman, M., Birk, Y., and Bondi, A. (1972). Interactions of lucerne saponins with sterols. *Biochim. Biophys. Acta 270*:181–187.
23. Segal, R., and Milo-Goldzweig, I. (1975). On the mechanisms of saponin hemolysis. I. Inhibition of hemolysis by aldactones. *Biochem. Pharmacol. 24*:77–81.
24. Seeman, P. (1967). Transient holes in the erythrocyte membrane during hypotonic hemolysis and stable holes in the membrane after lysis by saponin and lysolecithin. *J. Cell Biol. 32*:55–70.
25. Seeman, P., Cheng, D., and Iles, G. H. (1973). Structure of membrane holes in osmotic and saponin hemolysis. *J. Cell Biol. 56*:519–527.
26. Ohtsuki, I., Manzi, R. M., Palade, G. E., and Jamieson, J. D. (1978). Entry of macromolecular tracers into cells fixed with low concentrations of aldehydes. *Biol. Cellulaire 31*:119–126.
27. Lanier, J. P., and Torres-Pinedo, R. (1980). Interactions of soybean fractions with rabbit red blood cells. American College of Nutrition 21st Annual Meeting, Symposium on Nutrition and Child Health, Sept. 8–9, 1980 (Abstr. 54).
28. Gestetner, B., Birk, Y., and Tencer, Y. (1968). Fate of ingested soybean saponins and the physiological aspects of their hemolytic activity. *J. Agr. Food Chem. 16*:1031–1035.
29. Alvarez, J. R., and Torres-Pinedo, R. (1982). Interactions of soybean lectin, soyasaponins and glycinin with rabbit jejunal mucosa *in vitro*. *Pediatr. Res.,* in press.
30. Silverstein, S. C., Steinman, R. M., and Cohn, Z. A. (1977). Endocytosis. *Ann. Rev. Biochem. 46*:669–772.
31. Steinman, R. M. Silver, J. M., and Cohn, Z. A. (1978). Fluid phase pinocytosis. In *Transport of Macromolecules in Cellular Systems*, S. C. Silverstein (Ed.), Abakon Verlagsgesellschaft, Berlin, p. 167.
32. Walker, W. A., Cornell, R., and Davenport, L. M. (1972). Macromolecular absorption: Mechanism of horseradish peroxidase uptake and transport in adult and neonatal rat intestine. *J. Cell Biol. 54*:195–205.
33. Shary, S., Bernheimer, A. W., Grushoff, P. S., and Kim, K. S. (1974). Evidence for membrane cholesterol as the common binding site for cereolysin, streptolysin 0 and saponin. *Mol. Cell. Biochem. 3*(3):179–186.

34. Van Heyningen, W. E. (1976). Membrane receptors for bacterial toxins. In *Surface Membrane Receptors, Interface Between Cells and Their Environment*, R. A. Bradshaw, W. A. Frazier, R. C. Merrell, and D. I. Gottlieb (Eds.), Plenum, New York, pp. 147–167.

35. Carrasco, L. (1978). Membrane leakiness after viral infection and a new approach to the development of antiviral agents. *Nature 272*:694–699.

36. Whitington, R. P., and Gibson, R. (1977). Soy protein intolerance: four patients with concomitant cow's milk intolerance. *Pediatrics 59*(5):730.

37. Powell, G. K. (1978). Milk and soy-induced enterocolitis of infancy. *J. Pediatr. 93*(4):553.

38. Mortimer, E. Z. (1961). Anaphylaxis following ingestion of soybean. *J. Pediatr. 58*(1):90.

39. Ament, M. E., and Rubin, C. E. (1972). Soy protein—another cause of the flat intestinal lesion. *Gastroenterology 62:*(2):227.

40. Halpin, T. C., Byrne, W. J., and Ament, M. E. (1977). Colitis, persistent diarrhea and soy protein intolerance. *J. Pediatr. 91*(3):404.

41. Powell, G. K. (1976). Enterocolitis in low-birth-weight infants associated with milk and soy protein intolerance. *J. Pediatr. 88*(5):840.

42. Rothberg, R. M. (1969). Immunoglobulin and specific antibody synthesis during the first weeks of life of premature infants. *J. Pediatr. 75*(3):391.

43. Udall, J. N., Fritze, L., Pang, K., Kleinman, R., and Walker, W. A. (1981). Development of gastrointestinal mucosal barrier. 1. The effect of age on intestinal permeability to macromolecules. *Pediatr. Res. 15*:214.

44. Gunther, M., Aschaffenburg, R., Matthews, R. H., Parrish, W. E., and Coombs, R. R. A. (1960). The level of antibodies to the proteins of cow's milk in the serum of normal human infants. *Immunology 3*:296.

45. Eastham, E. J., Lichanco, T., Grady, M. I., and Walker, W. A. (1978). Antigenicity of infant formulas: Role of immature intestine on protein permeability. *J. Pediatr. 93*(4):561.

46. Gruskay, F. L., and Cooke, R. E. (1955). The gastrointestinal absorption of unaltered protein in normal infants and in infants recovering from diarrhea. *Pediatrics 16*:763.

47. Halpern, S. R., Sellars, W. A., Johnson, R. B., Anderson, D. W., Saperstein, S., and Reisch, J. S. (1973). Development of childhood allergy in infants fed breast soy or cow's milk. *J. All. Clin. Immunol. 51*(3):139.

48. Kjellman, N. I. M., and Johansson, S. G. O. (1979). Soy versus cow's milk in infants with a biparental history of atopic disease: Development of atopic disease and immunoglobulins from birth to 4 years of age. *Clin. Allergy 9*:347.

49. Butler, H. L., Byrne, W. J., Marmer, D. J., Euler, A. R., and Steele, R. W. (1981). Depressed neutrophil chemotaxis in infants with cow's milk and/or soy protein intolerance. *Pediatrics* 67(2):264.
50. Hill, H. R., Book, L. S., Hemming, V. G., and Herbst, J. J. (1977). Defective neutrophil chemotactic responses in patients with recurrent episodes of otitis media and chronic diarrhea. *Am. J. Dis. Child.* *131*: 433.

# STARCH INTOLERANCE

# 14

## STARCH INTOLERANCE IN INFANCY
### factors involved in a controversial area

EMANUEL LEBENTHAL and LEO A. HEITLINGER
*State University of New York at Buffalo
and The Children's Hospital at Buffalo, New York*

Glucose polymers including native and modified starches have, in recent years, been used with increasing frequency in infants for nutritional support. A number of formulas used routinely in nurseries for premature and compromised infants contain glucose polymers replacing or supplementing mono- and disaccharides in order to increase caloric density without a concommitant increase in osmolality. Term infants and young children with increased caloric requirements who are sensitive to increased volume, or intolerant of formulas with lactose, also receive these formulas. In addition, there has been an increasing tendency of early introduction of native and modified starches; many infants receive starch-containing foods as early as the first week. Native starches are in infant cereals and modified starches, for the most part, are in commercial strained and junior foods.

There are, however, several reasons for concern. First, there are several clinical reports of intolerance of glucose polymers and starches in the literature. Second, the laboratory investigations on which the starch digestibility was demonstrated were in mature, rather than immature animals (1-3). Both clinical and experimental experiences in the young developing infant or laboratory animal are extremely limited. In the young infant, amylase in resting duodenal fluid is low or absent, and the ability to stimulate release from the pancreas in the first month of life is poorly developed. Clinical methods to assess hydrolysis, absorption, and utilization of calories from these sources are not optimal. Moreover, the relative digestibility of starches, native or modified, do not seem to be uniform. For these reasons, it is possible that we may recognize only the most severe cases of intolerance and miss the more subtle manifestations and abnormalities of growth and development.

In addition, the effects of altering the relative caloric contribution from protein, fat, and carbohydrate on absorption of nutrients, vitamins, and minerals are not known. Similarly, the long-term effect of modification of starches with organic compounds that may be mutagenic or carcinogenic will not be evident in a short period. The effects on intestinal flora as related to nonabsorbed hydrolytic products of digestion of modified starches also require investigation.

We review what is known of the biochemical and physical properties of the glucose polymers, native and modified starches used in the infant diet, the clinical trials, the endogenous factors involved in digestion, the traditional and possible alternate pathways of digestion, the effect of dietary adaptations on pancreatic amylase, and in vitro methods of evaluation of starch digestibility. It must be stressed that there is an urgent need for additional data. Current practices, especially with modified food starches, should be reexamined, and their indiscriminate use in the first 6 months of life should be discouraged until further information is available.

## The Glucose Polymers, Native and Modified Starches Used in Infancy

Starch is a polymer of anhydroglucose units linked together to form either the linear polymer, amylose, or the branched polymer, amylopectin. Starches such as corn, tapioca, and potato contain 18–27% amylose, with the remainder amylopectin. When starch granules are heated in water with aggitation, the granules undergo irreversible swelling. Modified starches were developed primarily to overcome the high viscosity, opacity, and tendency to gel formation of native starch. They can be described as stabilizers: an essential component of baby foods, required to suspend the finely divided food particles. This provides the product with good consistency, texture, appearance, distribution of nutrients, and storage stability (1).

There are four basic types of modifying treatments: bleaching, conversion, cross-linkage, and stabilization (2,3). Waxy maize and tapioca starch are the parent compounds for the majority of modifications used in the United States. As currently used, modified starches constitute 5–6.5% of the net weight, and 10–32% of the total energy available in strained baby foods. Intakes as high as 29 g per day could be derived from this source (4).

Glucose polymers constitute a heterogenous population of linear chains from 5 to 100 glucose units in length. Corn syrup is the most common source. These compounds are extremely soluble and do not tend to form aggregates as currently used (1). Little is known of their digestibility; the available studies are reviewed below.

## In Vitro Analysis of Starch Digestion

The physical properties of starch determine the rate of hydrolysis in vivo. They include particle size, relative composition of amylose and amylopectin, degree of gelatinization (postcooking),  viscosity in solvent, presence of amylase inhibitors, and the nonstarch fibrous matrix. The relative composition of amylose and amylopectin contributes to the solubility of the starch in solution; the degree of cross-linking determines, to a large extent, the viscosity.

Amylase inhibitors occur in the following plants: acorn, buckwheat, colocasia, kidney beans, mangoe, oats, potato, rye, sorghum, wheat, yam (5,6). The inhibitors are active in vitro; some have been purified and characterized, but none have been tested, to our knowledge, in vivo.

The particle size, effects of cooking, and the hindrance of the nonstarch fibrous matrix were addressed by O'Dea and Snow (7,8). Cooking resulted in increased hydrolysis, as did grinding without cooking, both in vivo and in vitro. They claim good correlation between blood glucose and insulin response following a test meal, and in vitro estimation of hydrolysis. If this correlation can be confirmed, it may provide a new avenue of investigation in this area. One note of caution must again be mentioned. These data were collected in young, lean, healthy adults, not premature or compromised infants.

## Clinical Trials of Glucose Polymers and
## Starch Digestibility

Anderson et al. (9) studied 5 infants at 3 days of age with several corn starch derivatives at a dose of 2 g/kg and found a mean rise of 5–11 mg/dl in blood glucose. This compares to 46 mg/dl and 66 mg/dl with maltose and glucose, respectively. The authors interpreted these data to show that the infants digested some starch. We, however, interpret the data as within the margin of error of laboratory measurements for glucose and indicative of little or no digestion and absorption.

DeVizia et al. (10) challenged 1- and 3-month-old infants with a cow's milk-based formula containing starch derived from wheat, corn, tapioca, potato, or rice. Feces were analyzed for lactic acid, glucose, and dextrins, and a coefficient of absorption was calculated. They report a greater than 98% coefficient of absorption for the patients studied. Two infants, however, developed a fermentative diarrhea. We feel that the measurement of fecal excretion of the products of digestion is inadequate; intestinal microflora most probably utilize starch without allowing an increase in the substances measured.

Auricchio et al. (11) showed that infants less than 6 months of age hydrolyzed amylopectin incompletely by detecting dextrins greater than 30 glucose units in length in the jejunum. Studies of infants at 1 year of age revealed rapid hydrolysis to glucose, maltose, maltodextrose, and dextrins.

Lilibridge and Townes (12) report a young infant who had failure to thrive caused by starch intolerance. No amylase was present in duodenal fluid at the time of presentation. Removal of rice cereal from the diet resulted in catch-up growth. Repeat studies of the same patient at 1 year of age included a normal duodenal fluid amylase, and no difficulties following a starch challenge. This suggests that the physiological deficiency of amylase, associated with possible mucosal injury in early infancy, may result in an inability to digest starch.

Cicco et al. (13) performed tolerance tests with lactose and glucose polymers on premature infants. Both increased total plasma-reducing substances, but lactose increased serum insulin to a greater degree.

Fisher et al. (14) reports an infant who was tolerant of a casein hydrolysate formula with glucose, but intolerant of the same formula with glucose and glucose polymers, following a mucosal injury to the small bowel. At 7 months of age, amylase was still barely detectable in the duodenal fluid but the mucosal injury had improved. The infant tolerated the formula with glucose polymers and rice cereal, and grew normally. This report and the study by Cicco et al. (13) are clinical demonstrations of alternate pathways of starch digestion to be discussed below. At present, there are no clinical data available assessing modified starch digestibility in infancy.

## Endogenous Factors Involved in Starch Digestion and Absorption in Infancy

Many endogenous factors affect starch digestion: salivary amylase activity, gastric emptying rate, pancreatic amylase activity, physicochemical properties of the succus entericus and unstirred layer, intestinal motility, gluco-amylase, maltase, and isomaltase activities in the brush border, glucose absorption, and utilization (15). Pancreatic amylase has a potential rate-limiting effect. It is absent or barely detectable in duodenal fluids obtained from young infants. The apparent tolerance of starch by many young infants suggests the importance of alternate pathways (Chapter 15).

Salivary amylase (3.2.1.1) is present in a variety of mammals, including humans. Its molecular weight is approximately 69,000 (16). Multiple isozymes have been identified which segregate into two families on gel filtration and isoelectric focusing (17,18). In humans, most of the amylase originates in the parotid, one-fifth from the submandibular, and only trace from the sublingual glands (19). Various authors report that from 0 to 50% of ingested starch is partially hydrolyzed by this enzyme in adult humans (20,21). A study by Skude and Ihse (22) shows, however, that 75% of adults have active salivary amylase in the duodenum that contributes from 15 to 40% of the total concentration. The importance of salivary amylase in infancy has not been thoroughly investigated.

Pancreatic amylase (3.2.1.2) is thought to be the most important enzyme in the digestion of dietary starch, but is poorly developed in young children (23). Premature and term infants have little or no amylase in the duodenal fluid and do not respond to secretogogues (24-26). Auricchio et al. (27) described intestinal glycosidase activity in the fetus and newborn as being 10% of adult values in pancreatic homogenates, but not detectable in duodenal fluids. Several investigators report that the low or absent levels persist to at least 6 months of age, and that adult values are not reached until weights of greater than 12 kg are attained (25,26,28-30).

Glucoamylase (3.2.1.3) has been reported to be present in mammalian intestinal mucosa and may account for 25-30% of the latent maltase activity in the small intestine. By 1 month of age, this enzyme is present in quantities comparable to those of young adults (31). The role of glucoamylase in starch digestion in infancy requires further investigation.

## Possible Alternate Pathways of Starch Absorption

Persorption is the phenomenon by which solid, undissolved food particles enter the body from the intestinal lumen during normal digestion (32). Particles suitable for persorption enter the space between epithelial cells and are transported basally. Primary transport from the intestine is via the portal system and lacteals. Several investigators presented conflicting data on the persorption of starch granules and large glucose polymers (33-35). The data were collected in adults; no data concerning infants is available.

## Dietary Adaptation of Pancreatic Amylase

The arrival of food in the duodenum stimulates secretion of exocrine pancreatic enzymes at four to five times the resting rate, and 70% of the maximal capacity (36). At present, alterations in the relationship between the exocrine pancreatic enzymes appears to require a prolonged modification of diet (37-41). In the rat, dietary carbohydrates such as starch, sucrose, or glucose can increase the pancreatic content of amylase and decrease the content of lipase, while fatty acids can increase lipase (42). Feeding starch to premature infants increased amylase output 10-fold within 1 month but the amount was still negligible (25). It is possible that the introduction of starches early in life can induce amylase activity, but the data are inadequate at this time to confirm this hypothesis.

## Conclusion

We have reviewed the available studies in the literature regarding the digestibility of glucose polymers, native and modified starches; it must be stressed that there is an urgent need for additional data, particularly in the young or compromised infant and laboratory animal. Although reports of intolerance are few, the effect of feeding these compounds to large populations of infants remains unclear. Current practices, especially with the modified food starches, require evaluation. Further, the use of foods containing starches should be individualized with care until adequate data are available. As with any new drug, caution should be the rule until laboratory and clinical experience indicate the drug safe for use in patients of appropriate age and clinical indication.

## References

1. Lee, P. C., Nord, K. S., and Lebenthal, E. (1981). Digestibility of starches in infants. In *Textbook of Gastroenterology and Nutrition in Infancy,* E. Lebenthal (Ed.), Raven Press, New York, pp. 423-434.
2. The Subcommittee on Evaluation and Safety of Modified Starches in Infant Foods (1977). Safety and suitability of modified starches for use in baby food. *Committee on Nutrition,* American Academy of Pediatrics, Houston, Texas.
3. The Subcommittee on Safety and Suitability of Modified Food Starches and other Substances in Baby Foods (1977). Safety and suitability of modified starches for use in baby food. *National Research Council,* National Academy of Sciences, Washington, D.C.
4. Fomon, S. J. (1974). Voluntary food intake and its regulation. In *Infant Nutrition,* S. J. Fomon (Ed.), W. B. Saunders, Philadelphia, pp. 20-33.
5. Marshal, J. J. (1975). Amylase inhibitors from plants. In *Physiological Effects of Food Carbohydrates,* A. Jeanes, and J. Hodge (Eds.), American Chemical Society, Washington, D.C., pp. 244-266.
6. Shivaraj, B., Krishna Sharma, K., and Pattabiraman, T. N. (1979). Natural plant enzyme inhibitors. *Ind. J. Biochem. Biophys. 16*:52-55.
7. O'Dea, K., Snow, P., and Nestal, P. (1981). Rate of starch hydrolysis in vitro as a predictor of metabolic responses to complex carbohydrate in vivo. *Am. J. Clin. Nutr. 34*:1991-1993.
8. Snow, P., and O'Dea, K. (1981). Factors affecting the rate of hydrolysis of starch in food. *Am. J. Clin. Nutr. 34*:2721-2727.
9. Anderson, T. A., Fomon, S. J., and Filer, L. F. (1972). Carbohydrate tolerance studies with 3 day old infants. *J. Lab. Clin. Med. 79*:31-37.
10. De Vizia, B., Ciccimarra, F., De Cicco, N., and Auricchio, S. (1975). Digestibility of starches in infants and children. *J. Pediatr. 86*:50-55.
11. Auricchio, S., Della Pietra, D., and Vegnente, A. (1967). Studies on intestinal digestion of starch in man. II. Intestinal hydrolysis of amylopectin in infants and children. *Pediatrics 39*:853-862.
12. Lilibridge, C. B., and Townes, P. L. (1973). Physiologic deficiency of pancreatic amylase in infancy: A factor in iatrogenic diarrhea. *J. Pediatr. 82*:279-282.
13. Cicco, R., Holzman, I. R., Brown, D. R., and Becker, D. J. (1981). Glucose polymer intolerance in premature infants. *Pediatrics 67*(4):498-501.

14. Fisher, S. E., Leone, G., and Kelly, R. H. (1981). Chronic protracted diarrhea: intolerance to dietary glucose polymers. *Pediatrics 67*(2):271–273.
15. Lebenthal, E., and Shwachman, H. (1977). The pancreas: development, adaptation, and malfunction in infancy and childhood. *Clin. Gastroenterol. 6*:397–413.
16. Henster-Pettersen, A., Sonju, J., and DeBest, T. (1970). Human salivary alpha amylase purification and amino acid composition. *Scand. J. Dent. Res. 78*:40.
17. Rosenmund, H., and Kaczmarek, M. J. (1976). Isolation and characterization of isoenzymes of human salivary and pancreatic alpha amylase. *Clin. Chim. Acta 71*:185–189.
18. Joseph, R. R., Oliverio, E., and Ressler, N. (1966). Electrophoretic study of human isoamylases. *Gastroenterology 51*:377–382.
19. Jacobsen, N. (1975). Salivary amylase. II. Alpha amylase in salivary gland of the macaca irus monkey, the Cercopithicus aethrops monkey and man. *Caries Res. 4*:200.
20. Gray, G. M. (1978). Mechanism of digestion and absorption of food. In *Gastrointestinal Disease*, M. H. Sleisenger and J. S. Fordtran (Eds.), Saunders, Philadelphia, pp. 241–250.
21. Davenport, H. W. (1971). Intestinal digestion and absorption of carbohydrate. In *Physiology of the Digestive Tract*, H. W. Davenport (Ed.), Yearbook Medical Publishers, Chicago, pp. 183–190.
22. Skude, G., and Ihse, I. (1976). Salivary amylase in duodenal aspirates. *Scand. J. Gastroenterol. VII*:17–20.
23. Lebenthal, E., Lev, R., and Lee, P. C. (1981). Perinatal development of the exocrine pancreas. In *Textbook of Gastroenterology and Nutrition in Infancy*, E. Lebenthal (Ed.), Raven Press, New York, pp. 149–166.
24. Lebenthal, E., and Lee, P. C. (1980). Development of functional response in human exocrine pancreas. *Pediatrics 66*(4):556–560.
25. Zoppi, G., Shmerling, D. H., Gaburro, D., and Prader, A. (1970). The electrolyte and protein content and output in duodenal juice after pancreozymin and secretin stimulation in normal children and children with cystic fibrosis. *Acta Pediatr. Scand. 59*:692–696.
26. Zoppi, G., Andreotti, G., Pajno-Ferrara, F., Njai, D. M., and Gaburro, D. (1972). Exocrine pancreatic function in premature and full term neonates. *Pediatr. Res. 6*:880–886.
27. Auricchio, S., Rubino, A., and Murset, G. (1965). Intestinal glycosidase activities in the human embryo, fetus and newborn. *Pediatrics 35*:944–954.
28. Klump, T. G., and Neale, A. V. (1930). The gastric and duodenal contents of normal infants and children. *Am. J. Dis. Child. 40*:1215–1229.

29. Schwachman, H., and Leubner, H. (1955). Mucoviscidosis. *Adv. Pediatr.* 7:249.

30. Delachaume-Salem, E., and Sarles, H. (1970). Evolution en fonction de l'age de la secretion pancreatique humaine normale. *Biol. Gastroenterol.* (*Paris*) 2:135–146.

31. Lebenthal, E., and Lee, P. C. (1980). Glucoamylase and disaccharidase activities in normal subjects and in patients with mucosal injury of the small intestine. *J. Pediatr.* 97(3):389–393.

32. Volkheimer, G., Schulz, F. H., and Lehmann, H. (1968). Primary portal transport of persorbed starch granules from the intestinal wall. *Med. Exp.* (*Basal*)18:103–108.

33. Ugolev, A. M. (1960). Parietal (contact) digestion. *Bull. Exp. Biol. Med.* 49:12–17.

34. Jesuitova, N. N., deLaey, P., and Ugolev, A. M. (1964). Digestion of starch in vivo and in vitro in a rat intestine. *Biochim. Biophys. Acta 86*: 205–210.

35. Fogel, M. R., and Gray, G. M. (1973). Starch hydrolysis in man: an intraluminal process not requiring membrane digestion. *J. Appl. Physiol.* 35:263–267.

36. MacGregor, I. L., Parent, J., and Meyer, J. H. (1977). Gastric emptying of liquid meals and pancreatic biliary secretion after subtotal gastrectomy or truncal vagotomy and pyloroplasty in man. *Gastroenterology* 72:195–205.

37. Abdeljlil, A. B., Visani, A. M., and Desnuelle, P. (1963). Adaptation of the exocrine secretion of rat pancreas to the composition of the diet. *Biodhem. Biophys. Res. Commun.* 10:112–116.

38. Desnuelle, P., Reboud, J. P., and Abdeljlil, A. B. (1962). Influence of the composition of the diet on enzyme content of rat pancreas. In *Exocrine Pancreas*, A. DeReuch (Ed.), Churchill, London, p. 90.

39. Howard, F., and Yudkin, J. (1963). Effect of dietary change upon the amylase and trypsin activities of the rat pancreas. *Br. J. Nutr.* 17:281–294.

40. Snook, J. T. (1965). Dietary regulation of pancreatic enzyme synthesis, secretion and inactivation in the rat. *J. Nutr.* 87:297–305.

41. Snook, J. T. (1971). Dietary regulation of pancreatic enzymes in the rat with emphasis on carbohydrate. *Am. J. Physiol.* 221:1388–1391.

42. Christophe, J., Camus, J., Deschodt-Lanckman, M., Rathe, J., Robberecht, R., Vandermeers-Piret, M. C., and Vandermeers, A. (1971) Factors regulating biosynthesis, intracellular transport and secretion of amylase and lipase in the rat exocrine pancreas. *Horm. Metab. Res.* 3:393–403.

# 15

## ALTERNATE PATHWAYS IN STARCH DIGESTION
### their importance in premature and young infants

P. C. LEE
*State University of New York at Buffalo
and The Children's Hospital at Buffalo, New York*

Starch requires a combination of enzymes for its complete degradation to simple sugars. The key enzyme in the initial step of hydrolysis of starch is α-amylase (Fig. 1). Traditionally, it is assumed that the majority if not all of the active α-amylases present in the intestinal lumen is of pancreatic origin. In infants up to the age of 6 months it has been shown that pancreatic α-amylase activity in the duodenal fluids remains very low or nonexistent (Fig. 2). The same holds true in prematures of 32–34 weeks gestation during the first month of life (1).

Despite the lack of pancreatic amylase in their duodenal fluid, most newborns and young infants tolerate moderate amounts of starch. In an investigation involving prematures aged 2–3 weeks, results of glucose polymer tolerance tests show increases in plasma glucose levels comparable to feeding

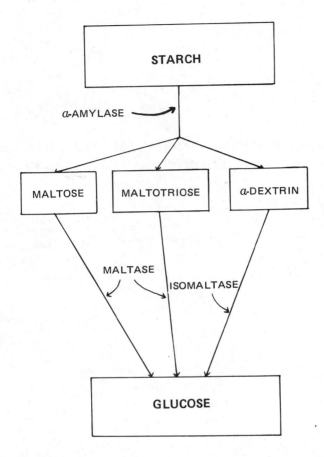

**Figure 1** Interrelationship of enzymes involved in starch digestion.

with isocaloric amounts of lactose (2). This observation suggests that premature infants, in spite of the absence of pancreatic amylase, can hydrolyze and absorb glucose polymers at least to the same extent as lactose.

These results have prompted us to look for other ways the body may have for the digestion of starch especially in prematures and other young infants. Our search revealed three enzymes that are potentially important in the hydrolysis of starch. As outlined in Figure 3, two of these are from endogenous sources and the third from an exogenous source. The endogenous ones

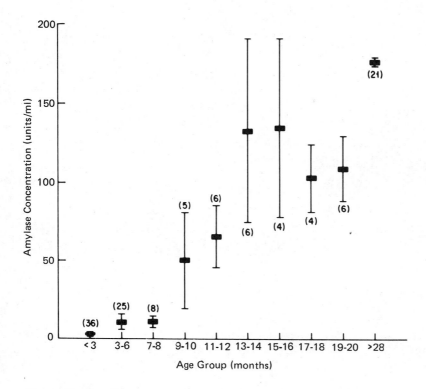

**Figure 2** Age-dependent increase in amylase concentrations in duodenal fluids of infants.

include the brush-border glucoamylase and salivary amylase and the exogenous one, the breast milk amylase.

## Glucoamylase

Glucoamylase has been shown to be present in the human intestinal mucosa in both the brush border (3–5) and lysosomes (6,7). This enzyme characteristically hydrolyzes starch to D-glucose by a stepwise removal of D-glucose residues from the nonreducing end. This enzyme has been estimated to account for 25–30% of the maltase activity in the small intestine. The pre-

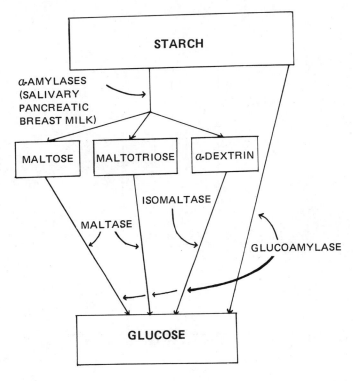

**Figure 3**  Interrelationship of enzymes involved in starch digestion showing possible alternate pathways.

ferred substrate is an oligosaccharide with 4-9 glucose monomers in a linear $\alpha$ (1-4) linkage. Its enzymatic activity decreases with smaller and longer polymer lengths and with increasing numbers of $\alpha$ (1-6) linkage. Glucoamylase is different from $\alpha$-amylases in terms of $Cl^-$ and $Ca^{2+}$ requirements, heat stability, pH optimum, and inhibition by high concentrations of glycerol. The contribution of glucoamylase to starch digestion in the presence of abundant $\alpha$-amylases is unclear because of the latter's more efficient and multiple point of attack on the starch molecule. On the other hand, glucoamylase may have an important role in young infants when their pancreatic amylases are extremely low. Glucoamylase is present in newborns at a level comparable to those of older children (4). The persistence of glucoamylase in a mild degree of mucosal atrophy has an added advantage for infants, since

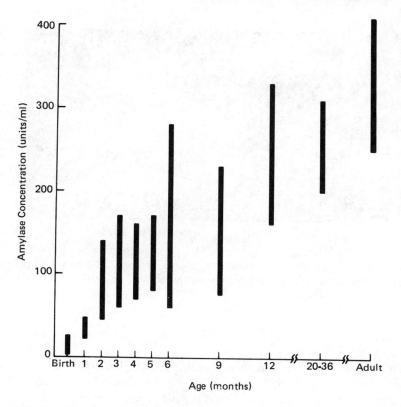

**Figure 4**  Age-dependent increase in amylase concentrations in salivas of infants. (Adapted from Ref. 9.)

neonates have been shown to be more susceptible to mucosal injury than adults. Although the physiological role of intestinal glucoamylase in newborns and infants is not fully understood, indirect evidence has begun to accumulate to show its importance. One such study with piglets shows retention of the capacity to hydrolyze glucose polymers in a resected jejunal segment devoid of any pancreatic secretion (8). Comparable studies in infants with proven severe pancreatic insufficiency may yield corroborative evidence and provide a better insight into the problem.

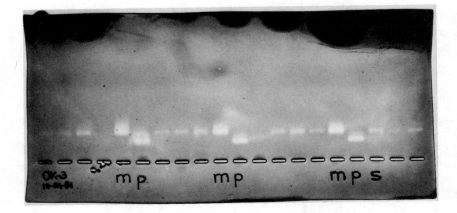

**Figure 5** Activity staining of acrylamide slab-gel electrophoresis of gastric aspirate, saliva (s), pancreatic secretion (p), and breast milk (m) showing relative electrophoretic mobility of different amylases.

### Salivary Amylase

Studies of salivary amylases and their availability during infancy have been few. Direct measurements of amylase in salivary secretion (9,10) together with studies of isoamylase patterns in sera (11) and urine (12) reveal the presence of salivary amylase in infants at birth. In a study by Collares (9), infants were found to have low salivary amylase at birth. The level of amylase in the saliva increases rather rapidly during the first few months, reaching one-third of the adult level by 3 months of age and further increases to the adult level by 1 year of age (Fig. 4). This relatively high level of amylase in the saliva of young infants may be of importance in starch digestion but has been the subject of controversy. One problem is the efficiency of oral digestion of starch and the second is the stability of the salivary amylase in gastric environment. In adults, it has been estimated that from 29 to 66% of starch ingested is hdyrolyzed to maltose and maltotriose after 1.5 min in the oral cavity (13). This suggests a relatively efficient amylolytic process in the mouth. However, ingested food very seldom stays in the mouth for more than 1 min and such degree of hydrolysis would not normally be achieved. More important then is the survival of the salivary amylase in the stomach and beyond. In order to investigate the role of salivary amylase in the digestion of starch and

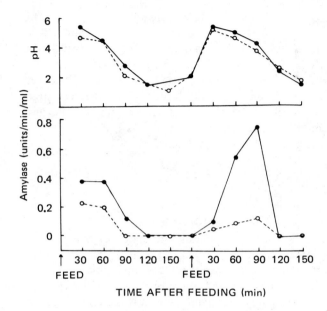

**Figure 6** Representative changes in pH and amylase activities in gastric aspirates of an infant born prematurely at 32 weeks of gestation. Gastric aspirates obtained at the age of 6 weeks (o---o) and 7 weeks (●——●).

other glucose polymers, we have examined samples of saliva and gastric fluid from fed and fasting infants of 29–42 weeks of gestation (14). Amylase activity was detected in the saliva of all infants as early as 29–30 weeks of gestation. The levels of amylase did not change from 29 to 42 weeks and seemed to relate to the secretory activity of their salivary glands. Gastric fluid was found to contain amylase activity with electrophoretic mobility on acrylamide gel identical to salivary amylase (Fig. 5). The presence of amylase activity in the gastric aspirate was pH dependent and was invariably present when the pH was higher than 3.5. More importantly, both pH and amylase activity in the gastric aspirates were closely associated with feeding (Fig. 6). In several neonates examined, up to 90 min after a gavage feeding the pH of the gastric fluid remained above 3.5 and amylase activity was invariably present. In vitro studies were also performed by incubating gastric aspirate with starch followed by analysis of degradative products by thin-layer chromatography. Thin-layer chromatograms revealed a consistent change in the distribution of glucose polymers of different sizes. The production of maltose and malto-triose was unquestionable. Thus, with the amount of amylase found in the gastric aspirate, hydrolysis of starch can be demonstrated at lease in in vitro incubation. Presumably, such hydrolysis could also happen in vivo; if not en-tirely in the stomach it should continue in the duodenum where the environ-ment would be more favorable for the action of salivary amylase. Further supporting evidence for the presence of gastric hydrolysis of starch has to come from in vivo gastric perfusion studies in infants.

## Breast Milk Amylase

The current return to breast feeding has renewed a host of interest on enzyme contents in breast milk. Of particular relevance to starch digestion is the breast milk amylase. Human breast milk contained levels of amylase in the range of about 10 to 50 times that of normal adult serum (Table 1) (15,16). Depending on the amount of milk ingested, the quantity of amylase may be far greater than that contributed by saliva and pancreatic secretion in young infants. Like salivary amylase, similar controversy exists regarding the survival of this amylase in a gastric environment and after its passage through the stomach. To investigate this aspect, in vitro experiments were performed using purified and unpurified mammary amylases by exposing the prepara-tions to acidity comparable to that found in the stomach of a young infant following a breast milk meal. The results showed that breast milk retained more than half of the original amylase activity after 4 hr and more than one-third of the original amylase activity after 6 hr of incubation at 37°C and at a pH of 3.5. Purified breast milk amylase, on the other hand, rapidly lost its activity at pH 3.5. Addition of bovine serum albumin or breast milk proteins stabilized the amylase activity to the extent very similar to that of raw milk, suggesting the importance of other proteins in protecting the amy-lase activity. Addition of physiological and higher concentrations of pepsins to the in vitro mixture at pH 3.5 did not lead to any greater decay of amylase activity despite the occurrence of a significant hydrolysis of proteins. These results give support to the potential role of breast milk as a source of amylase for young infants in facilitating starch digestion. Additional study into actual retention ratio of amylase activity in the stomach and small intestinal

**Table 1**  α-Amylase in Human Breast Milk

| Sample | Units/ml | | Units/mg protein | |
|---|---|---|---|---|
| Colostrum | 3.8[a] | — | 0.14[a] | — |
| Milk | 1.7[a] | 2–5 | 0.10[a] | 0.3–0.4 |

[a]Data from Ref. 15. Normal Serum = 0.08–0.3 units/ml.

lumen with time following a breast milk meal should give a better evaluation of the actual contribution of breast milk amylase to starch digestion in infants.

## Summary

Alternate pathways for starch digestion have been explored particularly in premature and young infants. Three possible sources of enzymes are present. Each of these may play a crucial role in starch digestion in the absence of pancreatic amylase. Brush-border glucoamylase is found in young infants in substantial concentration. Glucoamylase is capable of hydrolyzing both starch and corn syrup sugars in vitro. Indirect evidence suggests it acts similarly in vivo but more studies in this aspect are required. Salivary amylase is demonstrable in infants including prematures. Gastric environments in these infants are found to be favorable for the retention of salivary amylase activity. Since these infants all have low acidity especially after a meal, it may enable the passage of significant amount of salivary amylase unharmed. Human breast milk also contains amylase activity many times that found in adult sera. This mammary amylase is found to be relatively resistant to low pH and peptic action. It is likely that a significant percent of the activity of mammary amylase will be retained after passage through the stomach. The sites of action of both salivary and breast milk amylase are, however, not clear. Also, the contribution of these alternate sources of enzymes in starch digestion is still unknown. Because of their potential importance, further in vivo investigation is imperative in seeking the required answers.

# References

1. Lebenthal, E., and Lee, P. C. (1981). The development of pancreatic function in premature infants after milk based and soy based formulas. *Pediatr. Res. 15*:1240–1244.
2. Cicco, R., Holzman, I. R., Brown, D. R., and Becker, D. J. (1981). Glucose polymer tolerance in premature infants. *Pediatrics 67*:498–501.
3. Eggermont, E. (1969). The hydrolysis of the naturally occurring alpha-glucosides by the human intestinal mucosa. *Eur. J. Biochem. 9*:483–487.
4. Lebenthal, E., and Lee, P. C. (1980). Glucoamylase and disaccharidase activities in normal subjects and in patients with mucosal injury of the small intestine. *J. Pediatr. 97*:389–393.
5. Kelly, J. J., and Alpers, D. H. (1973). Properties of human intestinal glucoamylase. *Biochim. Biophys. Acta 315*:113–122.
6. Garland, G., and Forstner, G. G. (1974). Soluble neutral and acid maltases in the suckling rat intestine. The effect of cortisol and development. *Biochem. J. 144*:281–292.
7. Asp, N. G., Gudmand-Höyer, E., Christiansen, P. M., and Dahlqvist, A. (1974). Acid alpha-glucosidase from human gastrointestinal mucosa—Separation and characterization. *Scand. J. Clin. Lab. Invest. 33*:239–245.
8. Kerzner, B., Sloan, H. R., Haase, G., McClung, H. J., and Ailabouni, A. H. (1981). The jejunal absorption of glucose oligomers in the absence of pancreatic enzymes. *Pediatr. Res. 15*:250–253.
9. Collares, E. F., Brasil, M., Do, R. L., and Kawazaki, S. T. (1979). Secrecas saliva, concentracao e secrecao da amilase, saliva humana nopremenvo ano devida. *Arq. Gastroenterol. S. Paulo. 15*:91–94.
10. Rossiter, M. A., Barrowman, J. A., Dand, A., and Wharton, B. A. (1974). Amylase content of mixed saliva in children. *Acta. Paediatr. Scand. 63*:389–392.
11. Skude, G. (1975). Sources of the serum isoamylase and their normal range of variation with age. *Scand. J. Gastroenterol. 10*:577–584.
12. Tye, J. G., Karn, R. C., and Merritt, A. D. (1976). Differential expression of salivary (Amy 1) and pancreatic (Amy 2) human amylase loci in prenatal and postnatal development. *J. Med. Genet. 13*:96–102.
13. Mormann, J. E., and Muhlemann, H. R. (1981). Oral starch degradation and its influence on acid production in human dental plaque. *Caries Res. 15*:166–175.
14. Hodge, C., Lee, P. C., Topper, W., and Lebenthal, E. (1982). Digestion of corn syrup sugars in neonates: importance of salivary amylase and gastric hydrolysis. *Pediatr. Res.* (Abstr.), in press.

15. Jones, J. B., Mehta, N. R., and Hamosh, M. (1982). Alpha amylase in preterm human milk. *J. Pediatr. Gastroenterol. Nutr.* 1:43–48.
16. Heitlinger, L. A., Lee, P. C., Dillon, W., and Lebenthal, E. (1982). Human mammary amylase. A possible alternate pathway of carbohydrate digestion in infancy. *Pediatr. Res.* (Abstr.), in press.

# DIETARY MANAGEMENT

# 16

# INFANT FORMULAS FOR THE MANAGEMENT OF CARBOHYDRATE INTOLERANCE IN INFANCY

DAVID A. COOK
*Mead Johnson Nutritional Division, Evansville, Indiana*

One of the major concerns in the management of infants with chronic diarrhea is the prevention or treatment of malnutrition. Human milk is the preferred source of nutrition for normal, healthy infants as well as for many infants with diarrhea. However, human milk is not always available and the lactose content of milk-based infant formulas precludes their use in many infants with diarrheal disease (1). Therefore, various milk-substitute formulas have been used in the nutritional management of infants with diarrhea for more than 50 years.

In the past few decades much has been learned about the digestive physiology of the infant, and significant advances have been made in the clinical management of diarrheal disease. Many special formulas have been developed to aid in the nutritional support of infants who are intolerant of the carbohydrate or the protein in milk or milk-based formulas, or who may be allergic to the protein in some of the milk-substitute formulas (2). Most of these special formulas contain carbohydrate sources other than lactose, and some also contain medium chain triglycerides as a source of fat. Although the success of the early soy formulas in the management of infantile diarrhea was usually attributed to the absence of cow milk protein, many of these infants undoubtedly responded to the removal of lactose from the diet.

The primary purpose of this chapter is to consider the major factors in selection of ingredients used in formulas designed for the management of infants with diarrhea. These factors include nutritional value, digestibility and tolerance, osmolality, and functional properties.

## Selection of Ingredients for Formulas

### General Considerations

Carbohydrate is the major ingredient of concern in the design of infant formulas, since carbohydrate commonly provides 35–50% of the total caloric intake, and is the ingredient most likely to be involved in the pathophysiology of diarrheal disease associated with nutrient malabsorption (1). Nutritional considerations in selection of carbohydrate for infant formulas include (a) value as a source of available energy; (b) effects on mineral absorption, intestinal microflora, and stool consistency; and (c) reactivity with amino groups of proteins or amino acids in the formula.

Lactose is generally considered the preferred carbohydrate in the diet of healthy infants. It enhances the intestinal absorption of minerals, especially calcium and magnesium (3–5); however, adequate mineral absorption can also be achieved on lactose-free formulas. Lactose promotes the growth of lactobacilli in the intestinal tract which may, in turn, inhibit the establishment of less desirable intestinal microflora (6).

The potential reactivity with amino acids is another important consideration in selecting the carbohydrate source for infant formulas. Any carbohydrate which has a free, or potentially free, aldehyde group may react in an aqueous medium with the free amino group of amino acids or proteins. This reaction, known as the Maillard or "browning" reaction, may adversely affect protein quality by reducing the bioavailability of some amino acids. This nonenzymatic reaction occurs progressively over time, and the rate of formation is temperature-dependent. Reducing sugars such as glucose, maltose, lactose, and some forms of glucose polymers or corn syrup solids may react to varying degrees with the epsilon amino group of lysine in formulas containing intact protein or with any amino group in formulas containing free amino acids or small peptides. Consequently, the reactivity with carbohydrate source can be an important factor in the design of formulas, particularly those which contain high levels of free amino acids.

The carbohydrates in certain legumes, such as the raffinose and stachyose found in soybeans and navy beans, are not digested by enzymes in the human intestinal tract. The microflora populating the human gut, however, do metabolize these carbohydrates. This is thought to explain the gassy, foul-smelling stools of some infants fed the early formulas made with soy flour which contained these carbohydrates. It is now generally considered desirable to avoid the use of such carbohydrates in infant formulas not only from an esthetic standpoint, but because of concern over potential malabsorption of other nutrients as well.

The carbohydrate selected for an infant formula should not contain other components which may be detrimental to the infant. For example, patients with essential fructosuria or hereditary fructose intolerance cannot be fed a diet containing fructose, sucrose, or honey. Galactosemic infants must depend on diets which contain no lactose or galactose, as they are unable to metabolize these carbohydrates. Lactose is not used in formulas designed for infants allergic to cow's milk protein because commercially available lactose is obtained from cow's milk and may contain antigenic amounts of milk protein.

Infants who have diarrhea because of sensitivity to cow's milk have been successfully managed with milk-substitute formulas based on soy protein. Such products have been used for many years, and have been clearly demonstrated to support growth and development equivalent to that of infants fed human milk or formulas based on cow's milk. Some infants, however, develop sensitivity to formulas containing intact soy protein as well (Chapter 13). The clinical course of these infants may be very similar to that of infants with severe sensitivity to cow's milk protein. These infants are usually managed with formulas based on hydrolyzed casein or alternate protein sources. In some situations, it is essential to provide nutritional support by the intravenous route.

Significant malabsorption of fat is frequent in patients with gastroenteritis (7). It can be alleviated in many cases by use of a formula containing medium chain triglycerides. This source of fat is easily hydrolyzed and readily absorbed even by patients with subnormal digestive and absorptive capacity. However, the fecal energy loss caused by steatorrhea in diarrheal disease is usually transient and of little consequence, but it can be critical if dietary fat is limited. Low fat formulas may be associated with a worsened

Table 1    Contribution of Various Nutrients to Osmolality
of Human Milk and Milk-Based Infant Formulas

| Nutrient | Human milk | Milk-based formula |
|---|---|---|
| | (mosmol/kg $H_2O$) | |
| Lactose | 200 | 205 |
| Sodium | 7 | 11 |
| Potassium | 13 | 17 |
| Chloride | 11 | 15 |
| Protein | — | — |
| Fat | — | — |
| Other | 69 | 52 |
| Total | 300 | 300 |

Source: Modified from Cook, D. (1981). Carbohydrate content
of formulas for premature and full-term infants. In Textbook of
Gastroenterology and Nutrition in Infancy, E. Lebenthal (Ed.),
Raven Press, New York, p. 439.

nutritional state and may lead to chronic diarrhea (8). Proprietary formulas
now provide adequate amounts of fat to meet essential fatty acid requirements as well as energy to avoid these consequences.

Osmolality

Following reports suggesting that hyperosmolar formulas have adverse effects
when fed undiluted to preterm infants, the osmolality of infant formulas
has received considerable attention in the past few years. When fed undiluted
or too rapidly, hyperosmolar formulas may cause vomiting, diarrhea, or other
gastrointestinal complications in some infants (Chapter 1).

The type and level of carbohydrate in the infant formulas are very important determinants of osmolality. In human milk, for example, lactose ac-
counts for about 200 mosmol/kg water of the total osmolality of 300
mosmol/kg (Table 1). Sodium, potassium, and chloride account for a significant part of the remaining osmotically active solutes.

A formula containing free amino acids or protein hydrolysate instead of
intact protein would have an osmolality 90–100 mosmol/kg higher than a
similar formula which contains an intact protein such as milk or soy protein.

Table 2    Relative Effect of Various Carbohydrate Sources on
Osmolality of Infant Formulas

| Source | Osmolality from carbohydrate[a] |
|---|---|
| | (mosmol/kg $H_2O$) |
| Glucose, fructose | 400 |
| Lactose, sucrose, maltose | 200 |
| Glucose oligosaccharide, DE 40[b] | 160 |
| Glucose oligosaccharide, DE 30 | 120 |
| Glucose oligosaccharide, DE 20 | 80 |
| Glucose oligosaccharide, DE 10 | 40 |
| Starch | 0 |

[a]Estimated for formulas containing 1.5 g protein, 3.7 g fat, 0.36 g
minerals (ash), and 7 g carbohydrate per deciliter of formula (0.67
kcal/ml).

[b]DE, dextrose equivalent value.

Source: From Cook, D. (1981). Carbohydrate content of formulas
for premature and full-term infants. In Textbook of Gastroenterology
and Nutrition in Infancy, E. Lebenthal (Ed.), Raven Press, New York,
p. 440.

The osmolality of several hypothetical formulas containing the same total amount of carbohydrate but in the form of monosaccharides (glucose, fructose), disaccharides (lactose, sucrose, maltose), various types of glucose polymers or corn syrup solids, as well as corn starch are listed in Table 2. These figures illustrate one of the reasons glucose is not used in milk-substitute formulas and why various corn syrup solids are selected which provide a readily digested form of carbohydrate and yet result in a formula with low osmolality. Most of the commercially available infant formulas today have osmolality values in the same general range as human milk.

It is important to note that osmolality is usually of greater concern when the feeding is given in bolus or intermittent feedings than when it is given slowly by continuous infusion. Intact protein and undigested fat make essentially no contribution to formula osmolality. The water-soluble free fatty acids released on digestion of medium chain triglycerides are osmotically active in the gut prior to absorption.

## Product Functionality

Protein is not only a key nutrient in infant formulas based on milk or soy, but it also serves an important role in maintaining the physical stability of liquid formulas as well. In infant formulas with free amino acids or small peptides as the protein source, the stabilizing effect of protein must be achieved through the use of other ingredients in order to assure physical stability during shipment and storage of liquid formulas or during the interval between the preparation and feeding of powdered infant formulas. Carbohydrate sources commonly selected for their digestibility, tolerance, and nutritional attributes usually do not possess the functional characteristics necessary to provide a stable homogenous formula which does not contain intact proteins. Consequently, the most acceptable alternative at this time is to use certain types of food starches such as arrowroot starch, modified tapioca starch, or modified corn starch. Arrowroot starch was used for many years as a stabilizer in special formulas made with hydrolyzed protein. Since this source is no longer commercially available, modified tapioca starch has taken its place in recent years.

As noted below, the only forms of food starch used in commercially available formulas have been carefully evaluated, reviewed, and approved for such use. Such carbohydrates are included in formulas at the lowest possible level needed to achieve an acceptable, physical stability. In these cases, the minimal potential risk of using a small amount of carbohydrate that may not be digested and absorbed as readily as the smaller disaccharides or oligosaccharides must be weighed against the benefit of providing a nutritious homogeneous, and physically stable formula which is essential to meet the special nutritional needs of the infant.

## Starch, Glucose Polymers, and Modified Starches

It is generally recognized that young infants have a very limited capacity to digest intact starch (9-12). Consequently, this carbohydrate source is not used in significant amounts in infant formulas, and most formulas contain none. On the other hand, glucose polymers, corn syrup solids, or maltodextrins, which are partially hydrolyzed or digested forms of corn starch, are well digested and utilized by infants (Chapters 5 and 14). Furthermore, the intestinal enzyme glucoamylase appears to be very important in the digestion of these partial starch hydrolysates in the absence of a significant level of pancreatic amylase in the intestinal lumen (13). Anderson et al. have shown that newborns are able to digest and absorb corn syrup solids including those with a dextrose equivalent rating of 11 as early as 3 days of age based on blood glucose response curves following ingestion of various carbohydrates (9). Infants in their study, however, were not able to digest unhydrolyzed waxy maize corn starch even though it was heat treated prior to feeding. These results suggest that intact food starches should not be considered a good source of available carbohydrate calories in infants during the first few months of life.

Selected modified food starches are used in some special infant formulas, particularly those containing no intact protein (14). These modified food starches are used because of their functional properties and are included at relatively low levels, usually accounting for approximately 15% or less of the total calories in a formula. Modified food starches used in these special formulas have been deemed acceptable for use in infant foods by a Special Committee on GRAS Substances (SCOGS) of the Federation of the American Society of Experimental Biology and Medicine.

The digestibility and utilization of modified food starches by infants has been questioned. Although there is little direct clinical information on the digestibility of these starches as measured by blood glucose response curves, the appropriate growth and development of infants fed such formulas and the absence of diarrhea or reducing substances in the stools of these infants suggest that their digestibility is good. Against the concern about the bioavailability and possible effects of undigested starch, we must balance the benefit of providing a formula with a homogeneous distribution of fat, protein, vitamins, minerals, and carbohydrate for the nutritional support of infants with special needs.

## Formulas for Treatment of Carbohydrate Intolerance

A formula must be readily digestible and well tolerated by the infant if it is to be a good source of nutrition. Infants who lack the ability to digest and absorb specific carbohydrates may develop carbohydrate intolerance and thus require nutritional treatment (Chapters 1, 4, and 6). There are two types of patients: (a) those in whom the normal physiological systems have not matured sufficiently to handle certain carbohydrates, or where a congenital deficiency of a specific enzyme exists (15-19); and (b) those in whom the ability to digest or absorb carbohydrates is markedly reduced or entirely lost because of decreased enzyme activity associated with various medical conditions (20-24). In either type, carbohydrate malabsorption during infancy is clinically characterized by diarrhea and acidic, foul-smelling stools that contain reducing sugars and short chain organic acids.

Infants with severe carbohydrate malabsorption may also exhibit weight loss, failure to thrive, dehydration, and electrolyte losses (1,19,20,22,23,25). The secondary, or acquired, carbohydrate malabsorption syndromes may appear any time during infancy or early childhood. Lactose malabsorption is the most common and most significant in these clinical conditions (1,18–23), but there may also be malabsorption of sucrose (22,23) and, very rarely, monosaccharide absorption is impaired. Compared with lactase, intestinal sucrase develops earlier in gestation, and sucrase activity is usually higher than lactase activity at birth and shortly thereafter (16). In infants with intestinal atrophy, relative levels of disaccharidase activity are in the order of maltase>sucrase>lactase (27). There is also a rare recessive genetic condition characterized by the absence of intestinal sucrase activity (28). Sucrose ingestion by afflicted individuals results in the clinical response identical to that of lactose malabsorption.

Another important determinant of the suitability of various carbohydrates for use in infant formula is the functional maturity of the infant's digestive system. Since the fetal development of intestinal lactase occurs relatively late in gestation (16), some prematures may not be able to digest the amount of lactose in human milk or in commonly used dietary milk-based formulas (Chapter 5). Reports of transient lactose intolerance in premature infants, a condition which may be characterized by the clinical symptoms of carbohydrate malabsorption (15,18), has led to the development of formulas designed for prematures which provide a portion of their carbohydrate calories in the form of glucose polymers.

The primary goal of clinical management of carbohydrate intolerance in these conditions is the treatment of the underlying disease. When carbohydrate malabsorption is suspected, nutritional management usually includes avoidance of the offending carbohydrate. In diarrheal disease when there is lactose intolerance, removal of the offending disaccharide ususally is effective in reducing the number of watery stools (23). The lactose-free formulas most commonly provide carbohydrate in the form of corn syrup, sucrose, or combinations of these (Table 3). Infant formulas are available which contain neither lactose nor sucrose, but which provide carbohydrate in the form of glucose polymers or corn syrup, and in some cases, small amounts of modified food starches (Table 1). The lactose-free, sucrose-free formulas are useful in the management of infants intolerant of either or both of these disaccharides.

**Table 3**  Carbohydrate Sources in Selected Infant Formulas

| Formulas | CHO source |
|---|---|
| Milk-based | |
| Enfamil,[a] Similac,[b] SMA[c] | Lactose |
| Soy-based | |
| Isomil[b] | Corn syrup solids, sucrose |
| Nursoy[c] | Sucrose |
| ProSobee[a] | Corn syrup solids |
| I-Soyalac[d] | Sucrose, tapioca starch |
| Other | |
| MBF, meat-base formula[e] | Sucrose, modified tapioca starch |
| Nutramigen[a] | Sucrose, modified tapioca starch |
| Pregestimil[a] | Corn syrup solids, modified tapioca starch |
| Portagen[a] | Corn syrup solids, sucrose |

[a]Mead Johnson.          [d]Loma Linda

[b]Ross.                  [e]Gerber.

[c]Wyeth.

*Source*: Modified from Cook, D. (1981). Carbohydrate content of formulas for premature and full-term infants. In *Textbook of Gastroenterology and Nutrition in Infancy*, E. Lebenthal (Ed.), Raven Press, New York, p. 438.

Glucose polymers of glucose oligosaccharides, commonly known as corn syrup solids, are commonly used as carbohydrate sources in milk-substitute or lactose-free infant formulas designed for management of diarrheal disease. These glucose polymers are efficiently utilized as a source of energy even by stressed infants (20,25,26,29–32), based on biochemical studies as well as clinical performance criteria such as caloric utilization, absorption and retention of nitrogen and fat, and the absence of diarrhea or reducing substances in the stool. The use of carbohydrate-free diets should be reserved for those patients with monosaccharide intolerance (33). Carbohydrate-free feedings are not without risk, as hypoglycemia may occur. Parenteral glucose should be provided to infants who receive enteral feedings of carbohydrate-free formulas.

## Summary

A variety of ingredient sources are available and suitable for making formulas for infants with diarrheal disease. The most critical factors in the selection of ingredients include nutritional value, digestibility and tolerance, effect on product osmolality, and product functionality. In the design of formulas for nutritional management of patients with diarrheal disease, the selection of an appropriate carbohydrate source is the major determinant of nutritional adequacy and clinical tolerance. Many infants who are fed milk-substitute formulas for management of symptoms ascribed to "cow milk allergy" may actually respond to removal of lactose from the diet. Selection of protein and fat ingredients also depend on their nutritional value as well as their digestibility and tolerance. Some formulas have special sources of carbohydrates, proteins, and fat to aid in the nutritional management of patients with multiple problems of digestion and absorption. In special formulas which contain no intact protein, some carbohydrate sources are included for their physical or functional properties. The selection and use of all ingredients in infant formulas is done with primary attention to the overall needs of the infant for which the formula is intended.

## References

1. Lifshitz, F., Coello-Ramirez, P., Gutierrez-Topete, G., and Cornado-Cornet, M.C. (1971). Carbohydrate intolerance in infants with diarrhea. *J. Pediatr. 79*:760–767.
2. Sarett, H. P. (1981). The modern infant formula. In *Infant and Child Feeding*, J. T. Bond, L. J. Filer, Jr., G. A. Leveille, A. Thomson, and W. B. Weil (Eds.), Academic Press, New York, pp. 99–121.
3. Armbrecht, H. J., and Wasserman, R. H. (1976). Enhancement of Ca++ uptake by lactose in the rat small intestine. *J. Nutr. 106*:1265–1271.
4. Kobayashi, A., Kawai, S., Ohbe, Y., and Nagashima, Y. (1975). Effects on dietary lactose and lactase preparation on the intestinal absorption of calcium and magnesium in normal infants. *Am. J. Clin. Nutr. 28*: 681–683.
5. Kocian, J., Skala, I., and Bakos, K. (1973). Calcium absorption from milk and lactose-free milk in healthy subjects and patients with lactose intolerance. *Digestion 9*:317–324.
6. Barbero, G. J., Runge, G., Fischer, D., Crawford, M. N., Torres, F. E., and Gyorgy, P. (1952). Investigations on the bacterial flora, pH, and sugar content in the intestinal tract of infants. *J. Pediatr. 40*:152–163.

7. Jonas, A., Avigad, S., Diver-Haber, A. M. S., and Katznelson, D. (1979). Disturbed fat absorption following infectious gastroenteritis in children. *J. Pediatr. 95*:366–362.

8. Cohen, S. A., Hendricks, K. M., Mathis, R. K., Laramee, S., and Walker, W. A. (1979). Chronic nonspecific diarrhea: Dietary relationships. *Pediatrics 64*:402.

9. Anderson, T. A., Fomon, S. J., and Filer, L. J., Jr. (1972). Carbohydrate tolerance studies with 3-day-old infants. *J. Lab. Clin. Med. 79*:31–37.

10. Auricchio, S., Ciccimarra, F., Moauro, L., Ray, F., Jos, J., and Rey, J. (1972). Intraluminal and mucosal starch digestion in congenital deficiency of intestinal sucrase and isomaltase activities. *Pediatr. Res. 6*: 832–839.

11. Auricchio, S., Della Pietra, D., and Vegnente, A. (1967). Studies on intestinal digestion of starch in man. II. Intestinal hydrolysis of amylopectin in infants and children. *Pediatrics 39*:853–862.

12. Lilibridge, C. B., and Townes, P. L. (1973). Physiologic deficiency of pancreatic amylase in infancy: A factor in iatrogenic diarrhea. *J. Pediatr. 82*:279–282.

13. Gray, G. M. (1975). Carbohydrate digestion and absorption. *New Engl. J. Med. 292*:1225–1230.

14. Lebenthal, E. (1978). Use of modified food starches in infant nutrition. *Am. J. Dis. Child. 132*:850–852.

15. Abdo-Bassols, F., Lifshitz, F., Del Castillo, E. D., and Martinez-Garza, V. (1971). Transient lactose intolerance in premature infants. *Pediatrics 48*: 816–821.

16. Auricchio, S., Rubino, A., and Murset, G. (1965). Intestinal glycosidase activities in the human embryo, fetus, and newborn. *Pediatrics 35*:944–954.

17. Bartrop, R. W., and Hull, D. (1973). Transient lactose intolerance in infancy. *Arch. Dis. Child. 48*:963–966.

18. Jarrett, E. C., and Holman, G. H. (1966). Lactose absorption in the premature infant. *Arch. Dis. Child. 41*:525–527.

19. Lifshitz, F. (1966). Congenital lactase deficiency. *J. Pediatr. 69*:229–237.

20. Arasu, T. S., Wyllie, R., and Fitzgerald, J. F. (1979). Chronic diarrhea in infants and children. *Am. Fam. Phys. 19*:87–94.

21. Chandrasekaran, R., Kumar, V., Walia, B. N. S., and Moorthy, B. (1975). Carbohydrate intolerance in infants with acute diarrhoea and its complications. *Acta Paediatr. Scand. 64*:483–488.

22. Herber, R. (1972). Disaccharidase deficiency in health and disease. *West. J. Med. 116*:23–37.

23. Lifshitz, F. (1977). Carbohydrate problems in paediatric gastroenterology. *Clin. Gastroenterol. 6*:415–429.

24.  Paes, I. C., Searl, P., Rupert, M. W., and Faloon, W. W. (1967). Intestnal lactase deficiency and saccharide malabsorption during oral neomycin administration. *Gastroenterology 53*:49–58.

25.  Bury, K. D. (1972). Carbohydrate digestion and absorption after massive resection of the small intestine. *Surg. Gynecol. Obstet. 135*:177–187.

26.  Graham, G. G., Baertl, M. M., Cordano, A., and Morales, E. (1973). Lactose-free, medium-chain triglyceride formulas in severe malnutrition. *Am. J. Dis. Child. 126*:330–335.

27.  Lebenthal, E., and Lee, P. C. (1980). Glycoamylase and disaccharidase activities in normal subjects and in patients with mucosal injury of the small intestine. *Pediatrics 97*:389–393.

28.  McNair, A., Gudmand-Hoyer, E., Jarnum, S., and Orrild, L. (1972). Sucrose malabsorption in Greenland. *Br. Med. J. 2*:19–21.

29.  Graham, G. G., Klein, G. L., and Cordano, A. (1979). Nutritive value of elemental formula with reduced osmolality. *Am. J. Dis. Child. 133*:795–797.

30.  Powell, G. K. (1978). Milk- and soy-induced enterocolitis of infancy. *J. Pediatr. 93*:553–560.

31.  Roy, C. C., Ste-Marie, M., Chartrand, L., Weber, A., Bard, H., and Dorya, B. (1975). Correction of the malabsorption of the preterm infant with a medium-chain triglyceride formula. *J. Pediatr. 86*:446–450.

32.  Whitington, P. F., and Gibson, R. (1977). Soy protein intolerance: Four patients with concomitant cow's milk intolerance. *Pediatrics 59*: 730–732.

33.  Lifshitz, F., Coello-Ramirez, P., and Gutierrez-Topete, G. (1970). Monosaccharide intolerance and hypoglycemia in infants with diarrhea. I. Clinical course of 23 cases. *J. Pediatr. 55*:595.